THE INTERNATIONAL ECONOMY SINCE 1945

The International Economy since 1945

W. M. Scammell

St. Martin's Press   New York

ISBN 0–312–42191–5

Library of Congress Cataloging in Publication Data

Scammell, W   M
   The international economy since 1945.

   Includes bibliographical references and index.
   1.   International economic relations.
2.   Economic history—1945–   I.   Title.
HF1411.5292   337'.09'04   79–27416
ISBN 0–312–42191–5

Contents

Part Three
The Years of Crisis, 1964–80

List of Tables

Abbreviations and Acronyms[1]

AFL	American Federation of Labour
AID	Agency for International Development
Basle Club	Group of Central Bank governors meeting in Basle for monthly meetings of BIS
Benelux	Belgium, Netherlands, Luxembourg Economic Union
BIS	Bank for International Settlements
CACM	Central American Common Market
CAP	Common Agricultural Policy of EEC
CEEC	Committee for European Economic Co-operation
CIO	Congress of Industrial Organisations
COMECON	Council for Mutual Economic Aid – An Eastern bloc trade organisation
DLF	Development Lending Fund
ECA	European Co-operation Administration
ECAFE	Economic Commission for Asia and the Far East
ECE	Economic Commission for Europe
ECU	European Currency Unit
ECLA	Economic Commission for Latin America
ECM	European Common Market
ECOSOC	Economic & Social Council of the United Nations
ECSC	European Coal and Steel Community
EEC	European Economic Community
EFTA	European Free Trade Association
EMS	European Monetary System
EPU	European Payments Union
ERP	European Recovery Programme
EXIMBANK	Export–Import Bank of Washington
FAO	Food and Agriculture Organisation
FTA	Free Trade Area
GAB	General Arrangements to Borrow from the IMF
GATT	General Agreement on Tariffs and Trade
Group of Ten	Ten largest countries in IMF, pledged to lend to the Fund under GAB

[1] The forms used in this list may be found in E. T. Crowley and R. C. Thomas (eds) *Acronyms and Initialisms Dictionary* (Detroit: Gale Research Company; 4th ed., 1973).

IBRD or World Bank	International Bank for Reconstruction and Development
ICA	International Co-operation Administration
IDA	International Development Association
IDB	Inter-American Development Bank
IFC	International Finance Corporation
ILO	International Labour Organisation
IMF	International Monetary Fund
ITO	International Trade Organisation
LAFTA	Latin American Free Trade Association
MSA	Mutual Security Agency
NATO	North Atlantic Treaty Organisation
OECD	Organisation for European Co-operation and Development
OEEC	Organisation for European Economic Co-operation
OSA	Overseas Sterling Area
OPEC	Organisation of Petroleum Exporting Countries
RSA	Rest of the Sterling Area
SA	Sterling Area
SDR	Special Drawing Rights of the IMF
U.N.	United Nations
UNCTAD	United Nations Committee for Trade and Development

Except where it is otherwise indicated the words 'America' or 'American' in this book refer to the United States

Preface

This book reflects my belief that the history of the international economy is an essential supplement to the large body of theory which economists have in the last half-century provided to illuminate its working. The period selected for attention is the most interesting and dramatic, demonstrating the clash of nationalism with the realisation of the need for international co-operation and with the dispute between collectivism and private enterprise still unresolved. Any such book has to choose between a voluminous and detailed treatment at great length and an outline sketch which selects for attention the most fundamental influences. We have here chosen the latter route, keeping the narrative short and concise and confining the annotation mainly to bibliographical references.

I am indebted to my university for study leave and to the Social Sciences and Humanities Research Council of Canada for a grant of research funds. My wife has been helpful in ways too numerous to mention.

Hamilton, Ontario   W.M.S.
December 1979

ACKNOWLEDGEMENTS

The author and publishers wish to thank the Publications Board of the United Nations and the Controller of Her Majesty's Stationery Office for permission to quote from official sources.

While every effort has been made to locate owners of copyright, in some cases this has been unsuccessful. The publishers apologise for any infringement of copyright or failure to acknowledge original sources and will be glad to include any necessary acknowledgements in subsequent printings.

'Remember that what you are told is really threefold:
shaped by the teller, reshaped by the listener,
concealed from both by the dead man of the tale.'

NABOKOV

I
Introduction

'. . . there is no view except from a viewpoint and no
answers except to questions'.   GUNNAR MYRDAL

I

It is just over a hundred years since Bagehot, writing his *Lombard Street* and
looking out upon the world scene, drew attention to features which we now
recognise as distinctive of the modern international economy. In the forty
years which separate the publication of *Lombard Street* (1873) from the First
World War, the international economy established itself. As distance shrank
with the revolution in transport and communication, international trade
grew swiftly in volume. Financial services for payments and the mechanisms
of foreign exchange ramified. Loans and investment, both direct and
portfolio, moved with increasing ease along smooth channels from the affluent
savers of the old world to the risk-takers and entrepreneurs of the new. The
financial centres – London, Paris, Frankfurt, Amsterdam – became institutional nerve centres for an increasingly self-conscious international community. Gold, long recognised as a leading form of national money, became
established as an international unit of account and a vehicle for the holding of
reserves in world payments.

The international economy, in its modern form, is but a century old and
since its inception we have recognised problems which before its establishment either did not exist or existed only in such magnitude as not to demand
serious attention – problems of foreign balance adjustment, the choice of an
international monetary unit, the adaptation of monetary institutions to
changing conditions and the control or administration of the system from the
centre. These problems and others related to them have pressed upon us since
the international economy came to maturity.

This book is concerned with the most interesting and exciting years in the
record of the international economy, those between the end of the Second
World War and the end of the 1970s – thirty years of swift change,
intensification of strains and a growing realisation on the part of economists
and politicians that in the international, as in the national economy, there
must be control, policy and knowledge, if crisis is to be averted. This then is
the justification of choosing so short and so recent a period for study – that it
has shown a greater pace of economic change, that it has been more dramatic

in events, more formative in tendencies and more instructive in example than the seventy or so years which preceded.

Historical divisions are arbitrary but necessary. The period with which this book deals falls into three recognisably distinct periods: the years of recovery from the war, 1945 to 1955; the years of growth and comparative stability from 1955 to 1964; and what we may style the years of crisis, from 1964 on into the seventies. This division, the author would argue, is not only a necessary convenience, providing a form upon which to build a narrative, but is meaningful in itself as indicating the trend of development in the international economy over the whole period.

Across all historical studies of recent times the Second World War cuts its wide swathe, a great dividing-line. The old Europe and much of the rest of the world lay in ruins, its private and social capital devastated, its institutions shattered, its political and economic relationships destroyed. For the first and last time in modern economic history there was to be a fresh start in which the new could be planned without thought for the presence or vested interests of the old. The axis of power had shifted to the only major nation whose territory had not suffered damage and whose economy had been strengthened rather than weakened by war: to the United States. On a quickening, peace-oriented economy the United States had superimposed between 1941 and 1945 an efficient war economy which had enabled her to supply not only herself but her allies with war material. She emerged from the war dominant in economic power and political influence – a model for what other western nations believed they wished to achieve and their sole source of supply during the years of recovery.

The main source of weakness in the international economy was the scale of physical destruction. In Europe fighting had been more widespread than in the First World War and air bombardment had extended to every country except Spain and Sweden. Production and transport had seen great losses. Moreover, physical destruction did not stop at Europe. The Far East had had its share and Asiatic export surpluses were not available to Western countries. Apart from physical destruction, political disruption interfered with recovery in many countries. All this perverted the normal trade flows.

Confusion and discrimination in the real trade flows were reflected in the payments field. With the exception of the United States the ability of countries to export had been suspended and been replaced by a voracious appetite for imports both of capital and consumer goods. Of these the United States became the dominant supplier, thereby creating a massive surplus in its balance of payments. This surplus, constituting the first phase of the so-called dollar problem, dominates the period 1945–55. The traditional tools of balance-of-payments adjustment, exchange-rate variations or changes in relative prices, were useless in a world of acute physical shortages where prices meant little and where the price system as a measurement of relative values was in abeyance. It is with the policy measures devised to deal with this first phase of the dollar problem that we are mainly concerned in Part One of this book. Other matters will concern us, the changes in the distribution of national power, commercial policy and the period of unprecedented growth and prosperity which began in the middle fifties as the dollar shortage yielded to treatment.

One word aptly characterises the international economy in the period 1955 to 1964: growth. Indeed, these years were the apogee of postwar economic development where at a rate faster than in any earlier period for which figures are available the world got richer. Between 1938 and 1964 world national product increased by over 85 per cent; industrial production more than doubled. We must consider this growth of the developed economies in conjunction with the expansion of international trade which was complementary to it. In this period we move out of the shadow of the war and its confusions and new trends of development become discernible. Relative economic strengths change in the international economy, the dollar establishes itself as the leading key currency, new developments in commercial policy appear and economic integration on a regional basis becomes the planning vogue for the future. This is a period of excitement and abundant optimism. The old problems of reconstruction have been vanquished. Such problems as there are, are those of adjustment. In the buoyant atmosphere of prosperity and expansion anything seems possible.

The last period of this historical study, that from 1964 to 1980, has been a period of uncertainty and crisis. Changes began to occur which have not conformed to established patterns and experience but seem to indicate changes more fundamental than any which have taken place since the war. Thus a period, which began tranquilly enough with the main parameters known, has produced flux in which neither position, aim nor direction is easily discernible.

While the events of these years were many-faceted and sprang from a variety of causes, they lay mainly in the field of international finance and to give an account of them is to describe how the Bretton Woods system failed as an operational system, giving way after the Smithsonian Agreement of 1971 to a hybrid system, vestigial of Bretton Woods, bolstered up by a series of *ad hoc* arrangements some of which still obtain. To this ramshackle structure was administered the shock in 1973 of the oil crisis and of sharp rises in other primary commodity prices, bringing higher rates of price inflation in Western countries than had ever been experienced. The inflation problem compounded the balance-of-payments problem and, with the conjuncture of high rates of unemployment in the industrial countries, produced in 1974–5 the most menacing economic conditions since the Second World War. Although these problems were met without major disaster they were succeeded in the years 1975–9 by uneasy conditions. There is, it seems, to be no early or easy return to the buoyant growth and prosperity of the later fifties and the sixties.

Through all three periods, which we distinguish in this book, certain features have persisted which form a background to the march of other events. First among these has been the political division between East and West. As the Soviet Union and the United States became estranged and as the former country pulled under her influence Eastern European countries exhausted by the war and by German occupation, 'an iron curtain descended from the mid-Baltic to the Adriatic' cutting off trade and commercial intercourse between Eastern and Western Europe. This division did much to fashion the nature of economic events and the international economy. It led to American leadership in the West, to the American support of allies through the Marshall Plan and military and economic aid, to vast outlays on defence and defence-sponsored research and it held the Soviet Union aloof from the economic planning of the United Nations and its functional agencies.

A second divisive feature appeared more slowly but grew to a magnitude which at the close of our period can hardly be exaggerated. The decay and collapse of the old colonial world of the nineteenth century revealed in the post-Second-World-War period a large group of countries, augmented continually by new political creations, fermented by militant nationalism and assertive to produce the life-styles and living standards of the rich industrial countries. The acceptance of this dichotomy of rich and poor among the nations generated many economic problems which were to haunt the whole of the period – aid flows and development, tariffs and trade policy, currency and the role of the new countries in planning and moulding the future. The demand for a New International Economic Order is, as we write, the latest expression of this problem.

A third feature lay in an institutional change in the international economy which acquired great significance in these years. Even by the interwar period it was apparent that there existed, within the grouping of sovereign states, private corporations whose manufacturing, trading and financial interests cut right across national boundaries. Such corporations, while having been originally founded and operated in one country, had grown to acquire interests in many countries and to locate their functional activities in many centres. Often they were so large and diversified as to lose any original national allegiance. By the postwar period they had become so numerous and large as to constitute a group in trade and finance making them a force no longer to be ignored. They were now a force capable of challenging governments and of being a law unto themselves. Their financial transfers affected exchange rates; their placing and distribution of assets altered the aspect of capital movements; their decision-making was becoming a force influencing, and perhaps at variance with, the external policies of governments.

International finance will inevitably be an important part of our history and in this field two strands appear again and again. These, too, form part of our changing background. The first was the phenomenon of world inflation. Postwar growth had a cost which was the rise in world and national price levels by which it was accompanied – the creeping inflation of the fifties and sixties which in time was to creep no more, but to walk briskly and latterly, in the seventies, to run. Inflation became to the postwar world the elusive and all-pervasive economic problem which unemployment had been between the wars. The problem was tolerated. Whatever its causes it was generally regarded as a trade-off for growth and high employment and, at least until the seventies, a doubling of the price level every twenty years or so seemed a small price to pay. When, in the seventies, inflation rates in many industrial countries rose to 10 per cent and beyond and when asset values, money markets and financial institutions became unstable the trade-off argument is no longer tenable.

Finally, in the field of balance-of-payments policy we begin in 1945 with the dollar problem; we end in 1979 with a disequilibrium involving that currency, the key currency of the system. From 1945 to the mid-fifties the problem manifested itself as a chronic scarcity of that currency, a reflection of a great surplus in the U.S. balance of payments. From mid-fifties to 1971 the dollar acted as reserve currency and centre of the Bretton Woods system, but it was the growing deficit in the U.S. balance-of-payments which destroyed that system. The deficit still continues and to reconcile the economic policies of the United States as a deficit country and those of a group of powerful surplus countries, including Germany and Japan, is, as we write, the central dilemma in international payments.

In the chapters which follow, the main developments of this brief outline will be amplified and analysed. For the immediate postwar years there is ample material. The events of the forties and early fifties have already been documented by many writers and by the commentaries and reports of international organisations. As we come on to the sixties and seventies there is no lack of data or commentary but perspective becomes increasingly difficult to achieve. Writing now in the late seventies one sees events as incomplete, as the problems of one's own time. Their outcome is uncertain. They cease to be history but are the matter of current affairs. For this reason the account, as it approaches the present, will become more factual than analytic. That is the price we must pay for writing history too soon.

Part One
The Years of Recovery, 1945–55

2

International Economic Policies at the End of the Second World War

'things could be kept together by accepting the similarities, not the differences of men'. E. M. FORSTER in *The Longest Journey*

(i) THE BASIS FOR CO-OPERATION

The international situation in the summer of 1945 was unique in modern history; unique in that it gave to nations and to the world as a whole an opportunity for a completely new start. In certain fields, notably the economic, it was possible not only to reform international relations, but to start again virtually from scratch. This was the case with the international payments system, redrafted by the United States and Britain while the war was still in progress. In other fields changed relationships and relative strengths called for complete reassessment of policy aims and for different criteria of economic judgement. It is, therefore, a necessary preliminary of any examination of the postwar international economy to examine this problem of realignment.

Another unique feature of planning the new international order lay in the fact it was carried out dominantly by two governments, those of the United States and Britain, working to a plan which went back to the general statement of war aims known as the Atlantic Charter in early 1942. The growth of this plan and its ramifications need not concern us. It is sufficient to note that the Charter stated the intent 'to bring about the fullest collaboration between all nations in the economic field'. The political realities were approached when, in February 1942, Article 7 of the Mutual Aid Agreement committed Britain and the United States to international economic co-operation after the war and to embody in that co-operation two obligations, the freeing of trade and the pursuit of full employment.[1]

There were, of course, two reasons why these early economic manœuvres

---

[1] See Agreement between the United States and the United Kingdom, 23 February 1942, Article 7, Cmd 6391 of 1942.

were restricted to the Americans and British. First, these two countries led the allied group of what was later to be called the United Nations and were the only two countries within that group with any immediate control over their own destinies, the others being currently under German occupation and represented only by token governments in exile which were consulted more from courtesy than with any sense of political reality. Second, and apart from wartime co-operation as comrades in arms, the British/American relationship was clearly the focal point of future economic planning in the West. Upon agreement on certain key issues, yet to be defined, the stability of the postwar economy would depend. To this dual control of the economic planning operation there were some minor qualifications. The British had to cast a wary eye on the views of the larger and older Commonwealth countries such as Canada, Australia, New Zealand and India. Of these, Canada, already playing her now familiar role of honest broker in international relations, was watching Anglo-American relations and negotiations carefully; Australia, remote in the south Pacific, looked beyond the removal of the Japanese menace only to hope for full employment after the war; while India looked for political independence and, in the economic field, hoped for free and constructive use of the large sterling balances which she was acquiring during the war period. The United States, on the other hand, was unconstrained in pursuit of her economic policies. Emerging from a quarter-century of isolationism she had neither colonies nor allies to placate and in such relationships as might be important, such as that with Canada, she could rely on her great power and influence to prevail. The wartime negotiations between the United States and Britain (the Mutual Aid Agreement – including Article 7 – was signed on 23 February 1942) had produced no formidable difficulties. As long as negotiations were confined to principles there was a firm basis of common ground between the two countries which made the early negotiations easier than later when they moved to specifics. Both countries agreed that the confusion and national individualism which had marked the international economy of the thirties should not be repeated, that national self-interest, which had been the leitmotiv of the thirties, would have to be replaced by forms of international economic co-operation and that these forms would have to be innovated by the two leading Western nations. Moreover, it was agreed that in the Tripartite Monetary Agreement of 1936, which had ended the competitive exchange-rate manipulation of the early thirties, a useful start had been made to co-operation in the currency field and that this could serve as a basis for further international action. In a wider context co-operation would have to be extended into all fields of international economic affairs. There would have to be a fresh look at tariffs and at the new phenomenon of directly controlled trade which that brilliant villain Schacht had perfected for German use. There would have to be smoother flows of international investment to secure both stability and growth and not only would 'beggar-my-neighbour policies' have to cease but international machinery to prevent the transmission of unemployment from country to country would have to be pioneered. But all this, in 1942, lay far in the future.

Consider both sides of this partnership. In 1941 only eight years had elapsed since the United States withdrew from the London Economic Conference. Isolation and a back turned against the responsibilities of a creditor nation followed. Now there was to be a political *volte face*, a return not only to participation but to unprecedented leadership. To classify the complex web of motivation which underlay American policy at this time is impossible, but one may single out threads, traceable in these early negotiations and running through all later relations on economic matters.

First, the Americans conscious, of their wealth, their creditor position and the powerful bargaining levers which events had placed in their hands, held mixed views on the prospects of international economic co-operation. In essence it appealed to them for that tincture of idealism which captured the American mind. But power has other attractions than the pursuit of idealism and that it was usable to mould the world in the American image of *laissez faire* and that it was an advantage in pursuing old rivalries did not escape notice. Moreover, it was apparent that American assistance to her allies would be required on a great scale during the postwar period. The United States should not be the compliant donor for a host of squabbling mendicants. Her position meant that her will could settle all quarrels.

It is perhaps pertinent at this point to consider briefly wherein the great economic power of the United States lay in the immediate postwar years. In 1942 expectations of the American position in the international economy of the future hinged on two facts. First, it appeared certain that, when the war ended, the United States would be, for some considerable time, the dominant supplier of goods and money capital. Physical destruction in Europe made this inevitable. Second, was the knowledge that, while U.S. trade with the world was large absolutely, relative to the U.S. national income it was very small.[2] In short, while U.S. trade was of great importance to the world, the world was of slight importance to the United States. Domestic economic decisions had little or no connection with decisions in the foreign trade field. This was in sharp contrast with Britain, where all economic policy centred around British trading interests. The American situation compounded in British and European minds the fear of isolationism. The United States seemed to be emerging from isolationism. Fear that she might return to it was ever present and made her partners for many years compliant under that implicit threat.

Second, the Americans leaned at this time in the direction of freer trade. But it was a qualified free trade. To tariffs they had no aversion. But the incidence and application of barriers to trade were other matters. Discrimination and preference were, in the American mind, linked with

[2] The American economy accounts (at the time of writing) for 16 per cent of the world's trade and 42 per cent of world GNP, while U.S. trade equals only 4 per cent of U.S. GNP.

exchange control as engines of economic warfare. Hostility to them had been the text of Cordell Hull and his trade policies; now discrimination was symbolic of Hjalmar Schacht, Nazism and Anti-Semitism – things for the extirpation of which the war was being fought. Hostility to trade discrimination was perhaps the strongest American feeling in 1941. The Americans pressed the point of non-discrimination in world trade to the British in and out of season – in the discussions on the Atlantic Charter, in the Mutual Aid Agreement, in the Bretton Woods negotiations, in the Anglo-American Loan Agreement, in the negotiations for the establishment of an International Trade Organisation and through their influence on the policies and views of the General Agreement on Tariffs and Trade (GATT) and the International Monetary Fund (IMF). As with discrimination so was it with inconvertibility of currencies. American trade policy for the postwar period was clear: an immediate end to discrimination, gradual tariff reduction on the most-favoured-nation principle and, in the currency field, immediate restoration of multilateral trade with convertible currencies. Not only was this a reflection of belief in multilateral trade but a belief in the primacy of economic factors in international relations and, by 1941, a belief that the key to peace after the Second World War lay in economic order and economic planning in the international economy. With the American penchant for formal arrangements, this implied international organisations to regulate the main sectors of the international economy.

Third, American officials carried into all negotiations the traditional American distrust of banking and 'big money' interests. This mental attitude had in the past done much to shape America – to decentralise the American domestic banking system, turning the Federal Reserve into a twelve-headed hydra and dispersing commercial banking among thousands of small concerns. Now it was to influence the postwar financial institutions. Moreover, their activities and spheres of influence must be defined to the letter in written constitutions covering all contingencies.

Fourth, there was the ticklish question of American relations with Britain. The American attitude was made up of many strands. Initially, that is, in 1941 and 1942, there was great American admiration for Britain, for her fight against Germany in the face of air bombardment and military isolation, for her total war effort and determination to prevail. Moreover, in those years the personal relationship between Roosevelt and Churchill was in its high summer. Co-operation in war was as yet unsullied by wrangles over strategies or the precedence of objectives. But behind all this lay many other feelings and attitudes which would emerge with time. The crudest was a frank distrust by some influential Americans of Britain, of her policies, her attitudes and her capacity to rise again to the status of a great world power. Roosevelt was critical of her 'colonial' policies, Cordell Hull had long believed that in trade and general economic matters a special relationship with Britain was not only unnecessary but was to be avoided. White and others believed that in the postwar world, Russia would be the emergent power and in partnership between her and the United States, the future would be moulded. But Britain was there and for the moment the co-operative effort perforce must be with her and her alone.[3]

Lastly, there was one aspect of the American political scene pertinent to all who negotiated with the Americans: the fact that the administration was subject ever to the revisionary or annulling power of Congress. American negotiators were always aware of the limitations of their brief. Everything had to wear a good face before Congress. Foreign negotiators had to be aware that in making concessions they were not assured of a *quid pro quo* but had to be content with promises which might evaporate in practice.

The British approach to postwar economic problems was very different. It was shrewder, based more on political reality and far more flexible than the American. As a nation dependent upon foreign trade and as the only nation which, in the nineteenth century, had gone all the way to free trade, it was realised that when the war ended the country would face the most critical conditons in its history. It seemed probable that the structure of world trade, by which Britain had found equilibrium under a system of multilateral clearing and which had been deteriorating in the decade before 1939, would be destroyed by the war and the prospect of a general deficit in her overall external account was only surpassed in gloom by the threat of severe sectional deficits with particular countries, especially with the United States.

Side by side with a realisation of the foreign balance problem there was in Britain a determination that the prewar economic disease of involuntary unemployment should not reappear on the postwar scene. Keynesian economic teaching was achieving great popularity in Britain in the war years and with the desire to prevent unemployment was coupled the belief that we now possessed means to do this. There was, after 1940, a reversion from the frustrations and mistakes of the thirties, growing enthusiasm for active and positive policies and an end to the spiritless fatalism of governments. One feature of interwar Britain which shared in this rejection was the gold standard. At a popular level it was regarded as the creator of many woes, of flagging industries in the later twenties, unemployment in the thirties, even of the world depression itself; at a more sophisticated level, economists rejected it as a system of international adjustment.

Finally, British attitudes towards postwar monetary planning were conditioned by the characteristic British distaste for elaborate *a priori* planning or rigid systematic arrangements. British preference in 1941 was for a framework around which later arrangements might fructify; the American preference was for detailed planning and written constitutions.

Having assumed mutual postwar obligations it was now necessary for the

[3] Such naïve efforts as the Americans made to bring the Soviet Union into the postwar planning discussions were either rebuffed or ignored.

two governments to turn principle into practice and define the precise steps to implement Article 7. In an American memorandum, prepared probably in the spring of 1942, the following lines of action were laid down:[4]

1. An international organisation for maintenance of exchange stability and to deal with balance of payments problems.
2. An international organisation to deal with long-term international investment.
3. An international agreement on primary commodity price control.
4. International measures for the reduction of trade barriers.
5. The international organisation of relief and reconstruction, and
6. International measures to maintain full employment.

This comprehensive programme of international economic planning was to remain the basis of numerous initiatives during the next five years. As a structure it was never fully completed. Items 3 and 6 were not embodied in any institution, although efforts of various sorts were made. Items 1 and 2 came to fulfilment in the IMF and the International Bank for Reconstruction and Development (IBRD), while GATT partially met the requirements of 4 when the Havana Charter and the proposal for an International Trade Organisation failed. Item 5 brought the first operational organisation when the United Nations Relief and Rehabilitation Administration (UNRRA) was established in November 1943.

The history and problems of most of these organisations will be dealt with later. At this stage it is sufficient to note the form and strategy of postwar economic planning for the two main participants.

(ii)   BRETTON WOODS

The history of the negotiations which took place between the British and Americans between 1941 and 1944 and which led at Bretton Woods to the establishment of the IMF and the IBRD has already been written and it is

---

[4] See E. F. Penrose, *Economic Planning for the Peace* (Princeton, N.J.: Princeton University Press, 1953) pp. 39–40.
[5] The best account of these negotiations is to be found in R. Gardner's *Sterling–Dollar Diplomacy*, 2nd ed. (Oxford: Oxford University Press; New York: McGraw-Hill, 1969). An excellent recent book is Armand Van Dormael, *Bretton Woods: Birth of a Monetary System* (London: Macmillan, 1978). Briefer accounts are to be found in W. M. Scammell, *International Monetary Policy*, 2nd ed. (London: Macmillan, 1961) chs 5–8; and J. K. Horsefield, *The International Monetary Fund 1945–65* (Washington: I.M.F., 1969), vol. I: Chronicle, chs 1–6. R. F. Harrod, in his *Life of John Maynard Keynes* (London: Macmillan, 1951) chs XIII and XIV, provides an excellent account of the negotiations and interesting personal portraits of the main participants. Canadian aspects of the negotiations are dealt with in A. F. W. Plumptre, *Three Decades of Decision* (Toronto: McClelland & Stewart, 1977) chs 1–5.

unnecessary to repeat it here.[5] We shall be content to give the reader a brief account of such features of those events as is necessary to interpret later developments.

Although conforming to a wide and grandiose plan the institutions of the new economic order were created piecemeal. The Fund and Bank were planned and determined while the war was still in progress. The International Trade Organisation died stillborn and was replaced in 1948 by the more modest GATT. Side by side, in the political field, the United Nations Organisation emerged as a concert of the victorious powers and the economic institutions were grafted on to it as functional agencies, reporting to its Economic and Social Council, but in fact having virtual independence, each in its field. Looking back in 1950 the structure bore a family resemblance to the master plan but events, power changes and the come and go of personalities had altered many things, not least the fact that the Communist half of the world stood outside these arrangements. The split between East and West was the major reality from 1945 onwards.[6]

International currency planning began soon after the signing of the Mutual Aid Agreement (February 1942). It was based upon two documents, the American White Plan, whose author was Harry D. White; and the Clearing Union Proposal or Keynes Plan.[7] These plans had features in common but differed in certain important respects.

For the features in common: both provided for control of exchange rates by an international agency; both provided for supplementation of national stocks of international liquidity; both placed some supervisory powers in the hands of the agency in regard to national actions which might threaten international equilibrium; and both provided for a mechanism of multilateral clearing. Both took up the work of international monetary co-operation from the point where it had been interrupted by the war, moving from co-operation by treaty to co-operation through an international agency.

The Keynes Plan was the more ambitious, more daring in conception, of the plans. Thirty years ahead of its time, it anticipated the SDR plan accepted by the Bretton Woods powers and embodied in the Rio de Janeiro Agreement in 1968. A Clearing Union was to be established to administer a 'quantum of

[6] Only in the regional commissions of the United Nations, in particular in the Economic Commission for Europe (ECE) based in Geneva, did East and West face one another. Since the regional commissions were organisations designed to discuss and initiate policy only in the broadest terms, Soviet/Western posturing and bickering was of little practical consequence. ECE produced useful research material in its early years (when it was under the direction of Gunnar Myrdal), but declined into impotence and obscurity as the cold war became less bitter and as the functional agencies claimed most of the limelight.

[7] White was, in 1941, assistant to the Secretary of the Treasury, Henry Morgenthau. He became Assistant Secretary in January 1945, joined the Fund as U.S. Executive Director for a brief period and died in August 1948. Keynes was during the war years an Honorary Advisor to the British Treasury. He was chief British negotiator with the Americans on many matters, including Lend-Lease and the negotiations before and at Bretton Woods. He too did not survive to see the plans put to the test. He died in April 1946.

international currency'[8] suited in amount to the needs of world trade and capable of deliberate expansion and contraction in order to preserve an appropriate level of world effective demand. This quantum of world currency was to be the aggregate of a series of overdrafts in favour of the member countries, each country's maximum overdraft or quota being determined according to a stipulated formula. A member's quota with the Union would serve to supplement its own gold and currency reserves as a means of meeting deficits in its balance of payments. The most innovative aspect of the Clearing Union proposal was that it required no initial deposit of gold or currencies from its members. For the first time the principle of created fiat-money was to enter international finance. The quotas of members and the aggregate resources of the ·Union would be flexible, capable of being increased by agreement if the general level of prices were to rise or the volume of trade increase with the passage of time. Finally, as if such features as these were not sufficient to frighten the unimaginative or the faint-hearted, the total quotas of members was to be a large sum, far larger than the Americans cared to contemplate.

Such a plan was foredoomed to failure. Coming as it did from one of the mendicant nations, it was not surprising that it inspired American opposition and criticism. Not least, and certainly not without reason, the Americans argued that in the immediate postwar period the full blast of this international credit creation ($30 bln) would be turned upon their economy as other members used their credits to buy from them. In this likely event the U.S. economy would be exposed to considerable inflationary pressure. In any event the Americans had their own plan, and, in such a situation, who does not fight for the implementation of his plan simply because it is his own.

The White Plan was a sober, prosaic document[9] – its material presented in a form businesslike and direct. It showed a shrewd political sense in that it did not surpass the tolerance-limit of Congress or public opinion in the United States. It provided for the establishment of an 'international stabilisation fund with resources contributed by members according to quota' – paid partly in gold but dominantly in members' currencies. From this fund a member nation whose balance-of-payments was in deficit might purchase the currencies which were for the moment scarce to it, in exchange for its own. To such purchases a limit was set, but before the limit was reached, the member nation would be obliged to 'carry out measures recommended by the fund designed to correct the disequilibrium in the country's balance of payments'. There was to be no automatic supply of currencies, but in all cases the Fund was to have the right to place conditions upon the supply of currencies to deficit countries. Like the Clearing Union the Stabilisation Fund was to

[8] *Proposals for an International Clearing Union*, Cmd 6437 of 1943, p. 5 (London: H.M.S.O., 1943).
[9] The full title of the plan was 'A United States Proposal for a United and Associated Nations Stabilisation Fund'.

provide a pool of gold and currencies to augment national gold and currency reserves. Unlike the union, however, the Fund was to be the aggregate of member subscriptions and was capable of augmentation only by further subscriptions or borrowing from members. There was no credit element, no provision for creation of international liquidity.

It would be misleading, however, to brand the White Plan as conservative and unprogressive. In two respects it went beyond its rival. The first was that it was more militant on the subject of exchange rates. These were to be fixed by the fund in its own currency dealings and were to be changed 'only when essential to a correction of a fundamental disequilibrium and be permitted only with the approval of four-fifths of member votes'. This view reflected an American attitude on exchange-rate management much sterner than the British. Throughout the 1943–4 negotiations Washington pressed for a rigid international management of exchange rates denying the right of any country to change its exchange rate unilaterally. A second interesting feature of the White Plan was the section which proposed a means of liquidating the blocked sterling balances which had accumulated during the war as a result of Britain's necessity to obtain primary commodities, equipment and services from certain countries. In attempting, at such an early stage, to devise means of dealing with this problem, White showed great shrewdness and rare appreciation of the sort of currency problems which would have to be met when the war ended. Had such a proposal been adopted and acted upon it would greatly have assisted Britain in the immediate postwar period while it would have brought the IMF into the centre of postwar currency discussion in a period when, for a variety of reasons, it was relegated to relative obscurity.

Last but not least, the White Plan was typically American in that it prescribed for the Fund a board of directors each of whom was to be appointed by a member government. In the taking of major decisions the voting power of the directors was to be proportional to the size of their country's quota and, under the formula suggested, the power of the United States would be preponderant. It required little foresight to see that, if the Fund were located in the United States, the American directors, conscious always of their government's watchful eye, would discharge their duties with vigilance and use their large block vote to good (American) purpose. Couple this with the close scrutiny to which members' demands for accommodation were to be subjected and it will be clear that from the outset the international character of the fund was in jeopardy. In contrast to all this, Keynes had envisaged his Clearing Union as managed by a non-political, economic and financial intelligentsia – not full time, not resident in the Fund's place of location. The Union was to be much more a functional than a political organisation.

It was on the basis of an amended White Plan that one year later at Bretton Woods (July 1944) the IMF and the International Bank for Reconstruction and Development were established. The IBRD, or World Bank, was an

American initiative reaching back to 1942, but refurbished and reduced in scale for British approval and Congressional acceptance. Its role of supplying development project loans was specific and less controversial than that of the Fund and its inclusion as the second 'Bretton Woods twin' was regarded as at worst innocuous and at best desirable. The Fund was the more interesting twin, for around it was implicit a payments system which it was hoped would replace either the gold standard or the confusion of the thirties which had followed the breakdown of that system. In fact, the Bretton Woods system in its essentials was to endure for a quarter of a century and its monetary relationships and political motivations will be a continual preoccupation in the monetary discussions of this book.

On 27 December 1945 the IMF and the World Bank were formally established at a signing ceremony in Washington attended by thirty countries. This ceremony marked in many senses a climacteric. It was the end of the golden period of Anglo-American economic co-operation. It was peace at last and from the singleness of purpose created by war had been wrought foundations on which the new international economy might be built. While the builders had had their differences about the structure, there had been sufficient common ground on which to build. At least the achievements outweighed the defects and discrepancies.

This then is where our story of the international economy in the postwar period must begin. With our long perspective it is easy to see the harsh new realities which were soon to present themselves: the intensified American drive to achieve its economic objectives, impelled by the new Truman Administration; the weakness of the British economy to live up to its newly assumed obligations; all this against the background of deepening division between East and West. In December 1945 one feature was, however, dominant: the reality of American economic power. This, for better or worse, would be the formative influence of the next decade.

3

The International Monetary System: Imbalance and Recovery

(i) INTRODUCTION

The international payments system between 1945 and 1955 was dominated by what quickly came to be called 'the dollar problem'. Sir Dennis Robertson, writing in 1954, defined it as 'a persistent tendency on the part of the populations of the world outside North America to spend more in that region than the sum of what they are earning in that region and what the inhabitants of that region are disposed to lend to them or invest in their borders under the play of ordinary economic motive. The symptoms of the disease are a continuous pressure on the monetary reserves of the extra-North American countries. . . .'[1]

Although the United States, by reason of its wealth and growth, developed an export surplus at an early stage in its nationhood (*circa* 1874), and although it became a creditor nation in 1918, this did not in itself precipitate a dollar problem. During the interwar period means existed whereby the U.S. surplus could be accommodated in the world payments system. It was in part the removal of such means as a result of the Second World War which left us with the problem. Thus the full impact of a developing structural change in world trade was suddenly and rudely thrust upon us.[2] To this structural imbalance was added by 1945 the effects of the war itself.

From 1945 until the middle fifties the dollar problem was acute and continuous. It may conveniently be divided into three phases: the years of immediate postwar reconstruction from 1945 to mid-1948, when the problem was most acute; the years of the European Recovery Programme (1948–52), when the problem was being met by a flow of dollars from the United States and when internal economic stability was being restored in the deficit countries; and the years from 1953 to 1955 when the dollar shortage was

---

[1] See *Britain in the World Economy* (London: Allen & Unwin, 1954) p. 53.

[2] One factor thought to have been at work in the payments relation of Europe and the United States before the Second World War was the relative decline in the economic importance of the former. Europe's share of world export trade shrank from more than 50 per cent before the First World War to about 45 per cent in the interwar period and 35 per cent in the years 1948–50. See I. Svennilson, *Growth and Stagnation in the European Economy* (Geneva: United Nations, 1954).

TABLE 3.1

Balance of Payments of the United States, 1947–55

($ bln)

	1947	1948	1949	1950	1951	1952	1953	1954	1955
Exports of goods and services[1]	19.7	17.1	16.0	14.4	20.3	20.7	21.3	20.8	21.8
Imports of goods and services	8.2	10.3	9.7	12.1	15.1	15.7	16.4	15.8	17.6
Balance on goods and services	+ 11.5	+ 6.8	+ 6.3	+ 2.3	+ 5.2	+ 5.0	+ 4.9	+ 5.0	+ 4.2
Unilateral transfers to foreign countries (net)[2]	− 2.7	− 4.8	− 5.8	− 4.5	− 5.0	− 5.1	− 6.7	− 5.3	− 4.6
Balance on goods, services and transfers	+ 8.8	+ 2.0	+ 0.5	− 2.2	+ 0.2	− 0.1	− 1.8	− 0.3	− 0.4
U.S. capital: net outflow of funds (−)	− 8.0	− 1.9	− 1.2	− 1.4	− 1.2	− 1.6	− 0.6	− 1.4	− 1.2
Foreign capital: net outflow of funds (−)	+ 0.2	+ 0.35	+ 0.7	+ 1.9	+ 0.6	+ 1.6	+ 1.1	+ 1.4	+ 1.5
Gold sales (+) or purchases (−)	− 2.1	− 1.5	− 0.2	+ 1.7	− 0.05	− 0.4	+ 1.2	+ 0.3	+ 0.04
Total	− 9.9	− 3.05	− 0.7	+ 2.2	− 0.65	+ 0.4	+ 1.7	+ 0.3	+ 0.34
Errors and omissions	+ 1.1	+ 1.05	+ 0.2	−	+ 0.45	+ 0.5	+ 0.1	−	+ 0.06

[1] Including military transfers under aid programmes.
[2] Including private remittances and government payments for military supplies and services.

Source: U.S. Department of Commerce and *Survey of Current Business* (Mar 1956).

diminishing, before reversing itself to create a different sort of dollar problem in the sixties and seventies. This historical division of the dollar problem is arbitrary, but it serves as a basis for what follows.

Before going on to discussion, we must outline the magnitude of the dollar problem to 1955. Table 3.1 shows the balance of payments of the United States with the rest of the world during the years 1947–55. Table 3.2 shows how the dollar deficit of the non-dollar world was financed during the most acute phase of the problem.

TABLE 3.2
Financing of Dollar Deficit, 1946–9
(*$ bln*)

	1946	1947	1948	1949
Overall balance of United States on current account	+7.8	+11.5	+6.8	+6.3
Means of financing:				
U.S. Government grants	−2.2	− 1.9	−4.2	−5.3
U.S. Government loans	−2.7	− 3.9	−0.9	−0.6
U.S. private gifts	−0.7	− 0.7	−0.7	−0.5
U.S. private capital	−0.4	− 0.8	−0.9	−0.6
International Bank	0.0	− 0.3	−0.2	−0.04
International Monetary Fund	0.0	− 0.5	−0.2	−0.1
Foreign gold and dollar assets	−1.9	− 4.5	−0.8	0.0
Total	−7.9	−12.6	−7.9	−7.2
Errors and omissions	+0.1	+ 1.1	+1.1	+0.9

Source: U.S. Department of Commerce, *The Balance of Payments in the United States 1946–8, 1949–51* and *Survey of Current Business*, (Mar 1950).

(ii) THE FIRST DOLLAR PROBLEM, 1945–8

Few countries in the world escaped the economic effects of the Second World War. In the combat zones there were checks to production and destruction of private and social capital. With shifts in the location of world production went shifts in the pattern of trade. No country, not even the neutrals, escaped the price inflation which accompanied and followed the war.

Of the shifts in production and trade the most dramatic were those which favoured the United States. By the war's end more than half of the world's manufacturing and a third of the world's production of all goods were centred in the United States. In spite of shipping losses during the war the world total of merchant tonnage had risen by 6 per cent and the United States owned half of the total as compared with 14 per cent in 1939. By 1947 the United

States was providing a third of world exports but taking only a tenth of world imports.[3]

Inflation rates differed widely. Comparing price levels of late-1945 or 1946 with those of 1938 or 1939, rises of only 30–45 per cent were recorded for Canada, the United States, Australia, South Africa and Venezuela. Rises of 50–100 per cent occurred in Britain, New Zealand, Norway, Sweden, Denmark, Argentina and Switzerland; of 200–600 per cent in Finland, France, Holland, Portugal, Spain, Belgium, Czechoslovakia, Chile, Paraguay, Brazil, Bolivia, India, Egypt and Turkey. Spectacular rises of 10-fold occurred in Japan and Lebanon and 25-fold in Italy. In Hungary, Greece, China and Romania price levels passed out of control into hyperinflation. The German currency collapsed and the monetary system was virtually in abeyance until the currency reform in 1948. In 1946 the postwar inflation was by no means over. At varying, but generally much lower, rates it continued into the fifties and sixties.

The years 1946 and 1947 were periods of extreme difficulty and confusion. Fighting, particularly in Europe, had been widespread; aerial bombardment, again in Europe, had been continual. In Greece, fighting and civil war outlived the larger conflict. In many Far-Eastern countries liberated from the Japanese, Burma, Indo-China, Malaya and Indonesia, new wars or revolutions prevented a return to peaceful production. To the destruction of factories and transportation systems in industrial Europe was added the effects of arrears of maintenance, the destruction or running down of inventories, the dispersal of workers and technicians, the lapse of research and development, and the breakdown of trade and financial relationships. A painful beginning to reconstruction in 1946 ran into new difficulties in 1947. An exceptionally severe winter in Europe revealed serious shortfalls in fuel and energy supplies. Transport bottlenecks contributed to the winter misery and crop failures followed the drought of summer. Nor was trade faring any better than production. Exchange rates and prices had little effect in a world where physical procurement and survival were dominants. To conserve small reserves of gold and dollars was the main aim of the exchange-control systems set up by import-hungry countries. The bilateral trade agreements which ramified during this period could only cater for minimal trade volumes. They provided no basis for expansion.

Europe was the hub of the problem. Not only did lagging production retard the resumption of trade, but trade patterns reaching back to the nineteenth century and the industrial revolution were warped by the political cleavage between East and West. Before the war Western Europe had had a large import surplus from Eastern Europe – an import surplus greatly increased in the late thirties by Nazi economic policies towards Hungary, Romania and the Balkans. In 1947 the imports of Western European countries (other than

[3] See *18th Annual Report of the Bank for International Settlements, 1947–8*, p. 15.

Germany) from the Soviet Union were only 16 per cent (by volume) of 1938, and from other East European countries only 50 per cent. The Soviet Union took only half the exports of 1938 and the rest of Eastern Europe only 75 per cent. The effect of restricted trade between Western and Eastern Europe was to balance such trade but at a low level. The import surplus had disappeared and thereby increased European dependence upon the United States.

By 1947 the seventeen countries of Western Europe, later to form the Organisation for European Economic Co-operation (OEEC), had pushed their index of GNP at constant prices to 93 per cent of its 1938 level. Consumption and investment outlays at \$148 bln were \$7 bln in excess of the value of aggregate production. This \$7 bln almost exactly matched the European deficit on current account. A cut in domestic absorption of approximately \$7 bln would, it seems, have brought Western Europe near to external balance.

In the economic and political climate of the times even such a small reduction in absorption was not feasible. To adjust what seemed at the time to be the greatest trade imbalance in recorded history by checking the production of impoverished countries to suit the simple macroeconomic equations was unthinkable.[4] In order to achieve the required average reduction of 5 per cent, some countries, such as Germany, Italy, France and Greece, would have had to check production levels which were low and slow to recover, while others, such as the Scandinavian countries, which had already passed their prewar levels of production, would have suffered no great hardship. A second objection to the simple macro method of reducing the deficit lay in the fact that it provided only a partial solution, even if countries agreed to use it. To follow it, it would have been necessary to remove controls on prices, both domestic price controls, which almost certainly were bottling up inflation rates much higher than the indices of prices suggested, and exchange rates, which were in most cases polite fictions, giving no real indication of relative costs. To have removed these controls in 1946 and 1947 would have caused a massive redistribution of real income among populations, offending against ideas of social justice and equality running high at the time. Moreover, to end external controls and allow exchange rates to find new levels would probably have intensified inflation as inelastic import demand at devalued exchange rates passed its effect to domestic prices. Finally, it is arguable that adjustment of the deficit via reduced absorption and resort to the price system would, with so many physical rigidities and bottlenecks, have been unworkable in the confused conditions of the immediate postwar period. The year 1947 was horrendous, the nadir of European economic fortunes. It would have been a brave follower of price

---

[4] It was not unthinkable for some groups and for critics of loans and aid programmes in the United States, who questioned the failure of European countries to reduce the pace of their economies, and the propensity of some, particularly Britain, to expand domestic absorption in the form of government outlays on social programmes rather than to contract it.

and income adjustment who would have chosen that year to test the working of his policy weapons. The route by which, over seven or eight years, Europe stumbled to recovery and external balance was quite different than by planned use of policy weapons. In the first phase, from 1945 to early 1948, the aim was survival without disaster, the latter being seen as mass-unemployment, hyperinflation or even bloody revolution. The three-pronged defence was tight domestic controls,[5] bilateral trading and exchange control and a meagre flow of American aid. In the second phase, from 1948 to 1950, with production in most Western European countries higher than in 1939, balance-of-payments deficits were met by the more ample and methodical assistance given under the Marshall Plan, and from 1949 onwards to the mid-fifties as the dollar shortage subsided, revisions of exchange rates, the freeing and widening of international trade and tighter monetary disciplines in domestic policies ended the dollar shortage.

Thus far we have been concerned with the dollar shortage on the European side. Let us retrace our steps to 1945 and take up the story on the western side of the Atlantic.

The Americans, like the British, had been aware that the long-term monetary plans, finalised at Bretton Woods in July 1944, would not be sufficient in themselves to handle the payments problems which would follow the war. The two countries differed, however, in their assessment of the scale of the problem; the British believing that the period of recovery and reconstruction, particularly for their own country, would be long and arduous; the Americans believing that, after a transition period during which loans and temporary accommodating arrangements would suffice, the new Bretton Woods arrangements could take up the strain for the longer haul. The British, while believing in Bretton Woods, approached problems in piecemeal fashion; the Americans thought in terms of a steadily unfolding plan from which there need be few deviations. Central to their design was the need for an early return to multilateral trade.

We take up the tale of European payments problems with Britain, their storm-centre, during the war itself. During the first two years of war, while American supplies of arms were, under the Neutrality Act, available only on a cash-and-carry basis, Britain had paid $6 bln in cash on imports from the United States, thereby reducing her exchange reserves from about $4 bln virtually to vanishing-point. From the American entry into the war, and under the Mutual Aid Agreement, Britain received from the United States about $27 bln worth of Lend-Lease supplies giving 'Lend-Lease in reverse' of about $6 bln. This huge assistance kept the British balance-of-payments problem in abeyance during the war years, but the very dependence of the country upon such supplies could only increase British anxiety as to what

---

[5] Domestic controls consisted of food and consumer-goods rationing, capital-investment controls and price controls and subsidies, combined, in many cases, with high taxation.

would happen when the flow ceased and Britain was forced to rely on ordinary commercial external earnings.

The most difficult aspect of Lend-Lease administration for the British thus lay in the duration of the programme. Its late beginning and its uncertain tenure were both causes of disquiet. By 1942, when the programme began, the British had already been at war three years, during which they had exhausted their reserves and sustained considerable war damage. It would be an exaggeration to say that the British demanded compensation for these lone years, but it was arguable, they felt, that Roosevelt's 'equality of sacrifice' principle implied that some part of Lend-Lease should be regarded as retrospective to cover outlays in those years. This the Americans refused to concede, probably because it would have been impossible to justify such beneficence before Congress. Congress began to make a sharp distinction between the war itself and the reconstruction period which would follow. It was felt that Congress had had insufficient control over Lend-Lease, for the administration of which they had given a blanket approval to the executive. This mistake would not be made when it came to money granted for postwar reconstruction. There was to be no blurring of the distinction between Lend-Lease and postwar relief. On 19 August 1945, immediately after the capitulation of Japan, it was announced in Washington that Lend-Lease had been stopped. From now onwards Britain would have to pay for all supplies, including those already in the pipeline. The dollar shortage in its most acute form had begun.

The cessation of Lend-Lease posed grim questions for the British. The massive tasks of re-equipping British industry and repairing and renewing social capital all lay ahead. Now it was clear that to maintain a level of imports sufficient to meet these requirements from the only country capable of supplying them was impossible. With the then level of exchange reserves, imports could only be sustained for a few weeks. The alternative was, at best, intensified rationing, chronic scarcity, unemployment, and inflation; at worst, all these plus social unrest and political crisis. Nor would there be any chance of honouring the British commitment to the United States to establish multilateral trade. It seemed probable that Britain's external affairs would remain for a long time locked in a clamp of exchange control and Schachtian direction. Some there were in Britain[6] who would have opted for the 'siege economy' but to the Government, still more to Keynes at the Treasury, the solution was plain: to ask the American Government for a massive accommodation loan to tide over the reconstruction period.

The story of the negotiating of the Anglo-American Loan has been told elsewhere.[7] We need not repeat it. We are concerned with certain features of

---

[6] A group on the left-wing of the Labour Party and a mixed body of uninformed opinion who denied the need for American assistance, either because it was American or because they denied the need.

[7] Harrod, op. cit. pp. 586–623 and Gardner, op. cit. pp. 188–207.

the final agreement which had a profound influence upon events in the payments field in the years which were to follow.

After weeks of hard bargaining the Anglo-American Loan Agreement was signed on 6 December 1945. It provided for a line of credit of $3.75 bln to be drawn upon between the effective date of the agreement[8] and the end of 1951. Interest was to be levied at 2 per cent and repayment was to be in fifty annual instalments beginning 31 December 1951.[9] In respect of size and burden of repayment the loan fell short of British hopes and expectations, but was, in fact, with the aid of a loan of $1287 m. from Canada, not inadequate in relation to the needs for which it was intended.[10]

Two features of the Loan Agreement claim our attention. The first was the political 'strings' woven into the agreement; the second was the attitude of the Americans to the so-called sterling balances, their appreciation of this problem and their anxiety to take them away from Britain and into the wider forum of international manipulation. In the first of these features the Americans showed themselves as doctrinaire, short-sighted and incapable of relating a long-term aim to the confusion of immediate events. For their lack of judgement, Britain, in particular, and Europe and the world at large paid a heavy price. In the second feature the roles were reversed. It was Britain who insisted that the sterling balances were a British and Commonwealth problem outside the scope or jurisdiction of the United States. The Americans instinctively felt that this great weight of quick capital liabilities was a millstone which the British economy could not carry. Their attitude was economically sane, enlightened and generous. But it was in vain. The British, for several reasons, most of them wrongheaded, wished to solve their problem in their own way. It remained a problem which retarded their recovery.

The political strings to the Loan Agreement were the reaffirmation of Article 7 undertaking to collaborate with the Americans in the re-establishment of multilateral trade. All of the Bretton Woods negotiations had been based upon this assumption and had been acceptable to the British, partly because in principle they accepted it, but also because under the Bretton Woods Agreement, five years were to elapse before there was pressure to implement it. The Americans took a stricter view. To them multilateral trade, freedom from exchange control, an end to discrimination and bilateral agreements, was the primary purpose of that agreement. It had been accepted by Congress on those terms. There must be no backsliding by the wily British

---

[8] Later established as 15 July 1946.

[9] See *Financial Agreement Between the Governments of the United States and the United Kingdom*, 6 Dec 1945. Cmd 6708 of 1945 (London: H.M.S.O., 1945).

[10] Together the American and Canadian loans provided Britain with dollar credits amounting to $5037 m. It is interesting to note that the total British adverse balance of payments on current account for 1946, 1947 and 1948 was $4554 m. The inadequacy of the loan to meet the events of 1946–7 was, of course, due to (*a*) the looseness of certain sterling area financial arrangements which threw upon the loan the burden of dollar deficit for the wider sterling area, and (*b*) the liquidation of part of the sterling liabilities imposed on Britain by borrowing during the war.

who now were pleading that their temporary difficulties might delay this freedom, in particular, that their currency might have to remain inconvertible for years. The Americans were irritated by the British approach. They lacked any public understanding or congressional base from which to negotiate further aid to Britain than Lend-Lease had afforded. Moreover, the death of Roosevelt, the new-look of the Truman Administration, the end of Lend-Lease differently interpreted in the two countries, the inexperience of the new Labour Government in Britain and the pressing need of the British to act quickly – all these provided a negotiating atmosphere fertile in disagreement, and misunderstanding.

The political strings were drawn tight. The multilateral obligations of the Loan Agreement were much more exacting than those in the Bretton Woods Agreement. The provision concerning the current transactions of the sterling-area countries provided that:

> The Government of the United Kingdom will complete arrangements as early as practicable and in any case not later than one year after the effective date of this Agreement . . . under which . . . sterling receipts from current transactions of all sterling area countries will be freely available for current transactions in any currency area without discrimination.[11]

Thus the transitional period of five years granted in the Bretton Woods Agreement, during which Britain might adjust her balance of payments to assume the obligations of full sterling convertibility, was reduced at a stroke to one year. Moreover, the clause was not only aimed at attaining free convertibility of current sterling in the exchange markets, but was directed at the dollar pool of the whole sterling area. This was, in American eyes, an engine of discrimination against American exports inasmuch as sterling-area countries were required to deposit dollar earnings in London and any use of the dollar pool on their part to acquire U.S. goods was viewed askance by the British authorities.

The American pressure to make sterling convertible within one year of the first British drawing on the loan was seen by the American officials as a logical extension of their cut-and-dried arrangements for the postwar world. It showed a complete failure to grasp the economic implications of basing an international currency on a crippled economy. With no early prospect of even balancing her external accounts Britain was to be forced to make her own currency convertible into dollars. The currencies which she herself earned in third currencies would probably remain inconvertible and of little use to purchase the imports which she required. The sterling earned by third countries, on the other hand, would quickly be converted into dollars to

[11] See Article 7, Cmd 6708 of 1945, op. cit.

finance third-country imports from the United States. Britain would become the funnel through which would flow the demand of half the industrial world for dollars.

The convertibility undertaking was intended to apply only to sterling earned in current transactions. It was supposed that the great sum of sterling balances, swollen by the transactions of the war years, could be insulated and held in abeyance for separate treatment. But a suspicion remained that, in some way, illegal capital transfer might occur and a protection against such a contingency was provided in clause 8 of the agreement. Under Article 8 (ii)a postponement of convertibility to a later date might be sought; under Article 8 (ii)b convertibility could be suspended at any time during the Fund's transitional period. This latter option was, of course, invoked by the British in August 1947 when the convertibility experiment failed.

We turn now to the question of the so-called sterling balances. In June 1945 these amounted to £3355 m. of which £3052 m. were composed of net banking liabilities and funds held in Britain as cover for overseas currencies. Of the total, £2723 m. was owing to the overseas sterling area; £632 m. to North and South America and the rest of the world. Since total quick liabilities in August 1939 had amounted to only £476 m., the accumulation of short-term debt (of £2879 m.) was dominantly the result of the war.

The American demand was that the British should accept in the Loan Agreement a specific undertaking to freeze her sterling debts by a given date thus making it impossible to use the Loan proceeds to liquidate them. Another suggestion was that the United States should join with the British in negotiations with the sterling balance holders and that the United States should shoulder part of the cost of immediate releases in return for a substantial reduction in the balances. But the British would have none of this. Their attitude was simple: the sterling balances were a British problem, which they should be left to handle in their own way. They argued that American participation or any arrangement with the Americans would tie their hands in the negotiations which would soon take place with sterling balance holders. Ultimately a compromise was reached, clause 10 of the Agreement laying down that the sterling balances would be divided into three categories: some to be released at once and made convertible into any currency for current transactions; some to be released over a period beginning in 1951 and some to be written off. There were no declared figures for this division. Clause 10, in fact, embodied American wishes but provided no specific machinery for carrying them out.

On 6 December 1945 the Loan Agreement was signed. Later the same month the Bretton Woods Agreement was ratified by the United States, Britain and other participants. The framework of the postwar monetary system was complete. It was a ramshackle framework, but as 1946 began, there was no alternative but to live with it. The negotiators on both sides had their qualms. It would certainly have darkened their thoughts had they known that multilateral trade, the great purpose of the Agreement, was still fourteen years away and that the path to it would be impeded by the wreckage of their Agreement.

The story of the wreck can be quickly told. Britain the one country and sterling the one currency around which a multilateral payments system had to be built bravely attempted to honour her obligation of convertibility within one year. In one thing at least the Americans had been right: it was around sterling that multilateral recovery had to be built.

The final step towards sterling convertibility was taken in February 1947 when the sterling earned by Transferable Account countries[12] was made fully convertible into dollars. Moreover, between February and 15 July, an increasing number of countries was placed on the Transferable Account list. By 15 July 1947 sterling was fully convertible for current transactions within the dollar area, the sterling area and much of Western Europe.[13]

The results of this freedom were immediate. Between spring and autumn a payments crisis exhausted the loan, shattered the American objective of multilateralism and profoundly changed the nature and prospects of the Bretton Woods system. Like many such crises, the onset was swift and to some extent unforeseen. The year 1946 had been one of good recovery. By May 1946 British exports had passed the prewar level and by the year's end they were running 11 per cent above. The external deficit was £344 m., well below the estimate made by the British negotiators at Washington in the Loan negotiations. But the real nature of the dollar shortage had yet to declare itself. In company with most of Western Europe, Britain's main source of supply was the United States, from which she was importing heavily. Despite the better-than-expected balance of payments, drawings on the Loan were high.[14] Imports from non-dollar sources were low simply because such sources could not supply needed materials. At the same time much of the rise in British exports was to non-dollar countries in return for inconvertible currencies. The overall deficit was therefore a faulty indicator of payments recovery. The dollar deficit was the real key to the deteriorating external position. For 1947 the dollar deficit of the sterling area as a whole exceeded $4 bln. By mid-1947 $2050 m. of the Loan ($3.75 bln) had been drawn. Its exhaustion by the end of the year seemed certain.

The second source of payments disaster was, however, the loan condition of convertibility. In making a series of agreements with holders of sterling balances outside the sterling area and including these balances in the system

---

[12] Transferable Account countries were those within which the British exchange-control system might use sterling earned in current transactions for settlement with one another.

[13] The only exceptions to general current account convertibility on 15 July were a few countries (e.g. China, Greece and Hungary) where political conditions made it difficult to negotiate suitable agreements.

[14] $600 m. in 1946. See *U.K. Balance of Payments, 1946 to 1950*, Cmd 8065 of 1950 (London: H.M.S.O., 1950).

of Transferable Accounts, great reliance had been placed upon the competence and integrity of the monetary authorities of these countries, who were to regard only currently earned sterling as convertible into dollars. What actually happened is obscure, but it may be inferred from the statistics. Before convertibility in late 1946, the monthly dollar drain was $75 m.; up to June 1947, the monthly drain was $315 m.; at 15 July, the due date of convertibility, it was $498 m. and in the last three weeks of convertibility in August it was $650 m. Through the funnel of sterling, the proceeds of the loan were conducted to a dollar-hungry world, in return for sterling, both currently earned and formerly accumulated. On 20 August 1947 the British Government suspended convertibility.

The failure of convertibility had, in the longer view, two facets: its effect on the American drive for multilateral trade and the establishment of the Bretton Woods sort of world; and the narrower question of the effect of the experiment on British postwar recovery. Of the first, there can be no doubt. By overplaying their hand and forcing sterling convertibility at too early a stage of British recovery, the Americans created a situation in which after one failure the British were not prepared to risk a second. As to the effects of the convertibility crisis on British economic recovery, it is difficult to be precise. Certainly the loan was partly squandered in conversions of capital-account sterling and to that extent was not available to finance much-needed imports. But the fact was that in 1947 Britain would, even without convertibility, have seen the trough of her postwar fortunes and, even with the interest-free loan with no political strings which Keynes had sought, would have been in difficulties. But it must be remembered that, by late 1947, the Marshall Plan was already in the making. Without the capital drawings on the loan,[15] it might well have been possible for Britain to have covered current-account conversions up to the beginning of Marshall Aid.

(iii)   THE MARSHALL PLAN, 1948–52

The history of the various means whereby the postwar dollar problem was met is largely a history of American realisation of the dimensions of the problem. At first it was thought that a series of stabilisation and reconstruction loans, similar to those made after the First World War, would be sufficient to augment the Bretton Woods organisations. If these loans could carry political conditions which would strengthen the American drive for multilateral trade, so much the better. As it became apparent that the payments problem was formidable, and as it became intertwined with new political

---

[15] By 20 August 1947 $3.35 bln of the $3.75 bln total had been drawn. Of these drawings $410 m. were estimated to be for conversions of capital account sterling. See *The Banker*, Oct 1947, p. 15.

situations, the U.S. Government changed the nature and scale of its assistance and embarked upon the European Recovery Programme.

As has so often been the case in recent history, different departments of government in the United States were, in early 1947, pursuing different policies. While the Treasury, under the secretaryship of John Snyder, was impelling full British compliance with the convertibility requirements of the Loan Agreement, the wider-viewing State Department under George Marshall and his under-secretary, Dean Acheson, was assessing the European political and economic scene with that realism of which the Americans are capable in crisis, and which is perhaps their greatest political strength. The turning-point was a visit to Europe in the early weeks of 1947 by Will Clayton, Assistant Secretary of State for Economic Affairs. He saw Europe at the depth of her fortunes. He assessed Britain's prospects and found them grim. With Communist parties strong in France and Italy, Germany still in ruins, there was a power vacuum which could only be filled by the United States or Russia. Russia filling the vacuum would inevitably mean war.

American action was prompt. President Truman requested immediate economic and military aid of $400 m. for Greece and Turkey and in doing so personally enunciated what came to be called the Truman Doctrine. While couched in high-sounding generalities, the thrust of the doctrine was clear. It faced the political realities inherent in the economic weakness of uncommitted countries, it pledged the United States to economic aid to such countries and it linked that economic aid to the necessities of the Cold War. The doctrine was a watershed in American foreign policy, economic, political and military, and it rested on decisions taken in Washington months before sterling convertibility (15 July 1947) and the British payments crisis which followed it. The Marshall speech at Harvard which ushered in the European Recovery Programme was made on 5 June. The new approach was launched even before the old approach had been shown to have failed.

It has been necessary to make this slight detour into political history to lay by the heels the prevalent and oft-repeated assertion that the Marshall Plan was an act of magnificent philanthropy, a mighty enlargement of the principle of aid for reconstruction and recovery which had been the purpose of the stabilisation loans. It was indeed that, but it was much more. It was the price to the United States of building a ring of containment to Soviet territorial ambition. To describe it as such in no way denigrates it, but places it in correct perspective.

Marshall's speech at Harvard implied a new American realisation of the scale of the problem. It promised help adequate to that scale and it did so on the condition that Europe itself work out the detailed plan of needs and the means of achieving them. At one stroke it took the weight off the older organisations set up at Bretton Woods and moved to a regional planning conception for aid, payments and economic development.

The American offer was quickly taken up in Europe. Under the initiative of

Ernest Bevin, the British Foreign Secretary, a group of sixteen countries (roughly Western Europe less Spain, plus Turkey and Greece) was formed which became the Committee of European Economic Co-operation (CEEC) and which in September 1947 completed a report which, on the basis of national forecasts of production, import requirements and export possibilities, gave an account of what Western Europe might do and what external help it would require for the period 1948–51. The report called for higher than prewar production levels and reasonable balance-of-payments equilibrium within four years. It stressed the need to free intra-European trade from bilateralism and sketched the framework of what was later to become the Multilateral Compensation Agreement. It also estimated that in order to achieve output targets, a balance-of-payments deficit of $22.4 bln would be incurred of which about $16.5 bln would be with the United States. The American response was quick. The Marshall Plan took shape in the Foreign Assistance Act of April 1948, which established the Economic Co-operation Administration (ECA) to operate the aid programme on the American side. It was followed by an Appropriations Act in June and by subsequent annual appropriations. In April 1948 seventeen European countries (the group now included West Germany) signed a Convention of European Economic Co-operation launching the programme. The Committee for European Economic Co-operation was promoted to the Organisation for European Economic Co-operation (OEEC), as a working agency with a secretariat, to carry on research and allocate American aid.

The period from the summer of 1947 to mid-1948 was a difficult one for European payments. The dollar shortage was still acute, the American stabilisation loans were almost exhausted and Marshall Aid had not yet begun. The IMF had opened for currency transactions on 1 March 1947 and between 1 July 1947 and 30 April 1948 it had sold $544 m. to member countries, almost all to Western Europe. During this period dollar sales amounted to almost a quarter of the American quota in the Fund. Without the Marshall Aid which progressively became available in late 1948, the Fund's dollar resources would soon have been depleted. With the inauguration of ERP, however, the burden of demand for dollars was lifted from the Fund, who made it known 'that ERP members should request the purchase of US dollars from the Fund only in exceptional or unforeseen circumstances'.[16]

Three aspects of the Marshall Plan are important: the aid aspect; the trade aspect; and the contribution which it made to European economic recovery.

Originally intended to last for four years from 1948–52, the outbreak of the Korean War in 1950 interrupted the Plan and changed its character, switching emphasis from general economic aid to military aid and assistance on a wider geographical basis. The ECA was superseded in 1951 by the Mutual Security Agency but OEEC and much of the trade and payments

---

[16] See *Annual Report of IMF for 1948* (Washington: I.M.F., 1949) p. 49.

arrangements were continued and became a background to European trade and economic affairs throughout the fifties. Over the period of pure Marshall Aid $13 bln was appropriated by Congress. By the end of 1951 $11.5 bln had been disbursed, of which 10 per cent had been in the form of loans and 90 per cent in grants. According to one reliable source ERP financed a quarter of Europe's total imports of goods and services in the years 1947–50 and nearly two-thirds of its merchandise imports from the dollar area.[17]

Since we have no means of knowing how Europe might have muddled through in the absence of Marshall Aid, no precise evaluation of its assistance can be given. Other factors were at work, notably the realignment of exchange rates which followed the sterling devaluation of September 1949, the French devaluation of January 1948 and the monetary recovery of West Germany after the currency reform of mid-1948. Moreover, high ERP coverage of import bills is a deceptive indicator unless we know how much of such imports were essential or what role they played in freeing domestic industries for essential production. Yet it is impossible to read the contemporary economic literature, as it is impossible to have lived through those years, without the impression that the role of ERP in the recovery of its five greatest recipients[18] was central and considerable. For the leading countries, particularly Britain, it gave an intermission from crisis in which recovery could be planned and contemplated rather than conditions which might deteriorate quickly to economic breakdown and political chaos.

In the trade field ERP, by sponsoring, and at first underwriting, European plans for wider convertibility, enabled steady progress to be made from the bilateralism and constricted trade of 1947 to the ultimate convertibility of all European currencies in 1959. True, progress was slow, but in the light of the events of 1947 it was better that the widening and freeing of international payments should come at the Europeans' own pace.

The European Payments Union (EPU), which was the culmination of the Western European co-operative effort for wider payments, far outlived the Marshall Plan. It spanned the fifties and was only dissolved in January 1959 when the OEEC currencies were made fully convertible, thereby rendering it redundant. It was, perhaps, the most successful international economic experiment ever made. It had a specific task to do; it did it effectively. When the task was completed, it was wound up. During its operations it met problems, some of them, like the German surplus of the later fifties, of crisis proportions, but they were surmounted by negotiation, compromise and good sense. Most notable, and fortunately, it was a highly technical operation, run by financial technicians and beyond the ken of politicians or the media so that it operated free from publicity or the embarrassment of ill-informed comment on its problems.

[17] See OEEC, *A Decade of Co-operation* (Paris, 1958) pp. 22–3.
[18] The United Kingdom, France, Italy, Germany and Holland received together 75 per cent of total aid.

The mechanism of EPU bore great similarity to the overdraft system advocated by Keynes in his Clearing Union Proposal before Bretton Woods. Equally the SDR scheme, still seventeen years in the future, was by EPU anticipated in a regional setting. In another sense the Union echoed Keynesian ideas: it was non-political, essentially a technical organisation operated by technocrats for economic ends which were limited but none the less important in the general setting of economic recovery in Europe. There can be no doubt that the greater flexibility of European payments, the growth of intra-European trade, the growing self-confidence of the participant countries and the mutual recognition of the Union's function which resulted in members renewing its life from year to year, all indicated success in its operation.

Finally, in this assessment of the European Recovery Programme, we have to consider what contribution was made by it to European economic recovery. Such a question is difficult if not impossible to answer since one side of any comparison, Europe's performance in the absence of Marshall Aid, must remain unknown. Already in 1948 there were, we can see in retrospect, signs of recovery both in production and in trade. Nor can we generalise in our judgement of the plan. For some countries, Britain and West Germany in particular, recovery was almost certainly accelerated; for others, the effect is harder to trace. In the trade field which we have traced in some detail, Marshall Aid was not only a provider of much-needed international liquidity and a relief from the dollar problem, but an encouragement to the progressive return of multilateral payments and functional co-operation in Europe. Moreover, the liberalisation of trade, which the IMF in its early days pursued so ponderously, was achieved more easily in Europe by OEEC liberalisation measures. From 1949 these were applied to trade between members and by them intra-European trade was steadily freed from quantitative restrictions. Moreover, discrimination against the imports of the United States, which the relatively soft settlement of EPU implied, was progressively reduced by the hardenings of the Union settlement which took place in 1954 and 1955. Although by the later fifties American critics of European discrimination were becoming restive and accusing Europe of featherbedding itself within the EPU–sterling area framework, it is arguable that the extent of such dollar-discrimination was slight and of little consequence to the United States itself.[19]

---

[19] By January 1959 the proportion of private imports free from quantitative restrictions in intra-European trade was high – Italy 98 per cent, Benelux 96, United Kingdom 95 and Germany 91 – while in trade with the United States and Canada – Italy 68, Benelux 86, United Kingdom 73 and Germany 78 – it increased considerably during the last three years of the Union. Following convertibility, leading European countries raised their percentages for free U.S. trade to 90 per cent by the end of 1959.

(iv) EUROPEAN RECOVERY

The European Recovery Programme, as a balance-of-payments stabilisation programme, ended in 1950 with the outbreak of war in Korea. Thereafter, U.S. overseas aid was openly addressed to supplementing military strategy overseas. But by 1952 the dollar problem was much less acute and the years 1952 and 1953 saw a marked improvement in the international payments position. Britain had at last moved into surplus and the favourable balance of £225 m. in 1953 was the highest since the war. In Europe the OEEC countries as a group maintained an annual current account surplus of $1.5 bln in 1953–4. Germany moved into surplus in 1951, but France, whose rate of growth was swift in the fifties, had recurrent balance-of-payments difficulties. Meanwhile, viewed from the opposite side, the export surplus of the United States shrank until in 1953 the trade balance was in approximate equilibrium.[20] The year 1954 was, in spite of the United States' recession, one of easy payments conditions and, although there was still a Western European trade deficit of $1.4 bln, this was more than covered by direct American military expenditure in the area.

During the later fifties the trend of improvement of the balance-of-payments of the non-dollar world with the United States continued – despite a slight recession in 1957–8 and emergency imports of oil from the Western hemisphere during the Suez crisis of 1956–7. The outflow of gold from the United States which had been running at an annual average of $554 m. from 1950–4 was temporarily reversed in 1956–7 by the sudden increase of U.S. exports and in those years the United States acquired $306 m. and $799 m. respectively in monetary gold. In 1958 there was a renewal of the gold outflow. In addition the year 1958 saw a sharp reduction of American exports, the fall being continued more gradually in 1959. It seems that a long-run deterioration of the American export advantage had been taking place throughout the fifties and that, once the special demands of 1956–7 were removed, the impact of this became apparent. On the opposite side of the merchandise trade account, a change was also apparent in that imports, the trend of which had been rising throughout the fifties, remained virtually steady throughout the 1957–8 recession. Thus, the apparently stable relationship between imports and income in the United States, which had obtained throughout the postwar period, had been broken. Both imports and exports were subject to changes which produced a trade balance quite insufficient to meet the external commitments of the United States on capital and military account. The result was a loss of gold in 1958 of $2275 m. and in 1959 of $1076 m. – this gold outflow reflecting not only the true balance-of-

---

[20] To be precise, if military deliveries are excluded, the U.S. current balance changed from a surplus of $1829 m. in 1952 to a deficit of $62 m. in 1953.

payments position but even some speculation against the dollar in anti-cipation of devaluation.

The end of the fifties thus brought a transformation of the international payments situation. The dollar problem had reversed itself and become a balance-of-payments problem for the United States. During the sixties this new dollar problem was to persist and intensify to crisis proportions in the seventies.

(v) CONCLUSION

We conclude this chapter by briefly summarising the main changes in world payments of the year 1945–55 – a formative and significant decade.

The ten years covered by this chapter were dominated by two develop-ments, one political, and the other primarily economic. The first was the hardening division between the super powers, the second was the turmoil, wrought by change and the war, in international monetary arrangements. The two were, of course, connected only at a superficial level. The division of Europe between East and West had its effects upon European trade structure and, hence, upon payments. It delayed the economic recovery of Germany. It forced the United States to intervene quickly and decisively in the payments difficulties of Western Europe when it was thought that that area might collapse economically and succumb to Soviet influence. Perhaps most notably the Cold War intensified the American hegemony in the West. Had Russia remained aloof and indifferent to westward expansion, it is impossible to say how far the United States would have intervened in Western European economic affairs. It seems likely that she would have been content to disburse aid through stabilisation loans and encouragement in the IMF. As it was, her immense economic power and wealth and her determination to limit Soviet expansion made her not only Europe's benefactor but also her master. That the power which this gave her was wielded, in the main, with responsibility is not denied; but that it was there and that it was not always encased in a velvet glove is equally undeniable.

In the purely economic field the years 1945–55 saw the waxing and waning of American economic power in Europe. Its course can be traced in the dollar problem which in the immediate postwar years placed the United States in virtual control of Western European recovery. Although forced by events to put the IMF in virtual abeyance as a central payments authority, the United States, by its influence and voting power, was able to dominate that organisation. In 1948, when the Marshall Plan began to operate, American influence reached its zenith. But as the American external surplus diminished and as Europe's economies recovered, the United States sank to a position of *primus inter pares* in Western economic affairs. Later, as the second phase of the dollar problem developed in the sixties and as the full weight of a gold exchange standard was thrown on the dollar, American policy in Europe and European policies towards the United States were to become complex. They will be dealt with in later chapters.

A second notable feature of this decade lay in the placing in abeyance of the international currency arrangements which had been made at Bretton Woods. The American scenario for the postwar period had been one in which after a brief transition period, possibly smoothed by special *ad hoc* financial assistance, the IMF would play a central role in establishing full convertibility of currencies, a multilateral system of payments free from discriminatory controls and would, when necessary, provide temporary assistance to member countries in balance-of-payments difficulties. At or near the centre of these affairs, the United States, through its voting power in the Fund, would exercise a beneficent but stern influence.

All this had been much too optimistic. The scale of postwar payments disequilibrium had been much greater than expected. Left to itself the IMF would have been unable to meet the demands made upon it for dollar currency. It would have been forced to declare the dollar a scarce currency and under Article 7 of the Fund Agreement sanction discriminatory controls against the United States. But for Russian ambitions, this might well have come to pass with who knows what consequences for the whole application of the Bretton Woods principle. As it was the IMF, after a brief flurry of activity in 1946–7, virtually retired from the payments scene, switching its main effort to trying to reduce discrimination and trade controls – an activity which, considering the balance-of-payments deficits of most of its members, was both useless and frustrating to all. The focus of attention in economic matters was switched from the Fund to the new organisations spawned by the European Recovery Programme. The period between 1949 and the autumn of 1956 was a 'phase of retirement' for the Fund. With this decline in practical participation in payments affairs the Fund's standing and moral authority with its members fell and it was apparent that if the retirement were to be prolonged, the Fund and probably the whole Bretton Woods conception would fade away. Only a return to active lending in 1957 and the establishment of convertibility for all major currencies in 1959 prevented this.

Finally, the years 1945–55 saw the emergence of the new power structure which was to fashion events and condition economic policies in the sixties and seventies. By 1955 it was apparent that British recovery was lagging, that sterling was in decline as a key currency and that if the Bretton Woods system, as envisaged by the founding fathers, was ever to be achieved, it would rest upon the dollar, which underpinned by mighty reserves and a banking system of growing strength and sophistication, seemed now to be the world's key currency. In Western Europe Germany had, by 1955, made good her economic recovery and was already launched on a course of expansion which was to make her the leading industrial nation in Europe. In the East, discernible only in retrospect, Japan was moving forward from recovery to a period of growth which was to make her the trading leader and financial giant of the Pacific.

4
Commercial Policy

(i) THE NEW APPROACH

Commercial policy has a dual motivation. Its creators pursue, or believe they pursue, the economic welfare of their countries by influencing the direction and flow of trade. There are few aspects of international economic affairs so mystifying, so traditional. While economic theory demonstrates the welfare-superiority of free trade, only Britain, in the late nineteenth century, has tried it. From the dawn of the nation state it has been the area in which power politics and economics have mingled to the detriment of both. In the century of liberal experiment free trade was the declared objective of the great countries while each manipulated trade impediments as bargaining counters in the game of the balance of power. As the world shrank in size in the twentieth century realisation grew that the classical economic optimum of free trade could only be achieved at costs in domestic economic adjustment which few countries would accept. At the same time the traditional commercial policy weapon of the tariff was augmented by a formidable battery of direct and monetary controls, often more potent and flexible for trade manipulation. From the high tide of trade liberalism marked by the Cobden Treaty of 1860, under the influence of industrial rivalry and competition in the 1930s for declining markets, protectionism and trade and payments control became an accepted fact of economic life in which the great powers differed only in the degree to which they made use of protective devices. By the outbreak of war in 1939 tariff protection, under the influence of the great depression, was high among the great powers. Britain concluded her unilateral experiment as an open economy in 1932. France was already protectionist. The United States intensified her protection with the Smoot–Hawley Tariff of 1930. Germany, under Hitler after 1933, demonstrated the uses and abuses of direct controls on trade and payments.

It was natural that, during the war, when the United States and Britain were drawing up plans for international payments in the postwar world, the planning of a new approach to commercial policy should be a complementary task. The monetary flows or exchange-rate changes which were to adjust balances of payments under the Bretton Woods plan could only function efficiently in a world relatively free from commercial and monetary controls. Conversely it was well understood that persistent balance-of-payments disequilibria, not capable of adjustment by the Bretton Woods prescription, would beget the repressive, as distinct from adjusting, measures of import controls, discriminating exchange controls and the like. The approach of the wartime planners to commercial policy was, therefore, compounded of several elements. First, there was a guarded reaffirmation of the merit, but not the overwhelming merit, of free trade. Typical was the view of the United States, which carried into the postwar period the spirit of Cordell Hull and the Reciprocal Trade Agreements Programme. The Americans believed in tariffs and in the general principle of protection. They frowned on unilateral tariff reduction. But they believed in tariff negotiation, in reciprocity and the most-favoured-nation principle. These views were also held by the British, although in different degree, the Americans believing that only by expansion of international trade could full employment be achieved, the British believing that only by wider access to foreign markets would they be able to balance their external trade account.

A second novel aspect of the new approach to commercial policy was that it was now to be conducted mainly through international agencies to be formed and set up within the burgeoning framework of international economic co-operation. Cordell Hull's dream of a comprehensive charter to govern the conduct of world trade was to be fulfilled. The American passion for legislating and codifying was to be given free rein. The core of the trade planning programme would be the negotiation among 'as many nations as possible' of a multilateral convention on commercial policy – this convention to embody agreements on tariffs, preferences, quota restrictions, subsidies and state trading. On the British side, proposals by James Meade[1] for a Commercial Union were similar to the American approach – the Union emphasising the need for the reduction of tariffs and minimal use of direct controls. The Union was to act as an international body to enforce the convention and act as arbiter in commercial disputes between member nations.

It is best before dealing with the changes in commercial policy during the period 1945–55 to place these changes in a broader setting by looking at the whole postwar period in perspective. In this, four sets of events seem to have been formative. The first is the series of Anglo-American negotiations on postwar planning which established in the IMF an institution to nurture multilateral payments and discourage the use of direct balance-of-payments controls. These negotiations failed to establish the Havana Charter and the International Trade Organisation (ITO) but managed, at the eleventh hour, to create the General Agreement on Tariffs and Trade (GATT). These events occupied the first postwar decade. Second, was the creation through the Treaty of Rome of the European Economic Community (EEC). With this, new elements appeared upon the scene: the trade diversion and trade creation of the customs union; and for the Americans, the dilemma that while they welcomed the EEC politically, they were forced to tolerate in its economic

---

[1] James Meade, later a Nobel prize winner and international economist of great distinction, was in the war period a senior official in the British Cabinet Office.

aspect their abhorred principle of trade discrimination. Third, the American Trade Expansion Act of 1962 ushered in a long series of tariff negotiations which reduced tariffs on industrial products considerably. Fourth, was the growing desire of the developing countries to use commercial policy in pursuit of their development aims. These have been the bench-marks of commercial policy in the postwar period. In this chapter we shall deal with the first aspect, leaving the rest for subsequent chapters.

(ii) THE FAILURE OF THE HAVANA CHARTER AND ITO

The dominant commercial policy feature of the immediate postwar years was the failure of the plan for the Havana Charter and ITO. Of this failure there was no sign when, in September 1943, British and American representatives met in Washington to survey the field. Four aspects of the question were discussed and on only one of them was there disagreement. On employment policy after the war each country agreed that only on a basis of expanding trade in relatively free markets could there be any prospect of avoiding cyclical swings of activity such as those which had characterised the interwar period. The Americans were aware of the British fear that an American recession after the war would be quickly transmitted to other industrial countries through an American reduction of imports. Such a fear was given point in 1943 by the famous Department of Commerce Study[2] and the Americans were anxious to impress the British with their determination to plan for full employment, of which the removal of trade barriers was, they argued, a prerequisite. The British, bound by their governmental pledge to provide a high and stable level of employment after the war and carried on the high tide of Keynesian optimism, were more inclined than the Americans to stress the roles of fiscal and monetary policy rather than of trade. But the differences between the two countries lay in the nuances and not in the central issue. On the second aspect of trade policy, that of quantitative restrictions, there was complete agreement. These must be banished from the postwar scene – no exceptions, neither for infant industries or ailing industries, not even for agriculture. The only contingency in which quantitative restrictions should be allowed was for dealing temporarily with balance-of-payments deficits. On the third aspect, that of establishing an international code of trade behaviour to be interpreted and enforced by an international agency, there

[2] *The United States in the World Economy* (Washington, U.S. Dept of Commerce, 1943). It was from this study, based on prewar statistics of consumption and saving that the famous error of extrapolating findings based on prewar data into the postwar period was made. On the basis of such an extrapolation, a forecast of 8 million American unemployed within a few months of the end of the war was made. On the basis of this forecast, the ability of the U.S. to preserve full employment and of other countries to save themselves from American deflationary influence was called in question. The first ten years of peace were lived under the fear of an American depression and its international effects.

was, again, no disagreement. Both sides had proposals but they were very close together.

There was a fourth sector of the problem and on this there was no agreement. How were tariffs to be reduced? The Americans, ever in pursuit of their goal of non-discrimination, demanded an end to the Imperial Preference system of tariffs which had been created by the Ottawa Agreement of 1932. They quoted Article 7 of the Mutual Aid Agreement and demonstrated by their persistence their determination to end what seemed to them an intolerable advantage for British manufacturers in new and expanding markets, particularly Canada. The British on their side were immovable. Imperial Preference they regarded as a British matter, moreover it had been created in the depression years, two years after the Smoot–Hawley tariff had almost closed the U.S. market to them. They even made preference a bargaining-point, demanding from the Americans tariff reductions so drastic that they would eliminate preference. The result was an impasse. But it was only on the tariff issue. Over the whole trade field it appeared after the September 1943 meetings that real progress could be made and that some solution to even the tariff problem could ultimately be worked out.

The necessary compromise was slow in coming. Financial problems filled the centre of the stage and it was the spring of 1945 before British and American officials met in London and September 1945 before a set of Proposals for Consideration by an International Conference on Trade and Employment was hammered out in Washington and published.[3] Much of the delay was caused by the British, among whom there was now dispute on several of the principles which had been discussed in 1943. In particular, full realisation of the British economic position and the abrupt end to Lend-Lease in August 1945 caused some members of the Government to ask whether Britain might not require import restrictions and exchange control for a lengthy period and whether it was not unwise to abrogate protective policies at such a time. Two aspects of the delay were unfortunate. First, postponement till after the end of the war meant that discussions took place in a very different atmosphere from that of the war years. The spirit of wartime co-operation had disappeared and had been replaced by the 'hard-nosed' bargaining of the Truman Administration and the relative inexperience of the new British Labour Government, feeling its way forward amid increasing difficulties. Second, the timing of the September 1945 meetings was unfortunate since the Proposals, delayed by the Americans, were published simultaneously with the Anglo-American Loan Agreement in December. This meant that the claim was made by the Americans, that the British had made concessions on trade policy as part of a package deal for the loan; while for the British, disappointed and frustrated by what they considered to be a

---

[3] *Proposals for the Expansion of World Trade and Employment* (Washington: Dept of State Publication 2411, 1945).

hard-driven bargain, the Proposals were tarred with the same brush as the loan and were never considered on their merits by the public. On all three sectors of commercial policy planning,[4] views on both sides had hardened and, although there was still considerable common ground, the principles on employment policy and on restrictions were hedged about with many nuances and qualifications, some new, some long-standing, while on the tariff issue, and particularly on tariff preferences, a gulf existed between the two sides which appeared to be unbridgeable. Nevertheless, when the Proposals appeared in late 1945 it seemed that a workable compromise had been reached. On the employment issue it was agreed that each country should pursue its own full-employment policies so long as such policies did not include measures inimical to the trade of other countries. Restrictions on imports were to be for the transition period only, and to be subject to IMF provisions. On the tariff issue bilateral bargaining accompanied by the application of the most-favoured-nation clause was to be the method of tariff reduction while, on the hottest question of all, Imperial Preference, the issue was fudged. Preferences were 'eventually' to be eliminated and in the meantime not increased. In return for this American concession to British views, the Americans succeeded in including provision for an escape clause in their tariff agreements under which they would be permitted to take temporary action to prevent serious injury to producers caused by tariff concessions.

The story of the failure of this compromise is part of the story of the change which took place in Anglo-American relations in the early postwar years. The trade proposals must not be seen in isolation but as part of the unfolding problem of British economic weakness and suspicion of the Americans on the one hand and the single-minded American thrust for multilateralism, embodying in this case an all-out attack on Imperial Preference, on the other. The Proposals were published in November 1945; the Loan Agreement and the Bretton Woods Agreement were unwillingly accepted by Britain in December. The débâcle of the Fund's first meeting in Savannah, Georgia, and the railroading of America's wishes through that meeting was in March 1946. In 1947 the failure of sterling convertibility brought acrimonious meetings between representatives of the two countries. Both the Fund and the Loan Agreement had failed in American eyes by 1948 to advance the world towards multilateral trade. It is clearly, in retrospect, too much to expect that in 1948 wide agreement was possible upon the early application of a principle which one country believed had redounded to its detriment and which the other had pursued too ruthlessly.

In April 1947 representatives of twenty-three countries met in Geneva for the round of tariff and preference bargaining, the results of which would be embodied in a General Agreement on Tariffs and Trade (GATT). This was

---

[4] Employment policy, quantitative restrictions and tariffs.

the meeting at which, in American eyes, Imperial Preference was to be eliminated. Armed with congressional approval to reduce American tariffs to 50 per cent of 1945 levels, the American officials of the State Department believed that it would be possible by large tariff reductions and application of the most-favoured-nation principle to eliminate at least those preferences which interfered with the American export trade. Success in these negotiations was then a prerequisite of success in the whole commercial policy initiative. With the Imperial Preference system in ruins the U.S. Congress would be encouraged to approve the Charter of the ITO and an impressive institutional framework would be created through which, side by side with the Fund and Bank, American foreign economic policy would operate smoothly and successfully.[5] But all this was not to be. The spring of 1947, with the Loan running out and American-dictated convertibility of sterling pending, was not the time to crowd the British, whose enthusiasm for Commonwealth Preference was burgeoning as American popularity in Britain waned. The British wanted massive American tariff reductions in return for scaling down of preferences and under the Truman Administration they did not believe they would get them. The age of Cordell Hull and American trade liberalism was over and American concessions, even when made, would be hedged by conditions and 'peril points' which might make British reciprocating concessions dangerous. Even ITO and the Charter which the British had shared in planning were now called in question by some political groups in Britain.

The agreement on preference which emerged from Geneva was a disappointment to the Americans. Initially the British attitude was so intransigent that complete failure seemed probable, but in the face of American alarm that the breakup of the Geneva conference would be disastrous for commercial relations generally, the British finally agreed to an arrangement under which modest concessions would be made at once in the preferences enjoyed by Britain in the Commonwealth and that, in three years, they would be prepared, without commitment, for further discussions. The Commonwealth agreed to reductions in the preferences which they enjoyed in the United Kingdom. The delegates in Geneva put the best face they could on this agreement, claiming that it had saved the Conference. In both countries clamour broke out, British critics insisting that Imperial Preference had been sold to American bullying; American backwoodsmen claiming that the wily British had once more outwitted the simple and sincere American negotiators.

Wider aspects were, however, important. The United States had made many tariff concessions – some up to the limit of 50 per cent – and brought the

---

[5] The determination of the American State Department to destroy Imperial Preference as a prelude to the Charter and ITO is borne out by evidence given by an American official, Mr Harry Hawkins, to the Senate Committee on Finance (*International Trade Organisation*, 80th Congress, 1st Session, Mar–Apr, 1947) p. 195. See also Richard Gardner, *Sterling Dollar Diplomacy*, op. cit. p. 350.

average American tariff to its lowest since 1913. The effect of this had been widely distributed by most-favoured-nation treatment and bilateral agreements had been made to abolish quantitative restrictions among contracting parties. Most important of all, a General Agreement on Tariffs and Trade (GATT) was concluded in October 1947 which was designed to be an interim measure pending the establishment of a functional agency of the United Nations to supersede it.

Between November 1947 and March 1948 an international conference on trade and employment met in Havana to draw up a charter for ITO. It was quickly involved in a wrangle on the issue of discrimination, in particular its allowable practice during a transition period and its permissible uses, which deepened existing divisions. Moreover, a new and wider issue, apart from the purely Anglo-American ones, now appeared. This was the exception to multilateralism which might be permitted to what were then called underdeveloped countries in order to foster their economic growth. The claim of such countries was that the mature countries should take heed of their demands for a place in the sun, in particular that the draft charter of ITO should acknowledge economic development as one of its major aims. To the annoyance of the United States and Britain, who speedily closed ranks, the new group[6] demanded controls on international investment, preferences to promote the trade of developing countries and the permitted use of quantitative trade restrictions. Despite determined and often heated resistance by the United States, the Havana Charter, as finally signed on 23 March 1948, embodied compromises which diluted still further the original compromise on multilateralism of Britain and the United States. ITO and the Havana Charter were signed by 53 of the 56 nations represented at Havana, but only one nation ratified the Charter and both it and ITO were abandoned.

Thus ended the great drive for non-discrimination in trade which had begun seven years earlier in the framing of Article 7 of the Mutual Aid Agreement – probably the greatest sustained effort in pursuit of a single principle ever embodied in American foreign economic policy. Its pursuit had expressed much that was admirable and constructive in the American vision, but the methods of its pursuit had been often ill-conceived, had at best been frequently ill-timed and over-pressed until to the rest of the world the aim itself was like a wine that had soured by the time it was ready for use. It was 1950 before Congressional hearings on the Charter began. They continued, irrelevantly, against the background of Korea and a new war. On 6 December 1950 an obscure press release announced that the 'proposed Charter for an International Trade Organisation should not be resubmitted to the Congress'.

In Britain there was much criticism of the Charter. The belief that the

---

[6] Led by Australia, India, Chile and Brazil.

country would have to defend its balance of payments by frequent recourse to direct controls and discriminatory measures was widespread. After a hostile debate on the principles of the Charter in the House of Commons it was decided to defer a decision on its ratification until the United States had ratified. Thus, abandoned by its original architects, the formal edifice of trade planning collapsed.

(iii) THE GATT – A MODIFIED APPROACH

With the end of ITO co-operation in commercial policy continued at a more modest and practicable level. Many countries, including Britain and the United States, were committed to the Protocol of Provisional Application of the General Agreement on Tariffs and Trade.[7] The GATT originally intended as an interim arrangement had now to serve in default of ITO and it was imperative that the less grandiose principles implicit in GATT should not be lost.[8] In 1949 at Annecy, 1951 at Torquay and in 1956 and 1961 at Geneva the agreement was greatly amplified and enlarged.[9] The original membership of 23 countries was increased to 37 (accounting for 80 per cent of international trade) by the conferences at Annecy and Torquay. By 1970 participation had grown to 91. The result of all this has been a loosely knit 'organisation', not operating with a constitution and membership, but an Agreement whose contracting parties meet periodically to review the working of the Agreement, if possible to extend it and to apply it. A small secretariat located in Geneva was added to organise the almost continuous tariff negotiations and in 1960 a permanent Council of Representatives was created. The result has been an international agency less ambitious in aim

[7] The General Agreement in its present form includes most of the commercial policy amendments which were added to the draft charter at the Havana meeting. It does not include the wider planning objectives of ITO, e.g. 'Employment and Economic Activity'; 'Economic Development and Reconstruction'; 'Restrictive Business Practices' and 'Inter-Governmental Commodity Agreements'. Equally, it does not include the original Charter's organisational and procedural provisions.

[8] The best and most up-to-date book on the GATT is Kenneth W. Dam, *The GATT* (Chicago, 1970). A fairly detailed account of the negotiations for the Havana Charter will be found in Richard Gardner's *Sterling Dollar Diplomacy*, 2nd ed. (Oxford, 1969). The best direct source material is in the Annual Reports of GATT published by the Secretariat in Geneva. The Agreement itself is to be found in *The General Agreement on Tariffs and Trade and Texts of Related Documents* (Washington, D.C.: US Department of State, Government Printing Office). Raymond Vernon's *American Foreign Trade Policy and the GATT* (Princeton: International Finance Section, 1954) is a good examination of GATT's first phase, while Dam's book is an excellent review of the institution from a legal and organisational standpoint.

[9] The so-called 'rounds' of GATT have been seven in number and were as follows: 1947 at Geneva; 1949 at Annecy; 1951 at Torquay; 1956 at Geneva; 1960–2 at Geneva – the so-called 'Dillon Round'; 1964–7, the Kennedy Round, at Geneva; and 1978, the so-called Tokyo Round at Geneva.

and scope but with considerable flexibility and influence and at least vestigial of the original conception of the ITO.

The Agreement has two main components. It comprises a lengthy schedule of specific tariff concessions for each contracting party – a series of tariff rates which each country has agreed to with its partners. By the mid-sixties, when the membership of GATT had risen to include over sixty countries, this schedule covered many thousands of commodities and tariff concessions had been made on approximately two-thirds of the total imports of GATT countries. The second component of the Agreement comprises a set of general principles for the conduct of international trade. These provide for unconditional most-favoured-nation treatment, the removal of direct quantitative restrictions on trade, uniformity in customs regulations and an obligation by any member to negotiate for tariff remissions at the request of another. GATT deals with tariffs, quotas, preferences, internal controls and regulations affecting trade, customs regulations, state-trading and government subsidies. Its goal is a multilateral and free system of trading.

One problem which was not foreseen by the original draftsmen of the Agreement was that of accommodating within it the regional tariff arrangements of the customs unions and free trade areas which came to be dominant features of the postwar world in the late fifties. In spite of GATT's hostility to discrimination and its emphasis upon the most-favoured-nation principle, it does not preclude the formation of customs unions, the very nature of which is discriminatory. The only proviso is that the formation of a customs union must involve no net over-all increase in barriers against countries outside the union and that, although such a union may require to establish itself by stages, the transition period should not be prolonged. This latter condition secures that a supposed customs union may not die still-born and leave a web of discriminatory tariffs to linger on in perpetuity.

With this view in mind the concern of the draftsmen became that of distinguishing between regional groupings, which GATT approved, and preferential arrangements, which it abhorred. One of GATT's most complex and deceptive provisions, Article 24, was the result. It was under this Article that all subsequent arrangements with the European Common Market and the European Free Trade Association were accommodated.

When we turn from tariffs to direct restrictions on trade (a formidable feature in GATT's early days), it should be noted that GATT's jurisdiction extends only to quantitative restrictions on imports. Exchange controls and restrictions on payments are the responsibility of the IMF. The initial hope of GATT was that all restrictions on trade except tariffs would be removed, but in the economic climate of the forties and early fifties this proved impossible. Countries could not and would not abandon direct supports to their balances of payments. As balances of payments improved in the later fifties quantitative restrictions were considerably reduced, particularly among the industrial nations.

The General Agreement includes a general prohibition on the use of quantitative restrictions except in specific circumstances. The major exception is when a country is in balance-of-payments difficulties. Quotas may then be applied as necessary 'to forestall the imminent threat of, or to stop, a serious decline in its monetary reserves', or 'in the case of a contracting party with very low monetary reserves, to achieve a reasonable rate of increase in its reserves'.[10] GATT members who invoke this waiver are required to consult the IMF as to the degree of adequacy of monetary reserves and if the Fund determines that the country concerned no longer needs to protect its monetary reserves, the country loses the right to the waiver.

Another exception to the anti-quota principle lies in the provision for a country to protect a new industry by the use of import quotas. In this case, however, there is not, as in the case of balance-of-payments difficulties, a general waiver but each individual case has to be submitted by members for approval. This exception was made in deference to the wishes of the developing countries who were anxious to support industrialisation policies by some measure of direct protection.

Yet another exception to the prohibition of quotas is in the case of agricultural products. Where these are the subject of support programmes within a country, quotas may, subject to certain conditions, be used to prevent imports from impairing the domestic support programme.

When quantitative restrictions are used under any of these waivers they must not be discriminatory. Import quotas allotted to countries must be based on typical quantities in some previous period. For a time after the war and during the period of dollar shortage, countries using quotas, under the balance-of-payments waiver, were permitted to discriminate against imports of countries whose currencies were for the moment scarce to them. This was necessary in order to allow GATT to conform to the principle implicit in the Scarce Currency Clause of the IMF. The passing of the dollar shortage, the end of widespread use of currencies with limited convertibility and the fact that the Scarce Currency Clause of the Fund Agreement has never been invoked, make this tolerated infringement of the principle of non-discrimination of historic interest only.

Thus far in this description we have been concerned with the regulatory framework within which GATT has worked. We must also glance briefly at the record of achievement. Foremost in this has been the successive rounds of tariff negotiations in which each contracting party negotiates with others on the tariffs for commodities of which they are suppliers. Six such rounds of tariff negotiations have so far been completed under GATT auspices. A further round is now in progress. If two negotiating countries agree upon a concession, this concession is extended to all other contracting parties. Such a concession may not always be a tariff remission but may be a

[10] See Article 12.

commitment to continue duty free treatment or not to increase the present tariff rate. The first round of negotiations at Geneva in 1947 set the precedent. At this the United States negotiated with 22 countries, some of which also negotiated with each other. Negotiations were thus conducted bilaterally on a product-by-product basis, the results embodied in schedules which were appended to the General Agreement and made applicable to all the contracting parties. In the early sessions of GATT progress in tariff reduction appeared impressive and member countries seemed surprisingly ready to reduce or remove tariffs. But, at this stage, many of the agreements were in respect of rare goods or of goods which, even in the absence of duty, rarely entered into trade. Some reductions were, however, planned concessions to be conceded for reciprocal concessions. By the early fifties these deliberate concessions had already been used up. As discussion moved towards those duties on goods which were important to member nations progress was slower, either because tariffs on goods were the subject of legislative enactments[11] or because members were unwilling to make reductions. It seems there is, for every nation, a hard core of tariffs which it is difficult for GATT to touch or upon which the attitude of members is implacable.

During the period with which we are concerned in this chapter, 1945–55, GATT established itself as a flexible international agency with a growing participation and acceptance of its usefulness within its modest limitations. It provided a forum for trade bargaining and it preserved the idea of international consultation on trade matters at a time when ideas and policies were changing and being moulded by new events and influences. The year 1955 is a suitable date to interrupt this account of its activities. Not only was a reassessment of its role undertaken in that year, but in the sixties, with the rise of the European Common Market and with the new Dillion Round of tariff negotiations it was to face problems and needs qualitatively different from those of its early career.

(iv) CONCLUSION

Taking stock at the midpoint of the fifties several of the important economic developments of the postwar international economy were clearly visible. First, the American drive for multilateral trade in a world economy steered by international agencies was over. Some of the agencies were in being and

---

[11] GATT has no power to make member countries dismantle controls or amend duties which are legislatively sanctioned in their own countries. Thus, it cannot force countries to abandon existing preferences. In this respect GATT falls short of the defunct Havana Charter. Had this been ratified, and the principles of ITO been accepted, member legislatures would, by such ratification, have given their sanction to changes in duties and/or practices even provided for by their own legislation.

functioning, others had perished along the way. The ideal of 'One World' had faded in face of the Cold War and the divisive economic problems of recovery. American foreign economic policy was moving towards *ad hoc* interventions in strategic areas. The political and military realities were taking precedence; economic policies were seen as buttressing American strength and influence. Into this pattern fell the Marshall Plan, support for the economic plans of Western Europe embodied in the Treaty of Rome and American aid policies for what were now euphemistically called the 'developing countries'. Thus the earlier conception and its creations had been too grandiose to be abandoned entirely. There was much debris lying around. The Bretton Woods aims were half accomplished and might yet come to full operation. But in 1955, with many currencies still inconvertible and with exchange controls and discriminatory trade and payments arrangements still rife, judgement was suspended.

Second, the world was at last emerging from the shadow of the war. The industrial economies were growing, trade was growing, and, except among the developing countries, balances of payments were more stable. In particular the dollar problem, in the shape of a chronic scarcity of that currency outside North America, was passing, although in 1955 it was still impossible to discern what it was giving way to. Perhaps most surprising of all, although perhaps ascribable to the new orthodoxy of Keynesianism, the formerly much-feared resumption of widespread unemployment had not taken place. Rather there was misgiving that creeping inflation would replace unemployment as the supreme macro-policy problem of the age.

Finally, it was increasingly apparent that a redistribution of economic power and political influence was taking place. It was too early as yet to discern the emergence of West Germany and Japan as industrial giants, but it was clear that, in the poor and economically less endowed countries, mainly located in the southern hemisphere, there was an economic grouping whose potential demands for a larger share in world trade and for massive transfers of development capital from the mature economies were to be an increasing force in the next decade.

5

Growth, Trade and Prices in the Industrial Countries

(i) GROWTH IN THE DEVELOPED COUNTRIES

The Second World War marked many changes. In a broad perspective none is more striking in the economic field than the beginning in 1948 of a long period of unprecedented economic growth for the industrial countries. Although somewhat obscured in its early phase by the effects of the war this strong growth trend emerged clearly in the late forties and was continued through the fifties and sixties, in varying degree for countries and at varying rates over time, but always strong and apparent – a dynamic background to the economic history of the period. Table 5.1 gives some indicators of this growth.

Although this economic growth has been described by one writer[1] as 'high and smooth' it had its discernible phases. The first phase was short and consisted of the first few years of postwar recovery, during which demobilisation of armies and switches of factors from war to peace production took place. Not surprisingly the neutrals (Sweden and Switzerland) were quickest to get on the growth path. They were followed by that group of countries in Western Europe which had been lightly damaged by the war and which could make their factor-switches relatively quickly. Germany, France and Italy, all heavy sufferers by war-damage and social and political upheaval, were slow to recover. From 1948 the tempo quickened in all countries. The currency reform in Germany in 1948 marked the beginning of sensational recovery for that country. France, although still suffering inflation and financial instability, increased her national product sharply in 1948 and Italy followed a year later. The Marshall Plan in 1948, the 44 per cent devaluation of the French franc in January 1948, and the 30 per cent devaluation of sterling in September 1949 all worked in favour of European recovery, which was well under way by 1950. Even the Korean War in 1950, although it had unsettling effects on prices and world trade, did nothing to impede economic growth, but rather stimulated output, particularly in the United States.

The period 1953 to 1957 brought a quickening of growth rates and a strong period of economic development in which swift growers – France, Germany,

---

[1] See M. M. Postan, *An Economic History of Western Europe, 1945–64* (London: Methuen, 1967) Part 1.

TABLE 5.1

Some Indicators of Postwar Economic Growth

	Compound annual rates of growth of GNP 1913-50	% Change in output in 1948 as compared with 1938	Compound annual rate of growth of total output 1950-60	Rate of growth of output per head of population 1950-60
Belgium	1.0	10.7	2.9	2.3
Denmark	2.1	29.2	3.3	2.6
France	0.7	− 1.6	4.4	3.5
Germany	1.2	−26.0	7.6	6.5
Italy	1.3	− 6.8	5.9	5.3
Netherlands	2.1	13.91	4.9	3.6
Norway	2.7	22.39	3.5	2.6
Sweden	2.2	30.08	3.3	2.6
Switzerland	2.0	25.52	5.1	3.7
United Kingdom	1.7	12.00	2.6	2.2
United States	2.9	65.1	3.2	1.6
Canada	2.8	74.32	3.9	1.2

Source: ECE, *Economic Surveys of Europe;* also Angus Maddison, *Economic Growth in the West* (London: Allen & Unwin, 1964) pp. 80 and 87.

Italy, Switzerland and the Netherlands – became distinguishable from slower growers – the United Kingdom, the United States, Canada and Belgium. Very high growth rates were recorded in the later fifties by Japan (averaging 9 per cent) and the Soviet Union (7 per cent), although at the time these rates did not seem phenomenal inasmuch as countries with heavy war damage had been slow to reconstruct after the war and their recovery in the ensuing decade was being reckoned from a lower base. An interesting feature of growth rates in the fifties was the low scores of the United States and Canada (3 and 4 per cent respectively) – the result partly of high immediate postwar growth and hence a high base from which to reckon growth in the fifties, and partly the impact on North American exports of discrimination by European countries against trade with the dollar area.[2] For partially industrialised countries – Australia, New Zealand and South Africa – moderate growth rates (3–4 per cent) in the fifties reflected mainly a high and steady external demand for their exports.

Economic growth as sustained and pervasive as this clearly sprang from many causes – a coalescing of expansionary factors unmatched since the last years of the nineteenth century. For purposes of discussion we can divide these forces into two groups: those associated with demand for output and those associated with trade.

Since the onset of the Keynesian Revolution it has been a commonplace to attribute high levels of economic activity and growth to high levels of demand. The period 1945 to 1955 seems to be a striking demonstration of this principle. In all the categories into which effective demand is conventionally divided, there were powerful expansionary forces. In the immediate postwar period this was hardly surprising. For six years demand for consumer goods (and particularly consumer durables) had been held in check by direct controls, fiscal policy and appeals to save. Emancipation from the grey world of rationing, monotony and shortages brought hopes of better and glossier living to those who left the armies and the munitions factories for their places in the offices and the new production lines. Accumulated savings were often available to make this demand effective. In some countries, relatively untouched by the war, such as the United States and Canada and where the war production economy had been built on top of a great productive system, the switch to peace production and the provision of a flow of consumer goods were quick and responsive. In others, such as Britain, France, Italy and Germany, it was slower and years were to elapse before supply came forward to match demand. The demonstration effect of the new higher life in the fortunate countries served to stimulate demand in the less fortunate.

As with consumer outlay so with the other categories of demand. Private industrial investment had its arrears to make up, arrears of deferred plant

---

[2] Between 1950 and 1959 the American share of world manufactured exports fell from 27 to 21 per cent – this at a time when Germany, Japan, Italy and the Netherlands were increasing their trade shares substantially.

replacement, replacement of war damage, plant changes appropriate to new product-runs, technological developments in production. In the field of government expenditure, both consumer and investment demands of the public sector followed the same stimuli as in the private sector.

That immediate postwar demand was high is not surprising. The interesting question is: why did demand continue for a quarter-century after the war to drive the industrial countries in continuing expansion, creating high levels of employment and increasing *per capita* income? The answer to this question can be had by looking briefly, in turn, at the conventional categories of demand – investment, government outlays and consumption, in which we shall find similar influences at work in every industrial country. Moreover, as the industrial countries grew, the great increase in trade, made possible by a lowering of tariff and other barriers and stimulated by the great expansion of industrial Europe, added its force to that of domestic demand, the two acting and reacting as growth forces.

The sharp initial recovery rates of the large economies, unimpeded after this war, as they had been impeded after its predecessor, by government-controlled deflations, gave confidence to the private sector. Much had been learned of the art of production management during the war and a legacy of management skills was one of the better aspects of its aftermath. As it became evident that high consumer demand was absorbing growing outputs and that governments were anxious to foster high employment levels, confidence and profit expectations were high. Nor was there lack of investment opportunities. Prewar growth industries such as automobile manufacture resumed their upward trend, bringing widespread secondary effects in highway construction, accessories, service industries and tourism, while new growth industries such as aviation, nuclear energy, plastics, synthetic fibres, television and electronics opened vistas for exploitation which seemed to have no end. The result was a high ratio of investment to national income, particularly in the West European economy (see Table 5.2); substantial additions to gross national product which raised demand, increased the capital intensity of industry and allowed widespread innovation. This last point should be underlined. High levels of demand need not, in themselves, result in high levels of productivity or investment. It may well be that by bringing into use less efficient labour and capital productivity may be lowered. Such a result would be typical of a fluctuating demand at maximum level. But when high demand is sustained and expectations of its continuance are high, then investment, research and product development all come into play with beneficial effects on productivity. It was because demand was high and sustained that investment levels in Europe were higher in the fifties than ever before. In Britain, where demand was often high, but, because of stop-go policies pursued in the interests of the balance of payments, never sustained, the investment ratio to GNP was the lowest among the industrial powers.

It seems then that differences in the levels of demand and in the degree of steadiness with which high demand was sustained, together with the

TABLE 5.2

Total Gross Domestic Investment as a Proportion of GNP at Current Prices

	Average of years cited		Output per man hour in 1960
	1914–49	*1950–60*	*1913 = 100*
Belgium	–	16.5	188.2
Denmark	12.6	18.1	223.5
France	–	19.1	237.9
Germany	14.3	24.0	239.5
Italy	13.5	20.8	255.7
Netherlands	–	24.2	209.6
Norway	15.4	26.4	–
Sweden	15.5	21.3	280.2
United Kingdom	7.6	15.4	237.4
Canada	16.0	24.8	278.3
United States	14.7	19.1	328.8

Source: Maddison, op. cit. p. 240, app. 1. Maddison's table is compiled from a wide variety of sources and writers for the individual countries concerned.

expectations engendered in the private sector by these factors was one cause of the variation from country to country in rates of growth. But there were other factors which we must mention in passing, all of which may be classed as influences on the response of the supply side to the increase in demand. Of these, three are notable: recovery from the war, elimination of disguised unemployment and ability to close the gap between American and European productivity. The first of these elements was important in the case of Germany and slightly less so in those of France and Italy. Otherwise recovery, as we have seen, was swift. The second was important in some European countries where prolonged unemployment in the thirties had resulted in uneconomic use of labour. An over-large concentration of workers in agriculture, the preference of workers for secure rather than productive jobs and the survival of the small and the family business all contributed to a less than optimum use of the labour force. There was then a once-over gain in output to be had from the elimination of such concealed unemployment. It is notable that in almost all the European countries agricultural productivity rose fast in the fifties, but was accompanied by a huge release of manpower to other industries. The third influence, that of the large lag in European productivity compared with American, is more problematic. The gap was of long standing and in postwar Europe the awareness of American productive superiority had great effect. American management method was discussed and studied, productivity teams toured the United States, the necessity for a higher capital-output ratio in European industry was admitted. Powerful also was the demonstration effect of higher American living standards and a desire by European workers for the American standard of life.

It might appear at this point in our argument that the unprecedented flow of investment is sufficient explanation of the growth of GNP which took place. Obvious causes in economic history should, however, be viewed with suspicion. Given that investment grew and with it the industrial economies grew, leaves open the question of which was the prime factor. Investment is one input in the production process; to increase it is to alter the quantity and the mix of various other inputs necessarily associated with it, changes in scale, management, institutional factors and the like. It has been argued by some writers[3] that the incremental effect of these so-called 'residual factors' upon productivity in the postwar period was perhaps twice as great as the effect of investment itself. In this view of things investment, admittedly a major injection into any economy, is regarded as derivative and we are driven to ask the further question: what forces acted upon investment? The variations in the power of these forces can then explain many interesting questions about investment, why it varied between countries, why it varied over time, and what was its distribution among the many sub-categories into which it may be divided? We can do no more here than mention a few of the residual factors which may have borne upon investment rates in the early postwar period. One such factor was the demand for money capital expressed quantitatively by interest rates. For a century it has been fashionable in economic theory to attribute to the interest rate a major role in determining the level of investment. It is, however, an attribution which like many another in economics is unbacked by empirical evidence and for the late forties and early fifties there is little to sustain the view that interest rates were important. Germany with one of the highest investment rates in Europe had also high rates of interest largely because of deficiencies in her capital market. France had high rates until the later fifties because the Government maintained such rates to check inflation. In Britain, rates were very low until the early fifties and rose only moderately after that. Statistically it is impossible to isolate the interest rate from the many other factors that bear upon investment, but from survey investigations among firms it seems clear that interest rates were regarded as almost irrelevant in an industrial climate where future markets, prices, levels of demand and product opportunities were dominant.

Another factor bearing upon investment is the availability of capital. In other words, were entrepreneurs in the private sector in the postwar period constrained in their investment plans by shortage of finance and were the intra-country differences in investment rates due to variations in the amounts

[3] See N. Kaldor, 'Capital Accumulation and Economic Growth', in *Theory of Capital* (International Economic Association, 1961); R. C. O. Matthews, 'Some Aspects of Postwar Growth in the British Economy in Relation to Historical Experience', *Manchester Statistical Society* (1964). The case for regarding investment as the prime factor of economic growth is given in Maddison, *Economic Growth in the West* (London: Allen & Unwin, 1964) pp. 80 and 87.

of investible funds? The answer is almost certainly no, for with the level of demand for investible funds the supply was such as to give rates of interest which, we have already argued, were irrelevant to investment rates. Apart from this, and on the basis of the simplest of macroeconomic theory, savings must have kept reasonable pace with investment in view of the low rates of inflation which obtained in Western countries down to at least the mid-sixties. There is certainly no evidence to support a view that the 3–4 per cent rates of price inflation of the period 1945–55 were the result of investment exceeding saving. For explanation of these inflation rates one might look rather to high rates of government outlay, and the pricing-policies of firms faced with increasingly powerful labour unions under conditions of full employment. Evidence supports the view that, from a very early stage in postwar recovery, private and corporate savings were flowing at a rate at least not far behind the needs of new capital.[4]

Another so-called residual factor in determining investment lay in the different attitudes, favourable or apathetic, towards investment itself; in what might be described as 'dynamism' or 'thrust' in this industry and a willingness to 'muck along' or 'return to normal' in that. Such differences between industries were very apparent, for in every European country the demand for new capital was highest in the new industries – chemical, petro-chemical, man-made fibres, plastics, electronics, automobile and aircraft – and lowest in old long-established industries like textiles, mining, shipbuilding, building and construction. Two influences suggest themselves as driving forces of investment fitting this pattern. The first is that of 'relative factor cost'; that is, that the rising cost of one factor, labour, drove a high demand for the factor which might most economically replace it, capital. Thus, either high wages, or the expectation of high wages, might serve to make industries more capital intensive. The second influence is obviously that of technical innovation, of which in the immediate and later postwar periods there was no lack. The replacement of obsolete capital was not by replicas of the old, but by technically superior substitutes. Thus, even in comparatively old industries like the automobile industry, new models of greater refinement requiring more elaborate design, tooling and manufacture replaced the old. The jet aircraft replaced the piston-engine powered, synthetic textiles grew up alongside but did not oust natural fibres. Thus it was either in new-product industries or in industries where the product was capable of great development and variation that investment was concentrated and in such industries technical innovation gave rise to technical research and further development. The fixed-capital base was constantly deepened rather than widened, although some widening did necessarily take place. In older industries where replacement and replication of capital took place, the drive for investment

---

[4] *The World Economic Survey for 1960* (New York: United Nations, 1961) pp. 9–10 and 33–8, argued that throughout the period up to 1959 the total supply of savings increased *pari passu* with increases in GNP.

was narrower and more short-lived. It was also a fact that the innovations of
the forties and fifties were labour-saving and that they required a high
investment of capital per worker. The opening up of capital intensive fields
such as computers or the production of nuclear energy spring at once to mind.
Equally the application of automated production processes which computers
made possible in a variety of industries changed the capital–labour ratio in
favour of capital.

It has been argued[5] that the different endowments of countries with
modern and innovating industries goes far to explain different rates of
investment, that Germany with a brand-new industrial structure and Britain
with an old decrepit one demonstrate this linkage. It may well be a partial
explanation but it leaves serious questions unanswered. France was not well-
endowed with new galvanic industries, yet she raised herself by her
technocratic boot-straps and registered very high industrial growth rates in
the early sixties. While Britain had many old and sluggish industries, she had
also many new growth-type industries and it seems a poor explanation to
attribute her low investment performance to her industrial structure.

The picture of investment and growth which emerged in the first postwar
decade is one in which both acted and interacted under the influence of high
and sustained demand, technological change and innovative enterprise. The
great initial thrust of the immediate postwar replacement and recovery boom
was the prime mover. From then on the boom continued, constantly fuelled
by investment demand and innovation on a scale unprecedented and, in
contrast to the past, uninterrupted by government-engineered deflations.

Turn briefly now to the influence which without doubt has driven the
economies of the West hard and continuously since the war, the policies of
Government. After the First World War the postwar-reconstruction boom
was ended in Western countries by purposive monetary policy. The boom,
once broken, gave way to fitful bursts of economic activity and a period of
relative expansion in the later twenties before the plunge into depression in
1930. Government economic policies were purely *ad hoc* and often served to
exacerbate conditions rather than to alleviate them. After the Second World
War it was different. Governments were pledged to high employment
policies. There was no attempt to check the immediate postwar expansion.
Monetary policy was in most countries in abeyance with interest rates at very
low levels and while the private sector surged ahead with replacement and
expansionary investment, the public sector had its own grandiose spending
programmes. Thus, government policies tended to overlay and neutralise the
cyclical propensities of the private sector. The maintenance of full employment and the relative stability of the industrial economies provided an
economic climate in which profit expectations promoted high investment and
expansion.

[5] See Postan, op. cit. p. 131.

It must not, of course, be assumed from all this that government policies were perfect. One evident shortcoming was that government policies were aimed dominantly at full employment in the short term and that the longer-term issues of the growth and balance of the economy were at first not considered. Another difficulty lay in the degree of success with which governments were able to cope with the problems which high employment and growth produced; in particular, with price increases and balance-of-payments deficits. Here countries differed considerably. The United States, Canada and Belgium did not maintain high enough levels of demand to preserve full employment, sacrificing thereby potential economic growth. Britain, obsessed by the aim of preserving high levels of employment, drove the economy too much, raising prices and creating balance-of-payments deficits. Germany, schooled by two hyper-inflations within living memory, aimed at price stability, accepting a somewhat lower level of employment. France, to whom the balance of payments was a marginal consideration, was able in the late fifties and early sixties to achieve prodigious growth rates and transform its industrial structure. Thus, there emerged among the industrial countries, fast-growers and slow-growers. In the first group were countries such as Germany, whose pace was steady and controlled like a long-distance runner who achieves the rhythm and pace he desires, or like France or Italy, prepared to tolerate inconvenience and transitory problems in the interest of high overall performance. In the second were Britain, faced with the task of handling an international reserve currency with an erratic balance of payments, inadequate reserves and large quick liabilities; the United States, in which policy allowed demand to flag and where in mighty affluence a modest measure of unemployment did not appear a waste; and Canada, linked firmly to the United States and incapable of independent action.

It would be an interesting but lengthy exercise to analyse the policies of individual countries in order to explain differences in their growth rates. All we can say here is that growth occurred and was encouraged because there was high demand and full employment which in turn encouraged growth. But growth policies by government hardly existed in the early fifties and would have involved much more than the mere maintenance of demand. As a minimum they would have included: controlling the long-term movement of demand; maintaining and fostering competitiveness in foreign trade; and encouraging high industrial productivity. By chance, intuition and favourable circumstance some countries came near to doing these things; others failed to do so.

We turn now from government policies to government spending, an item so large that it inevitably plays a major role in determining the momentum of the economy. As can be seen from Table 5.3, government expenditure on goods and services increased as a proportion of GNP in every major industrial country except Germany between 1950 and 1960. If to expenditure on goods and services are added transfer payments and interest on the public debt, the

TABLE 5.3

Government Current Expenditure on Goods and Services as a Proportion of GNP at Current Prices

	1950	1960
Belgium	9.8	12.1
Denmark	10.3	12.6
France	12.9	13.3
Germany	14.4	13.6
Italy	11.1	14.5
Netherlands	12.6	13.5
Norway	10.6	14.6
Sweden	13.9	17.7
United Kingdom	15.6	16.6
Canada	10.6	14.4
United States	10.6	17.2

Source: A. Maddison, *Economic Growth in the West*, p. 103. The table was compiled by Maddison from OECD sources.

proportion of total current expenditure to GNP, for the same group of countries as in Table 5.4, ranged in 1957 from 21 to 30 per cent. A constant increase in a category of total demand as important as this was clearly so great as to almost nullify the effects of variations in private sector outlays.

If we divide government outlays into convenient subdivisions – government consumption (including defence), transfer payments, capital outlay on public works, and spending in those parts of the economy which are publicly owned – we can locate the main sources of expansion in public-sector demand. From the realm of government consumption, two factors stand out: first, the relative importance of government consumption measured as a proportion of GNP had by 1960 increased in all countries save Germany and Italy[6] as compared with prewar; second, government expenditures on goods and services in the 1950s increased faster in money terms than private demand in all countries except Germany. The main reason for this twofold expansion lay in defence expenditures which were heavy and increasing throughout the 1950s and on into the sixties. The fact that Germany was curtailed in her rearmament was an economic advantage to that country.

Most transfer payments are designed to raise the consumption level of people in lower income groups. Pensions, family allowances, unemployment and sickness benefits and medical allowances are examples. The appearance and growth of these social payments has been a feature of most European countries since the war. One feature of such transfer payments was to give a

[6] The prewar totalitarian regimes in these countries were large spenders in both the military and public works categories.

TABLE 5.4

Matrix of World Exports, 1960

Exports to	Industrial countries	Other developed areas	Under-developed countries	Centrally planned economies	Total
Industrial countries[a]	37	5	16	2	60
Other developed areas[b]	4	n	1	1	6
Underdeveloped countries[c]	14	1	5	1	21
Centrally planned economies[d]	2	n	1	8	12
Total	57	6	23	12	100

[a] EEC countries, Austria, Canada, Denmark, Japan, Norway, Sweden, Switzerland, United Kingdom, United States of America.
[b] Other Europe, Australia, New Zealand, South Africa.
[c] Underdeveloped countries which were members of IMF.
[d] Europe and Asia.
n Negligible.
Discrepancies in totals due to rounding.

Source: IMF, *Direction of Trade*, vol. 2; *1960–4.*

stability to consumption which would have been lacking in their absence; this in its turn contributing to the confidence which favoured investment.

Public works expenditure was not, in the early postwar period such an important part of total demand as might be supposed. Its magnitude in most countries was varied to allow for the large size of other items and outlays on roads and infrastructure tended to lag behind the needs of the economy. Nevertheless, the existence of large waiting programmes of public works expenditure served to bolster confidence in full employment since such programmes could always be begun in the event of flagging demand elsewhere.

Even from the foregoing brief review of the main factors influencing demand and supply in the industrial countries it is evident that almost all worked towards expansion, full employment and growth. Indeed, for a concomitance of such favourable influences, modern economic history has no parallel. Yet, thus far, we have examined only the domestic influences, common to the industrial countries. Another and perhaps the greatest force was trade, which in the fifties and sixties grew and exerted its influence on the growth of its participants.

(ii)   TRADE

Although restrictions on trade were great and lingered on, in the postwar period, until 1960, the total value of the trade of non-communist countries rose from $53.3 bln in 1948 to $112.3 bln in 1960 – an average annual rate of growth of 6 per cent.[7] Not all countries shared equally in this growth. The industrialised countries of Europe, North America and Japan increased their relative share of world exports from 61 to 70 per cent. Other developed countries (Australia, New Zealand, South Africa and some smaller European countries outside the OEEC) saw their share fall from 9 to 7 per cent. The share of the developing countries fell from 30 to 23 per cent.

By the mid-fifties world trade, both in primary commodities and in manufactures, was expanding faster than world production. Between 1953 and 1960 (inclusive) world production increased by 44 per cent in volume with agricultural output growing by 22 per cent. During the same period the volume of manufactured exports rose by 83 per cent and of primary products by 44 per cent. This increase in the foreign trade proportion[8] continued into the sixties and in 1963 it was about 25 per cent higher than in 1953. It should be noted, however, that even by the latter date the proportion fell short of its 1913 and 1928 values.

At the heart of the increase in world trade was Western Europe which in

---

[7] This is the more impressive in that prices of traded commodities were approximately the same in 1960 as in 1948.

[8] The ratio of trade to GNP.

1960 accounted for 38 per cent of world exports. From 1948 to 1962 the index of export values (1958 = 100) rose from 40 to 138. Between 1948 and 1962 exports and imports of European countries grew at an annual average rate of about 7 per cent while GNP grew at an annual average rate of about 4 per cent. Moreover, European trade grew faster than that of the world as a whole. The index of exports of European countries by volume rose by 275 per cent between 1948 and 1962; for the world as a whole the increase was 230 per cent. In value terms for the same period European exports rose by 200 per cent and world exports by 150 per cent. Tables 5.4 and 5.5 show the relative importance of country groups in world trade in 1960 and the country rates of growth of exports for leading countries. Table 5.6 shows clearly that by 1960 two-thirds of the world's trading was done by the developed countries and that nearly half of such trade was with other developed countries. Time comparisons of the data from which Table 5.4 is compiled show that the trade growth of the industrial countries was at the expense of the developing countries. Moreover, the industrial countries provided by far the largest market for the products of the developing countries.

Tables 5.5 and 5.6 illumine the export performance of the trade leaders. The former shows the great difference in the rates at which countries increased their trade during the fifties. Seven countries had growth rates for exports in excess of that for the world as a whole and for at least three of these (Germany, Italy and the Netherlands) the rise in exports must have been a powerful factor in demand and a stimulus to the growth of their economies. Perhaps the most outstanding feature in Table 5.5 is the very low rate of growth of U.K. trade – making her the only country in which exports grew less than total output.[9, 10] This poor performance has been variously explained but never very satisfactorily. A number of hypotheses are: high pressure of demand for output drawing goods to the home market; fitful domestic demand policies born of the British desire to preserve sterling as a reserve currency; diminishing competitiveness due to long delivery dates and poor after-sales service; a concentration on commodities for which world demand was relatively stagnant; failure to concentrate export effort in the fastest-growing markets – but it is impossible to assign weights to these causes, all of which probably played some role in what was certainly a dramatic relative decline for a great trading nation.[11]

Turning to Table 5.6, we find that, with three exceptions, the trade shares

[9] For Canada the rates of growth of output and exports were the same.

[10] If we relate the level of British exports of manufactured goods to gross domestic product (at constant prices) the ratio is very stable. Between 1956 and 1966 it varied only within the range 13.8–14.3. Manufactured exports account for three-quarters of total exports. Imports varied within the range 4.1–7.9. Since the import/GNP ratio rose, the constancy of the export ratio implies a progressive deterioration of the British merchandise trade balance.

[11] For a good analysis of Britain's deteriorating trade position in the fifties and sixties see L. B. Krause, 'British Trade Performance', chap. v of *Britain's Economic Prospects* (Washington: Brookings Institution, 1968).

TABLE 5.5

Rate of Change in the Volume of Exports

	Average annual percentage growth, 1950–60
Belgium	7.7
France	7.2
Germany	15.8
Italy	11.8
Netherlands	10.0
Sweden	5.5
Switzerland	7.8
United Kingdom	1.9
Western Europe	7.0
Canada	3.8
United States	5.0
World	6.4

Source: A. Maddison, 'Growth and Fluctuation in the World Economy, 1870–1960', *Banca Nazionale del Lavoro Quarterly Review* (June 1962)

TABLE 5.6

Trade Shares of Some Industrial Countries, 1937–60

	Percentage of World Exports		
	1937	*1950*	*1960*
United Kingdom	20	20	14
France	7	10	9
Germany[a]	16	6	15
Other Western Europe[b]	20	20	21
Canada	8	9	7
United States	23	32	28
Japan	6	3	5
	100	100	100

[a] The geographical difference between prewar and postwar Germany affects the comparability of these figures.
[b] Belgium, Luxemburg, the Netherlands, Italy and Sweden.

Sources: IMF, *Direction of Trade, 1960–64*; A. G. Kenwood and A. L. Lougheed, *Growth of the International Economy, 1820–1960* (London: Allen & Unwin, 1971) p. 286.

of the major industrial countries were remarkably stable over the period 1937 to 1960. The first exception was Germany, which, for obvious reasons, dropped her share in the immediate postwar period and increased it spectacularly in the fifties. The second exception was the United States, which increased her share in the immediate postwar period because of her temporary position as almost sole supplier of a wide range of manufactured goods. The third exception was Britain, which continued in the postwar period a secular decline in her share of world trade which began in the nineteenth century.[12]

Finally, a glance at the commodity composition of world trade is necessary. Table 5.7 shows the changes over the same period as the last three tables in the shares of commodity groups in world exports. Manufactures increased in relative importance; primary products, both food and raw materials, declined. Within these broad classifications and not discernible in Table 5.7,

TABLE 5.7
Commodity Groups in World Exports, 1937–60

| | Percentage of Total Exports | | |
	1937	*1950*	*1960*
Food	23	23	18
Raw materials	40	34	29
Total primary products	63	57	47
Manufactures	37	43	53
Total trade	100	100	100

Source: D. W. Slater, *World Trade and Economic Growth: Trends and Prospects with Applications to Canada* (Toronto: Queen's Printer, 1968) p. 29.

there was a shift in the manufacturing group away from textiles and in favour of machinery and transport equipment. Chemicals continued a long upward trend. Thus, capital-goods trade accounted for much of the expansion in manufactures at the expense of consumer goods. The relative decline in food as a trade element in the 1950 to 1960 period can no doubt be attributed to a growing drive for self-sufficiency by the former large importers and a natural relative decline in the food element in expenditures in the rich countries as incomes rose. Within the raw-materials group, both agricultural and mineral products declined from 1937, despite notable increases within the minerals group reflecting rising world demand for fossil fuels.

The picture that emerges from scrutiny of the world, country and commodity trade of the period up to 1960 is one of spectacular growth

[12] Care should be taken in assigning too much significance to trade shares. It is, of course, quite conceivable that a country whose share of world trade is declining may still have a satisfactory balance-of-payments position even over a run of years. This is particularly true if the declining share is a share of a swiftly growing total. In the case of Britain, however, the fall in the trade share is usually taken as corroborative evidence of a deep-seated deterioration of the British trade position.

among the industrial nations in trade in their own products and of only modest growth (and declining relative importance) in the trade of the primary producers both with each other and with the industrial countries. Since the division of countries into industrial and primary producers is similar (but not precisely the same) as that between developed and developing countries, we come near to concluding that in this period the rich countries were getting richer, the poor were becoming relatively poorer. This unevenly distributed growth of the world economy, spanning as it has done more than a quarter-century, has been one of the most influential economic forces in our time, producing a great gap, politically, economically and strategically between the developed and the developing countries.

It remains in this discussion of the great trade resurgence to consider a number of general considerations which arise. The first of these lies in a discrepancy which exists, or appears to exist, between the trade growth which has occurred and the theory by which we are supposed to explain changes in real trade flows. On the basis of the pure trade theory of the thirties and of predictions made by some economists on other grounds, the great growth of intra-industrial trade, particularly in capital goods, in the fifties and sixties was anomalous.

The most widely accepted theory of international trade in the thirties was based on the so-called Heckscher–Ohlin theorem, a development by two distinguished Swedish writers[13] of the earlier Ricardian theory of comparative costs. By this theory trade was based on the country-to-country variation of factor endowments. The greater the differences in (*a*) factor quantities and (*b*) the intensity of factor use, the greater the volume of trade. With great precision the older theory of comparative costs, a mere elaboration of international division of labour, was extended. Differences in commodity values were the basis of trade, and differences in such values were the result of varying factor endowment. While some empirical investigations of the fifties somewhat clouded the purity of this ingenious analysis, it still holds its ground in the pure theory chapters of the international trade textbooks.

But the theory carried an evident corollary. If trade was indeed caused by unequal factor endowments, with time and economic development, trade itself would ensure that the more mobile factors, labour and capital, would cross frontiers and that in the long-run factor endowments (except unique land or climate) would tend to equalise and trade would diminish. This, however, clearly did not happen. Not only was there in the postwar period a strong secular growth in trade, but most of this change lay in increasing trade between the industrial countries of which the factor pattern was fairly

[13] See Bertil Ohlin, *Interregional and International Trade*, rev. ed. (Cambridge, Mass.: Harvard University Press, 1967); Eli Heckscher, *Ekonomisk Tidskrift*, vol. xxi (1919) pp. 497–512. The latter work, an article originally in Swedish, is reproduced in abridged form and in English in *Readings in the Theory of International Trade*, ed. H. S. Ellis and L. M. Metzler (Homewood, Ill.: Irwin, 1949) chap. 13, pp. 272–300.

uniform. Trade between the mature and the developing countries where factor patterns differed greatly was declining relatively. As interpreter of the postwar trade pattern, the Heckscher–Ohlin theory performs badly.

In such a situation one may abandon the theory and seek more plausible explanations or one may attempt to save the theory by attributing events to temporary aberrations not accommodated within the model. Neither of these courses will be followed here. To the writer the Heckscher–Ohlin theorem has always appeared more elegant and ingenious than useful in historical interpretation and empirical evidence and the wind of change may, therefore, blow where it listeth. In any event this narrative is concerned with historical facts and their interpretation rather than with fitting theory to the real world. It would seem that forces more powerful than differences in factor endowment took command of trade after the Second World War. What were these forces?

Probably the greatest was the progressive restoration by 1960 of a system of relatively free trade between major industrial countries. This change was confined to the industrial countries, but restrictions on trade in the rest of the world were not sufficient to retard the trade growth. In Western European countries trade in the immediate postwar period was severely constrained by bilateral trading and payments agreements. Not until 1948 did production make exportable surpluses available and at that time the Marshall Plan provided finance for higher levels of imports. Within Europe, the code of liberalisation of OEEC established targets for trade liberalisation while in 1950 the European Payments Union made European currencies convertible, not only with Europe, but through sterling in the sterling area and through the franc in the franc area. Thus, bilateralism withered away and was replaced by area convertibility and relative trade freedom. The areas of trade freedom became wider. Ultimately, in the late fifties, they were united and virtually the whole of the non-Communist industrial world was free from direct controls on trade and payments.

There were also tariffs. Progress in lowering these was modest upto the mid-fifties. GATT and the application of the most-favoured-nation clause was responsible for some alleviation. But in 1957 there was a big step forward. The Treaty of Rome of 1957 provided for progressive removal of tariffs within a customs union which accounted for a sizeable part of continental Europe. The European Free Trade Area (EFTA), set up in 1959, accounted for much of what remained and provided for internal tariff reductions which matched those of EEC. Somewhat later, in 1962, the 'Dillon Round' of GATT negotiations resulted in a general reduction of tariffs of 20 per cent in the industrial countries. The tariff reductions of the fifties and sixties were modest in amount but coupled with the disappearance of non-tariff trade barriers the stimulus to trade was considerable. It should be noted, however, that this stimulus was confined to the mature, industrial countries. The non-tariff barriers were considerable in the developing countries and lingered long after they had disappeared in the OEEC group, while tariffs against the exports of manufacturers by the developing countries were reduced little, if at all, by the industrial countries. Moreover, the effective rates of such tariffs in most cases exceeded the nominal rates and constituted a very considerable barrier to entry.

A second influence on the postwar trade pattern was that of the terms of trade. These, with the exception of a brief interlude during the Korean War, were uniformly in favour of the industrial countries. Such trade terms might have been expected to reduce the demand of primary producers for industrial products and to have thereby reduced the trade of the developed countries. In fact, it does not appear to have done so. Probably foreign aid and tied lending served to maintain such exports. In any event the steep rise in industrial imports by the industrial countries from one another was the mainspring of export expansion.

A third factor propelling trade expansion was the steady increase in *per capita* incomes in the rich countries. This ensured that the sophisticated products of such countries found ready markets in similar rather than in less-developed countries. Certainly the products of both capital and consumer goods industries were avidly exchanged by the rich countries, the exchange seeming to rest upon a fine differentiation of product lines rather than upon factor endowment or the intensity of factor use. Thus, between Britain, France, Germany and Italy, all having large automobile industries, trade in cars increased steadily. The same might be said of a wide range of consumer durables. All this was only possible because rising incomes provided expanding markets in all the industrial countries. There was also the general macroeconomic effect of rising GNP levels. Even if marginal propensities to import did not increase the amount of imports would rise fastest in the countries whose income rose fastest. Since these were the West European countries, it is evident that there was a constant trade impeller for such countries. In certain countries, where exports were the leading sector, trade itself was a main growth-force, in others income growth sprang from domestic causes pulling trade in its wake. In any event it is clear that the fastest-growing areas tended to generate trade increases and this was undoubtedly the case with Western Europe in the fifties.

Finally, technological change played a considerable role in trade expansion. Innovations and particularly their application to new-product lines conferred upon the innovating countries and on firms and industries within them, significant competitive power and potential for new market penetration. Technical innovations were not only cost-saving in the productive process; they were, when they led to new products, a generator of the new specialisation which lay behind much of the boom in industrial products in the fifties. Moreover, the larger European countries provided domestic markets large enough to nurture new industries producing such products and allowed them to grow to a scale at which they could operate economically.

All this was true of the early and later fifties but it soon became apparent that for many firms the growth potential was greater than the domestic market alone could sustain. In automobiles, civil aircraft, chemicals, synthetic textiles, electronics and (in the sixties) computers, the necessary scale of operations overspilled frontiers and generated trade either through the build-up of export markets or by trade-creating disintegration of production on an international basis.[14] The picture which emerges is one of growth industries, which through innovations, research and development on a great scale and early exploitation of market opportunities, added to national outputs and, soon outgrowing their home markets, expanded by export sales and ultimately by direct investment spread their activities over several countries.

(iii)　THE AGE OF INFLATION

Despite its greater scale the price effects of the Second World War were somewhat less than those of the First World War. Table 5.8 summarises the price records of a number of countries over the war period and in the first decade of peace. If we compare prices in 1945 or 1946 with those in 1938 or 1939 we may divide countries into groups according to the steepness of increase of their price levels over the period. In the first group, Canada, United States, Australia, South Africa and Venezuela had increases between 30 and 45 per cent; in the second group, the United Kingdom, New Zealand, Switzerland, Denmark, Ireland, Argentina, Norway, and Sweden had increases between 50 and 100 per cent. In a third group, consisting of the Netherlands, Portugal, Spain, Mexico, Belgium, Chile, Brazil and Egypt, the increase was two- to fourfold. In Japan, prices increased tenfold, in Italy, twentyfive fold, and in Hungary, Greece, Romania and China there were hyper-inflations.

　In most countries price inflation coming from war expenditures, consumer-goods scarcities and large pent-up consumer demand lasted well into the postwar period. Unlike after the First World War, there were no purposive deflations and prices tended to level out or take on more gradual rates of increase once the sharp rises of the immediate postwar period (1946–8) were spent. Countries which had succeeded in controlling their price levels well during the war (United States and Canada) removed some or all of the controls in this period allowing prices to rise. Those which had had very high wartime inflation rates, such as Germany, resorted to currency reforms, while a third group deferred decontrol until supply caught up, or nearly caught up,

---

[14] It seems probable that the scarce factor of efficient management, which economic theory tells us limited the optimum capacity of firms, was stretched in the fifties and sixties as firms grew ever larger. No doubt the techniques of scientific management, the advances in instant communication, the use of the computer and mechanised accounting processes all made this growth possible. That it also brought with it great new concentrations of economic power was also soon apparent.

TABLE 5.8

Wholesale Prices, 1938–55 (selected years)

(1953 = 100)

	1938	1946	1948	1950	1951	1952	1953	1954	1955
Belgium	24	80	94	93	113	107	100	99	101
France	4	24	65	78	100	105	100	98	98
Germany	46	–	90	85	100	103	100	98	101
Netherlands	27	67	75	87	107	104	100	101	102
Italy	2	55	104	93	106	100	100	101	101
Norway	37	62	66	76	94	101	100	102	104
Sweden	38	62	72	76	100	106	100	100	104
Denmark	33	62	74	86	109	107	100	100	103
United Kingdom	31	53	67	80	97	100	100	100	104
United States	46	71	95	94	104	101	100	101	101
Canada	46	63	88	96	109	102	100	98	99
Japan[1]	–	5	43	79	96	98	100	103	101
Australia[2]	31	44	53	69	85	98	100	99	102
New Zealand	41	62	72	78	91	101	100	99	100
Switzerland	47	94	102	95	107	104	100	101	101

[1] Consumers' goods only.

[2] Basic materials, home consumption of food, raw materials and farm products.

Source: United Nations, Statistical Yearbooks, 1938–55.

with demand. Finally, there were a few countries (United Kingdom, New Zealand and Norway) which retained controls for a longer period. In general, it may be said that the pattern of price level increases across countries in 1946–8 was conditioned by the choices of when price control and rationing was removed and of how the transition to prices in a free-market economy were handled.[15]

Before the price effects of this transition to free markets had run their course, two events occurred which tended also to raise prices in the leading countries: the first was the realignment (through devaluation) of exchange rates in 1949; the second was the boom in primary-commodity prices which followed the outbreak of war in Korea in 1950. Since these events occurred almost together it is impossible to separate their effects. It is, however, certain that both had inflationary effect and for most countries 1951 or 1952 were peak years for prices in the first half of the fifties.

The combined effects of the exchange devaluations and the Korean War provided the first worldwide inflation of the postwar period. While it was of modest dimension, it provided some interesting lessons and a foretaste of much that was to come. First of such lessons was that while price levels did subside after the boom there was not a complete reversal (see Table 5.8, p. 70). By 1953 wholesale prices had fallen in most countries but only to a high plateau from which they were later to resume a steady rise through the later fifties and early sixties. The 'ratchet effect' of prices was apparent: they could and did rise but they almost never fell. For this there were probably two reasons. The first was the concomitance of expansionary factors present in the whole industrial economy in the postwar period. In particular, after the Korean War, the general rearmament in the West added high defence outlays to the already strained level of demand. But beyond this was a second influence. While within the structure of costs of production, raw material costs might rise or fall, there was no such possibility with labour costs. The greater power of trade unionism and its extension in industry was coupled with a new realisation of its bargaining power under conditions of full employment. From henceforth wages might be expected to rise but never to fall. From then until now it has been merely a question of what the rise would be. In the annual round of wage increase in which unions jostle to get ahead and seize for their members a place in the sun, there emerged a powerful cost-inflationary force. This, with the pressure of buoyant consumer demand, high private-sector investment fed by profit and growth expectation and large and ever-expanding government outlays, was to provide through the whole of the period covered in this book price levels which rose and required careful fiscal and monetary management to control.

[15] Control of the demand side through rationing was ended at various times but tended to precede the ending of price controls. The United States and Canada ended price control and rationing almost simultaneously in 1946 and 1947. Between June 1949 and early 1950, Australia, Austria, France, Denmark and Sweden abolished or simplified their rationing systems. The United Kingdom, New Zealand and Norway lagged behind.

6

The Recognition of the Third World

(i) THE PROBLEM

Among the world's nations in the fifties the rich got richer and the poor, in most cases, got poorer. Between 1955 and 1960 real GNP *per capita* rose by 10 per cent in the developed countries; for the developing countries the comparable figure was, on the average, 4 per cent. This relative decline of the poor nations has been a feature of the period with which this book is concerned. It has revealed a fissure in the international economy the consequences of which in human, economic and political terms it would be hard to exaggerate. It is with us now: it will remain with us for decades to come. It is essential that we get it in perspective. This chapter attempts to do that for the first part of our period.

(ii) FORMS AND SIZE OF AID; DONORS AND RECIPIENTS

What has come to be called 'the problem of the Third World' was sensed rather than recognised before the Second World War. To those who thought about it, it presented itself in two forms. The first of these was a vague, tacit recognition that it would be economically advantageous for many countries, chiefly in the southern hemisphere, to develop their economies and to raise the standard of life of their populations. To do so would eradicate many social wastes and alleviate much suffering. As to method there was even greater vagueness. Infra-structure should be provided by foreign capital; social organisation, legal systems and land tenure should be reformed. Industrialisation and Western life-style might ultimately dispel poverty. The problems were dimly discerned. Colonialism had brought some of the benefits of Western life. Medical service, rudimentary public health and sanitation had lengthened life and enabled populations to burgeon. Minimal investment in ports and infra-structure had brought peripheral trading prosperity to cities or to fringe coastal areas. Traditional ways of life were often disturbed but seldom transformed in ways that increased productive effort. Education often created a small class attuned to Western values but with no opportunity to apply or diffuse them. Above all, the low rates of saving of traditional societies gave no basis for investment on a scale sufficient to meet rises in population. While the demonstration effect of the life-style of colonial administrators caused growing demands for a better material life, such countries were static, far short of Rostow's condition of take-off into self-sustaining growth.[1] For the economic dynamics of development, neo-classical economics had little help to offer. It was to be hoped that beneficent imperial powers would grapple with the economic problems of their dominions, for the rest, the draw of risk capital to exploit new resources would have to suffice.

The second conception of the development problem was more immediate and practical. The poor countries of the world are also producers of its primary products and hence the suppliers of food and raw materials to the rich industrial countries. In the trading nexus between primary producers and industrial users serious problems had been revealed. In the period between the two World Wars these problems had assumed crisis proportions. The inelastic nature of primary-product supply, the inelastic demand of the user countries, the destabilising effects of terms of trade changes upon the suppliers – all these had had their effects, their incidence falling most heavily upon the suppliers. The depression years of the thirties had been disastrous for the primary producers and despite innovative market schemes to control prices, smooth long-run supplies and stabilise incomes, the depression had wrought economic havoc in the primary-producing countries. There seemed every prospect that in the postwar period instabilities would reappear. It was thus in the form of the primary-product marketing problem that the developing countries impinged most on Western thinking in the prewar years.

This picture of Western attitudes to developing countries was transformed over the war period. By 1944 we find the Bretton Woods Conference setting up the World Bank and explicitly recognising the necessity for Western capital assistance to such countries; we find by 1947 a programme of foreign aid by the United States which by 1957 totalled $90 b.; while the other industrial countries, in varying degree, accepted the principle of the necessity for aid and and, as their rates of recovery allowed, made their contributions. It was in the United States that the forces of change were most at work for, in the immediate postwar years, that was the only country economically capable of giving expression to changing attitudes. What, in the course of a mere decade, wrought this change?

The answer lies in several factors. Of these by far the most powerful was a realisation of the importance of development aid as a strategy in the Cold War. From 1948, the year of the Marshall Plan, development programmes were conceived by the United States as part of a global strategy to contain communism and limit Soviet influence. Since the Korean War the American Congress has been unwilling to give foreign assistance apart from some wider pattern of political and military strategy. Aid was refused to countries trading with Communist countries. So widely recognised was the American motive

[1] See W. W. Rostow, *The Stages of Economic Growth* (Cambridge: Cambridge University Press, 1960).

that some developing countries (Burma and Indonesia) refused aid rather than take sides in the Cold War. A complete analysis of American aid policy in the fifties and sixties would be impossible without a concurrent review of the unfolding American political and military strategy. Not only does political strategy go far to account for the emergence of aid in the world scene, it accounts also for the American lead in aid policy.

A second important set of reasons for the new approach to the developing countries was economic, within which paradigm there are several facets. In the beginning of the postwar period when the United States was almost the only country capable of giving foreign aid, such aid was considered by Congress to be 'all of a piece', in the interests of promoting world trade, non-discrimination and the Bretton Woods ideals. The persistence of a foreign-aid bill of $4–5 bln a year was seen as a price to be paid for revitalising the international flow of goods in free channels. The watershed for the transformation of this approach to the strategic one of military aid and containment was the Korean War (1950–1) by which time aid to developed countries had ceased and been superseded by aid to what are now called 'developing countries'. From then a three-pronged economic argument justifying economic aid emerged. First, was the stressing of industrial countries' increasing dependence on foreign sources of raw materials. These must be ensured by keeping supplying countries economically viable and by ongoing interest in smooth marketing arrangements for key materials. Second, was the belief that the developing countries must be expanded as markets for industrial products and as such they could be developed through loans, particularly tied loans, and foreign aid programmes. Third, it was argued that world prosperity was indivisible and that it would be impossible for industrial countries to remain prosperous indefinitely in a world, half of whose population lived below the poverty level.

Finally, it is possible to say that there was a deep humanitarian base to the new study of economic aid to poor countries. It was not powerful nor widespread, nor would it, of itself, have been sufficient to generate change. But coupled with the other motivations, it played its part. It came from several sources: from some few politicians,[2] from prominent and influential economists such as Gunnar Myrdal, Arthur Lewis and Raul Prébisch; from wealthy foundations; from rich countries with low political commitments such as Sweden or Canada and from a growing mountain of data and empirical material collected by international agencies. Although often debased, as when humanitarian motives were piously claimed for economic policies which were in fact practical and hard-headed, human sympathy and disinterestedness has played its part.

We may also include as humanitarian the ongoing interests of former imperial countries in areas and regions in which they had laid a development

[2] It is difficult to explain the Truman Point Four Program without giving weight to its humanitarian aspects.

basis. Britain and France both showed a responsibility to former colonial territories in which the acquired legal and institutional backgrounds were akin to their own.

Thus far we have said little of the developing countries themselves and their changing attitudes towards their poverty and their place in the economic world. In its essence their emergence as a group of nations, as the Third World, has been an acceleration of processes long in being. Consciousness of relative poverty and economic stagnation is not new. It existed in the great colonial systems and in any dependent country in which the population was able to observe the life-style, wealth and ease of the ruling administrative class. But expression of this yearning for economic equality had to wait on the political ferment of the postwar period and on the emergence of dependent territories of the great powers as independent states. After the Second World War more than sixty new countries gained formal independence within fifteen years. With independence came a rising political consciousness in these countries and in other countries neither new nor developed. With this came clamant demands for modernisation and progress. The postwar history of developing countries in this context has been in three phases: first, a realisation of their own poverty and need; second, a demand for aid from the rich countries as of right; and, third, later consciousness of their power as a group and the development of a strategy to exploit that power. The first two of these phases falls into the time span of this chapter, the third, a development of the sixties, is the concern of Chapter 11.

(iii) TRADE IN PRIMARY PRODUCTS

The formative period of development-financing began in 1945 and ended with the conclusion of the European Recovery Programme in June 1952. This financing was dominantly done by the United States, but it was increasingly augmented by United Nations' functional agencies such as the Fund and Bank and by the Export–Import Bank of Washington. Early aid was not to the developing countries but was directed to the aim of European economic recovery. In the years 1945–8 only limited credits, mostly a continuation of wartime emergency programmes, went to developing countries. A few true development credits (only about $275 m. in the period 1945–8) were made by the Eximbank to Latin America. In the same period the World Bank made only one development loan but this was disbursed much later. This, with limited aid from the European colonial powers to their dependencies, was the sum total of development aid up to the beginning of the Marshall Plan.

In the years 1948–52 Marshall Aid to Western Europe dominated the aid scene and only small amounts of additional capital were made available through the World Bank and the Export–Import Bank of Washington.

Between 1952 and 1960 the aid programme gathered speed and volume. In perspective two aspects of it emerged: the increase in bilateral aid, at first by the United States and then by a growing number of developed countries; and increased and ramified lending by international agencies. It is worth glancing briefly at each of these facets in turn.

During the fifties the United States' policy on development shifted several times but the trend was continually towards the giving of liberal financial and technical assistance to countries with which America had military alliances or which, in the absence of aid, might defect to the Communist bloc. It was accepted that the aid programme to Western Europe was nonrecurrent and that, once postwar reconstruction was achieved, aid to developing countries would be available in adequate amounts from private investment and from the loans of specialised agencies such as the World Bank. This attitude was modified at the policy level by Truman's Point Four Policy statement of January 1949,[3] which announced 'a bold new programme for making the benefits of [United States] scientific advances and industrial progress available for the improvement and growth of under-developed countries . . .'. Although conceived mainly with an emphasis upon technical assistance in the fields of agriculture, health and education, the Point Four Programme did include modest grants of direct financial assistance.

The determination that after 1952 the United States should withdraw from the aid field was abandoned for non-economic reasons – the realisation that American political and military alliances would have to be cemented by liberal applications of dollars and that uncommitted countries would have to be wooed by this means lest they succumb to Soviet blandishments. Thus the European Recovery Programme was succeeded by the Mutual Security Programme and between 1952 and 1957 United States aid of $9.1 bln was given to a number of countries in the Middle and Far East which flanked the Soviet Union and Communist China. Only small amounts of aid went to Africa and Latin America. Part of Mutual Security Assistance was for defence, but there was also development and general economic aid – soft loans repayable in local currencies or loans derived from the sale of surplus commodities.

In 1953 the Eisenhower Administration made an attempt to withdraw from official aid-giving and leave the task in the hands of the U.N. functional agencies. Much in earnest, the U.S. Treasury even brought pressure on the Eximbank in 1953 to terminate its development lending with the result that the credits given by the Bank more than halved between August 1953 and August 1954. But the American attempt to withdraw was in vain. Aid was now hot politics. In the Economic and Social Council (ESC) of the United Nations the dissolution of colonial empires was adding new countries, many of doubtful economic viability, each with its demands. The Soviet Union was

---

[3] The programme was so called because it was enunciated in Point Four of Truman's Inaugural Speech in 1949.

ready with promises of economic largesse[4] which had to be matched. Moreover, the Americans were now too deeply involved in development financing to withdraw, and in the later fifties their foreign aid expanded steadily. Certain trends also became apparent: there was a shift from grants to loans and a growing emphasis on project aid. In 1957 the Development Loan Fund was established with an appropriation of $300 m. By the fiscal year ended 30 June 1959 loans by the Mutual Security Agency (MSA) and the Development Lending Fund (DLF) to developing countries totalled $530 m. By 30 June 1961 lending by the same two agencies topped $650 m. Meanwhile, the Eximbank, with restriction on its lending lifted in 1954, doubled its loans in 1955 to over $600 m. By the fiscal year 1961 lending from this source was running at an annual rate of more than $800 m.[5]

By the end of the fifties we find a situation in which the United States was committed, apparently beyond recall,[6] to the granting of large aid emoluments to developing countries. Moreover, she had been joined by an increasing number of other developed countries, some of which in their proportionate[7] (but not in their absolute) aid soon surpassed her. In 1957, out of a total official and private net flow of resources to developing countries and multilateral agencies of $7.6 bln, the United States contributed 54 per cent; in 1968 the comparable figure was 44 per cent. In 1957 the second and third places on the list of aid donors (by absolute amount) were occupied by France and Britain; in 1968 the order of precedence after the United States was West Germany, France and Japan. By 1969, judged in terms of official and private net flows related to GNP, the United States, at approximately 0.5 per cent, was at the bottom of the OECD list of seventeen aid-giving countries. The first development decade, as the sixties came to be called in United Nations' aid-policy circles, was then predominantly a period in which the granting of aid became a general, although variously honoured, responsibility.[8]

---

[4] It is impossible to quantify Soviet aid in this period. Lavish claims of aid given by the Soviet Union were made in U.N. committees and regional commissions, but there were counter-claims by developing countries that, though promises were generous, they were honoured more often in the breach than the observance.

[5] For a detailed account and statistics of American aid in this period, see R. F. Mikesell, *Public International Lending for Development* (New York: Random House, 1966) pp. 51–5.

[6] There was always a large and highly vocal anti-aid lobby in the United States and any aid appropriation bill was likely to be savaged in Congress. As one writer put it: 'Each year the Congress cast a thoroughly jaundiced eye at this "temporary" programme of assistance to the less-developed world. Each year we have had a round of appraisals and reappraisals, lamentations about the folly of "give aways" and protestations about the corruptibility of man. Nevertheless, . . . foreign aid has consistently enjoyed the support of a bipartisan majority in Congress and seems firmly embedded in our national budget.' See G. Ranis, *The United States and the Developing Economies*, rev. ed. (New York: Norton, 1973) p. vii.

[7] That is proportionate to GNP.

[8] It must be remembered that statistics of aid from developed to developing countries commonly includes several elements: official assistance supplied by governments, or concessional aid; and flows of private foreign investment. The inclusion of the latter, which take place in

Turning to the aid contribution of multilateral agencies, the record in the postwar period was one of growth and ramification. In the first postwar decade the aid structure was simple. The United States' bilateral aid programme and the Bretton Woods institutions dominated the scene. In the later fifties and sixties not only did the amount of bilateral aid increase but so did the number of agencies. The scope of the United Nations' aid effort was widened and the function of co-ordinating the aid effort gave rise to a number of co-ordinating agencies. At the same time there were efforts to regionalise and channel financial assistance through regional development banks.

By the end of the fifties aid and development had become a world business involving vast expenditures, requiring huge bureaucracies and transferring great amounts of money between countries. For the first time a planned effort was in progress to instil economic growth in economies, all of which were lagging, some of which had been static for centuries. How effective was this effort? To answer such a question would require a book in itself:[9] here it is possible only to mention a few of the general questions which arise.

An obvious preliminary is to look for some results from this effort. These there are. Between 1950 and 1967 the developing countries as a group increased their GDP at an annual rate of 4.8 per cent. This rate is considerably faster than the growth rates of the present industrial countries during their main periods of growth,[10] but not as fast as their growth rates in the postwar period. Moreover, when account is taken of the accelerating rate of population growth in the developing countries the average *per capita* rate of growth becomes 2.0–2.5 per cent per year. Since population growth in the advanced countries in the 1950s was small and the average rate of growth (5 per cent) was high, comparison between developing and developed countries *per capita* growth rates in the 1950s do not give an impression of high return on development aid. But this comparison is an extreme one. The spectacular increase in growth rates of the industrialised countries in the fifties was unprecedented. The comparison is, however, significant in that it has been constantly made and has conditioned the attitude in the developing countries and elsewhere that aid has yielded a poor result. We would argue simply that the aid input has had results, but that these are modest because of the swift rise in population in the recipient countries.

---

response to normal profit stimuli, is dubious. Other features, such as technical assistance, may not get into the statistics at all. A firm definition of aid is lacking and intra-temporal or intra-country comparisons are qualified and often approximate.

[9] An attempt was made to survey the whole aid and development situation in the late sixties by the Commission on International Development which was appointed at the request of Robert McNamara, President of the World Bank. The Commission's report was published as *Partners in Development* (New York and London: Praeger, 1969).

[10] The United Kingdom between 1790 and 1820, 2 per cent; Germany between 1850 and 1880, 2.7 per cent; the United States between 1820 and 1850, 4 per cent; and Japan between 1876 and 1900, 4 per cent.

It should also be remembered that averages are dangerous statistics and that, while average improvement has been modest, some countries have exceeded the average while others have fallen far below it and for some there has been a decline. The *Pearson Report*,[11] however, taking a longer view into the sixties, describes the growth record as 'good', arguing that for seventy low-income countries the average total growth rate reached 5 per cent while some twenty countries held a growth rate of over 6 per cent per annum in the sixties. If the rate of growth of the late sixties were maintained *per capita*, income would be quadrupled in sixty to seventy years. Countries now with *per capita* incomes of $400 a year or more (Mexico, Chile, Venzuela, Greece, Gabon, Cyprus) would reach levels of income near to those at present in Western Europe, while poorer countries (those with *per capita* incomes less than $100 such as India, Pakistan, Mali, Nigeria) would experience great improvement, although certainly not affluence.

The question inevitably arises: has the amount of aid given been sufficient and, in the absence of constraints on the supply side, could greater amounts of capital have been absorbed by the recipient countries? Such a question could only be answered by case studies for individual countries. No doubt in some cases aid could have been greater. More often, however, the impression is that the problem in each country lies not in maximising aid but in organising its effective use and matching types of aid to local needs. The trial-and-error process which inevitably attended the use of large aid expenditures in primitive countries during the early years of aid programmes produced some very odd results and public agencies such as the World Bank swiftly realised that planned application of strategic sectors was far more important to growth than the raw amount of assistance. The question of whether aid is adequate or not can only be determined in the light of the capital requirements of developing countries over a run of years and whether the flow of funds from developed countries is sufficient to meet such requirements. No machinery existed to determine this relationship in the fifties. Estimates might be attempted for individual countries in the light of the rate and nature of development and the resources available to meet it. But here also the need for external aid must be related to changes in commercial policy, to trade opportunities and to other factors (such as the efficiency with which aid is used) which may increase or diminish the need for external support. The aid equation of demand and supply is too complex for us to supply the coefficients with any accuracy, either in the early fifties or at present.

A second important matter determining the effectiveness of aid to developing countries lies in what we may call the 'aid relationship', the complex of points of pressure and friction between donor and recipient countries. Ideally, we may say at the outset, that the aid relationship depends upon the acceptance by both parties that aid's main purpose is for the

[11] See *Partners in Development*, op. cit. p. 28.

recipient country to achieve self-sustaining growth. This carries with it certain corollaries. Governments of developing countries must match the aid received with their own measures to remove obstacles to growth–political, social and traditional. Tax rates and savings ratios must be an earnest of their desire for further investment rather than quick gains in consumption patterns. Receipt of aid must not be accompanied by luxury political programmes and foreign policy adventures. On the donor's side, aid must be given in forms which do not smack of political or commercial penetration. The old colonialism must not be seen to be replaced by an economic stranglehold. We may sum the matter up: development policies must in the final resort be the prime responsibility of the recipient, but the donors have rights which lie in advice, consultation and tactful persuasion.

This ideal lies far from the relations which existed between donors and recipients in the fifties and early sixties. Much of the aid given carried political overtones. Recipient countries were, in many cases, breaking free from colonial status and spreading and testing their political wings in new conditions of independence. There was widespread suspicion of motives. A desire for the affluence of the developed countries was mixed with a desire to be free of their influence. One attitude, common in the developing countries, was to be formative. It was the belief that while the rich countries were ready to supply aid for development, they were not prepared to accompany that aid by changes in their external economic and trade policies which would, in themselves, be as growth-invoking as financial aid. Tariff policies, currency policies and the like were, it came to be argued, determined by the rich countries in their own interests and without regard for development. The lack of bargaining-power of the developing countries in GATT and the IMF were particular sources of annoyance. It was not surprising that even by the later fifties these countries were searching for means by which they could exert collective pressure upon the rich countries for the attainment of goals outside the bilateral aid setting which had been the first manifestation of the division between the rich and poor nations. There is now, looking back, a clear watershed set in the early sixties.[12] Up to that time aid was seen by the developed countries as a matter of individual responsibility, to be given bilaterally to countries and for purposes of the donors' choice. It was accepted on those terms by the developing countries because it was welcome, even on such terms, any aid being better than no aid. From 1960 onwards the demands of the developing countries were not only for an increase of aid and an insistence upon it as a moral right, but also for a concerted effort for economic development of what was now called the Third World, which would involve basic changes in economic, monetary and trade relationships to that end. By the mid-sixties the Third World had acquired uneasy cohesion and had emerged as a force in international relations.

[12] If it must be marked by an event, the first UNCTAD meeting in Geneva in 1964 is a suitable one.

Even as early as the fifties a special long-term problem was casting its shadow, the problem of the accumulation of external debt by the developing countries. In its most pressing dimensions this problem was one for the sixties and seventies but it was anticipatable from the simplest arithmetic. Much foreign aid is given in the form of loans on which recipients have to make payments of interest and repayment instalments until the loan is amortised. Given that the recipient is a developing country and continues to borrow, a part – and, as time goes on and borrowing continues, a growing part – of all new borrowing goes to offset repayment and servicing of earlier loans. The net resource transfer to the country declines with the increase of debt-service and repayment. If the process continues, unless gross borrowing rises, the net capital inflow will fall to zero and eventually become negative. On the worst assumptions, if interest rates are high, amortisation periods short and if there is a decline in gross borrowing, a developing country could find itself in a situation of having to meet a large net *outflow* of capital.

This simple model is alarming enough in its implication for the borrowing country but it takes no account of changes in the borrowing country's balance of payments which, by its deficit, measures the net transfer of resources. If there is a continuing deficit in the balance of payments the net borrowing will be further reduced, will fall more quickly to zero and then become negative.

It is possible, by assigning hypothetical coefficients to the variables determining the net resource flow, to construct capital-import debt-servicing models of various types and different degrees of complexity. It is however, unnecessary to present such models here. They vary as different coefficients are assigned to the variables. We need only summarise their implications, which are, to say the least of it, alarming. The inexorable pressure of compound interest, on the best assumptions, increases the debt burden considerably; on less favourable assumptions it may have catastrophic effects.[13] It is apparent that a sustained import of capital on hard terms will quickly provide a borrowing country with an unmanageable burden of debt-service and a strong improvement in the trade balance is required during the borrowing process, even if this process began in a condition of minor deficit. The practical implications are clear: when service on foreign debt grows more quickly than export earnings, foreign exchange budgets become constricted. New aid relieves the pressure only partially because the aid is usually tied aid, whereas the service is payable by the borrower in convertible currency. Where the models do not fit the actual situation is, of course, that borrowing countries do not go on borrowing their trade deficit plus servicing charges – a capital outflow which their creditors are not prepared to make – but rather seek to suppress their trade deficit or solve their foreign-exchange problem by direct controls on their balances of payments.

[13] The reader who is interested in testing the effects of various coefficients for the variables set out above should consult R. F. Mikesell, *The Economics of Foreign Aid* (Chicago: Aldine, 1968) pp. 105–15.

In the long-term aspect of a country's debt-servicing capacity, one fact stands out as overriding: the contribution of capital imports to the country's growth and balance of payments stability should be the criterion of judgement for both lending and borrowing country. More specifically, the additional capital resources should make possible an expansion of net domestic output corresponding to a net return on the investment well above the rate of interest in international capital markets. As long as a country continues to grow at a high enough rate, total indebtedness may continue to expand, providing the rates of growth of output and of exports are great enough to induce the ratio of import requirements financed by capital imports to decline. If this ratio continues to rise, however, it is because of a continuing adverse trade balance and shows an inappropriate distribution of investment as between domestic-oriented and export-oriented industries. If such a maldistribution of capital imports is allowed to continue, and particularly if such capital imports are on hard terms, interest payments would quickly come to absorb all of the country's export earnings and its net indebtness would grow quickly. Thus we can say that debt-service capacity is dependent upon the development of the economy judged by its *per capita* growth and export capacity and by the contribution which continuing borrowing makes to these two indicators.

In the practical world of aid policy the 'debt-burden problem' commanded only speculative attention in the fifties. It lay in the future: some stochastic term might enter the projection and all might be well. By the sixties it was apparent that the effects were imminent. Between 1957 and 1967 debt-service payments on official account alone increased by 17 per cent. In the decade of the 1960s the external public debt of the developing countries rose by 14 per cent. There was growing clamour by developing countries for debt-service moratoria and some debt deferments and defaults.

Another feature which was a source of rancour between aid donors and recipients was 'tied aid'. Few aspects of the aid relationship have been debated so hotly as the practice of arranging the aid terms so that all or some part of the aid flows back to the donor country. The condition may be imposed upon the borrower that aid proceeds must be used for purchase either of certain commodities or for purchases in the lending or donor country. For example, credits granted by the American Government were made available only on condition that they be used to purchase specified agricultural products. Export–Import Bank loans demanded that the proceeds be used to purchase in the United States the goods necessary for the project. Agency for International Development (AID) loans, save in exceptional cases, are tied to the purchase of goods in the United States. The advantages to the donor country of tied aid are readily apparent. Political approval for aid appropriations is more willingly given if it can be shown that some part of the aid redounds to the advantage of the donor. It is possible to argue for the stimulating effects of increased exports for the economy, the ability to unload unwanted agricultural surpluses by export, stimulus for the balance of payments and a number of other factors which make the role of donor more acceptable to critical electorates. The United States was the main trend-setter in tied aid and during the sixties tying spread until it became almost the norm.

Finally, it is appropriate to comment upon the changing constituents of total development aid over the years. Table 6.1 shows the shares of official disbursements and private investment in the aid flow for selected years in the fifties and sixties. This table shows clearly that while the net flow of resources

TABLE 6.1

Net Flow of Financial Resources by Category to Developing Countries and Multilateral Agencies, 1956–68

($ m.)

Disbursements	1956	1959	1961	1965	1968
Official disbursements[1]	3260	4311	6099	6290	6910
% share of total	(52)	(60)	(66)	(61)	(54)
Private investment and lending[2]	2998	2820	3098	4170	5843
% share of total	(48)	(40)	(34)	(39)	(46)
Total flow	6258	7131	9197	10 460	12 753

[1] Official disbursements encompass flows which are concessional and primarily intended for development and export credits extended by independent public institutions.
[2] Includes direct investment, bilateral portfolio, multilateral portfolio and private export credits.

Source: Recalculated from *Pearson Report*, op. cit. p. 378.

to developing countries was more than doubled between 1956 and 1968, the growth was shared (save in the early sixties when there was a relative decline) by public and private sectors alike. Since most of our discussion so far has been concerned with the growth and problems of public sector aid, it is appropriate to conclude with a few comments on the role of the private sector.

Direct investment is by far the largest constituent of total private investment, although it declined relatively in the sixties. It has been for historical and political reasons an emotive topic for the developing countries. Large corporations, preserving their own national enclaves and remitting their profits to the distant foreign capitalists, have long been a symbol of imperial exploitation. Foreign enterprises were acutely aware, in the postwar period, of the keen scrutiny to which they were subject and of the sanctions – expropriation, controls on remittance of profits, etc. – which might be used against them. This was one factor which kept the level of direct investment from rising. The risk element was high and the creation in the postwar years of militant nationalist governments in new independent states posed a threat to the independent operations of foreign corporations. Other factors served to check the growth of direct investment: restrictions on private capital outflow from the industrialised countries; high rates of returns in comparatively riskless domestic investment; ignorance of investment opportunities; and, for manufacturing investments, a limited market in the host countries. One final feature of the postwar direct investment by the mature in the developing countries was the low proportion (less than 30 per cent) of such investment which was in manufacturing industry and which benefited the consumption of people in those countries. 40 per cent was in the oil industry, 9 per cent in mining and just under 30 per cent in public utilities. The legend of the foreign corporation exploiting local resources and using cheap local labour was hard to dispel.

It is unnecessary here to debate the case for and against direct investment as an aid to development. Divested of the political overtones (but these are crucial), there are several factors which point to the productivity of such investment for the host economy. There are few cases in which such investment produces no net benefit to the host country. The case for and against direct investment in the aid context is one which balances in such a way as to indicate the need for policies rather than restriction. The guiding of foreign private investment into productive avenues and its co-ordination with local investment should be the object of these policies.

We may now sum up the aid situation as it evolved in the period we have been discussing. The problem of development had been recognised, aid was flowing, international agencies had been created and were functioning with some success. Some positive results in economic growth were attributable to this aid, but the variation of success was wide, varying from nil to what might be described as modest but promising achievement. Steadily burgeoning population was the greatest single impediment to success. In the developing countries themselves lack of progress and the disparities between the aid policies and the general economic policies of donor countries led to frustration and a determination to escalate the problem to a situation of confrontation with the rich countries on a wide range of economic issues in trade, commercial policy and currency fields.

(iv) COMMERCIAL POLICY

There is a tendency, partly justified by the facts, to regard the developing countries and the primary-producing countries as identical. While it is true that most of the developing countries are producers of primary products and that they rely on these for such stake in international trade as they may have, it is none the less true that a number of rich countries – the United States, Canada, Australia and New Zealand for example – are among the most important primary producers. All of these countries, however, have considerable industrial content in their production. None of them relies, as many developing countries do, on a narrow range of primary products whose situation in world markets is sole determinant of their prosperity. The interwar period had demonstrated clearly the intractable economics of their situation. Primary-product prices fluctuate more widely than those of manufactured products. The fluctuations of import prices take their effect on the incomes and balances of payments of producing countries. The effects are at their most extreme when a country has a narrow primary commodity export base where exports form a large proportion of national income. In summary, it is a grim generalisation that primary commodity prices, markets and conditions do much to condition economic growth in the developing countries.

The primary-product picture in 1945 was a varied one, but not one which gave cause for dismay. Some commodities (meat, animal fats, tin, jute and timber) promised to be in short supply for a long time; others (sugar and rubber) it seemed would soon be readily available. Over a wide range of products supply would be adequate to meet a normal peacetime demand, particularly if international regulation of supplies was maintained to meet the difficulties which might be expected from widespread replenishment of stocks.

Like so many economic forecasts of the time this one was dead wrong. For the period 1945–8 demand for primary commodities ran well ahead of supply and prices rose continuously and steeply. The terms of trade moved strongly in favour of the primary-producing countries. For this there appear to have been four main reasons.[14] The first was the insatiable appetite of the booming United States for primary products, particularly raw materials. The high tempo of American industry and its expanding demand for materials, despite rising prices, was quite unforeseen. American imports of many materials were double prewar and for a long list of others, 60 to 70 per cent greater. The increased demand for foodstuffs was less spectacular, but was in line with the 12 per cent increase in population over the war period. The second reason was the very poor harvests of grain crops and sugar in Western Europe and the United States in 1947. Third was the disturbed political condition of South East Asia which delayed the resumption of normal supplies of a wide range of products. Finally, supplies of wheat, maize and wool were all affected by Argentina's export policy under which these products were marketed by a state agency whose low price to producers resulted in low levels of production. Altogether the period 1945–8 was one of slow adjustment to new trends in world demand, the instability being accentuated by unstable supply conditions carried over from the war period. From 1948, when the general rise in prices eased, there were signs that the effects of the war had run their course and markets were moving towards stability. Ripples of demand and supply changes (including those wrought by the 1949 devaluation of sterling) moved

[14] We draw here on a long analysis of the postwar primary commodity situation by J. W. F. Rowe. See his *Primary Commodities in International Trade* (Cambridge: Cambridge University Press, 1965) pp. 96–100 and 155–209.

across the surface, but they were small and in early 1950 with postwar
recovery well under way there was, it seemed, every reason to expect a period
of stability in primary product markets. Such was not to be the case. The
outbreak of the Korean War later that year shook the markets to their
foundations.

The Korean War began in July 1950. By many it was interpreted as the first
phase of a wider conflict in anticipation of which there was a wild scramble to
acquire stocks of food and strategic materials. At a time when merchants and
manufacturers were rebuilding stocks, the U.S. Government entered many
raw material markets as a heavy buyer. Prices rose steeply and by the spring of
1951 some material prices were multiples of their prewar level. Food prices
rose much less, but those for which the United States was not itself a supplier,
nevertheless registered substantial gains. Wool, rubber, jute and the non-
ferrous metals were the most volatile prices. The fear that the north Asian
conflict would encompass the south, drove the United States to scramble for
the products of that region. The period July 1950 to March 1951 saw the most
remarkable short-period rise in primary-product prices ever recorded.

Two factors broke the boom: the fact that it was a procurement scramble
and was soon seen to be causing shortages and prices unjustified by events;
and the fact that the United States, as the leading buyer, soon began to order
its buying and introduce measures to check prices in markets which it
dominated. As early as January 1951 the U.S. Government imposed
maximum prices for a wide range of commodities. In February so-called
strategic stockpiling purchases were being reduced. By September a general
downward adjustment of prices was in progress. Some prices fell sharply,
others, particularly food prices, fell quite slowly. By the end of 1952 the
Korean boom had dissipated itself and the conditions and, in many markets,
the prices of the period 1948–50 were restored.

So far as any general movement may be attributed to prices in the years
1952–6, it was one of slow decline, but there were many individual market
adjustments and anomalies within this trend. The great boom of 1950–1 in
primary-product prices was to be followed by many years of relative recession.
Throughout the whole of the later fifties and much of the sixties – that is,
during the great period of growth and expansion of the industrial countries –
the primary-producing countries were to experience adverse terms of trade
and a recurrence of many earlier problems. So far as it is possible to describe a
complex set of relations for many markets and products in general terms, it
may be said that the period 1948–52 was one of shortage of primary products
following the war to which there was slow adjustment, broken by the
aberration of 1950–1, down to 1956. Thereafter, and for more than a decade
the story is one of normal adaptation to a changing economic world.

One feature of the commodity markets of the fifties was the reappearance of
commodity control schemes. In August 1949 came the International Wheat
Agreement, a multilateral marketing contract agreement whereby exporting

countries sold up to a quota at a defined maximum price while importing countries bought at a stated minimum price. Deals were negotiated between importers and exporters at any prices between these limits which were mutually agreed. The purpose of the agreement was to restrain price fluctuations within the defined limits. Further agreements of similar type were concluded in 1953, 1956 and 1959 and had a varied career. On the export side they were controlled by the major exporters, the United States and Canada. Britain, as the major importer, was critical of the schemes and ultimately withdrew in 1953, followed in 1956 by other importers until the third scheme controlled only a quarter of total world trade in wheat. In January 1954 an agreement covering exports of sugar was concluded among a number of countries supplying the 'free market'.[15] Prices were held within a certain range by export quota controls and until 1956 the scheme worked reasonably well. In that year the Suez crisis caused prices to soar. The quota restrictions were temporarily removed and not until 1958 was the agreement reactivated. Almost at once it ran into fresh difficulties as first the Cuban civil war and then the switch of Cuban exports from the United States to China and the Soviet Union had to be catered for. By December 1961 the scheme had broken down.

It would be tedious to describe even briefly the record of other international commodity agreements. A common and fairly familiar pattern emerges. So long as there is a common interest among participant countries to limit price fluctuations, and so long as the price fluctuations are modest, the scheme works well enough, although it may be asked whether, under such circumstances, it is justified. As soon as the price movements become large or the market becomes disturbed by strategic or political influences, the scheme is apt to break down and dissolve in market anarchy. The earlier record of the interwar period also bears out this experience. It is the 'normal' abnormality of market conditions which has ensured that the life of commodity control schemes is often violent and short.

(v) CONFRONTATION

By the end of the fifties the problem of the Third World was clearly defined. Enough had been done to see that there was no simple solution, nor even a set of solutions. Only a concomitance of factors could galvanise into economic growth a set of countries whose economic condition resembled, though only with a family likeness, the condition of Britain in 1700 or France and Germany a century later. Investment capital was needed, but was in itself not enough, if misdirected or misapplied. Industry was needed, but not such as to

---

[15] The free market in this context consisted of countries outside the United States, with its contract-bound suppliers (Hawaii, Puerto Rico, the Philippines and Cuba), and Britain and Canada supplied by certain British Commonwealth countries.

create enclaves of urban affluence in the midst of squalor. Trade expansion was needed but was balked by the refusal of rich countries to accept the trade pattern which was its corollary. Education and technical expertise were needed, but of a kind far subtler and attuned to need than the meagre amount that was given. In the developing countries themselves there was need of an ideological, all-pervasive drive for development, extending to all groups and classes and capable of sustaining itself for years. Instead there was, all too often, a new indigenous and well-heeled élite with a vested-interest in the *status quo*; beneath them the apathy and resignation of great populations as yet untouched by change.

By 1960 little had been achieved in narrowing disparity of *per capita* income between the rich world and the poor. In many cases disparities had widened. The creation of new sovereign states – the fragmentation of Africa and the Caribbean, the division of the old India and the new Pakistan, soon itself to divide – had bred a fierce nationalism which bedevilled the already complex economic issues. Moreover, the sources of aid were being eroded. Such idealism and sympathy as there had been in donor countries was being replaced by weariness and cynicism; hard-headed aid-givers no longer saw their concessionary aid as a strategy in the Cold War, private investors questioned the wisdom of making direct investments which were hostages to the fortunes of predatory local despots. By 1960 a watershed in the relations of the rich and poor world had been reached.

Part Two

Growth, Expansion and Experiment, 1955–64

7
International Economic Relations after 1955

(i) INTRODUCTION

It is appropriate at this point to notice certain changes in the political relations which had taken place in the world economy during the first decade of peace. The power alignments and relationships which had emerged were in some cases discernible from the end of the war; others were new. In any event they were, in essence, to remain throughout the next fifteen years and were to have great influence on economic events. In order to sketch in the outlines on this very large canvas we give our attention in turn to (a) the global scene, (b) the pattern of the new Europe and (c) other changes not within the first two categories but important in themselves.

(ii) THE GLOBAL SCENE

The central fact of international relations by the mid-fifties was the Cold War. Co-operation between East and West, such as it had been in wartime, had not survived the immediate postwar allocation of territorial occupation and spheres of influence. Polarised around the United States and the Soviet Union, the developed countries ranged themselves with one or other, or endeavoured to remain aloof as political or geographic circumstances allowed. The division conditioned alliances and shaped policies for leaders and satellites alike. Moreover, total collapse of Chiang Kai-shek's Nationalist China and its replacement by a Communist regime which, in Korea in 1951, demonstrated formidable military potential, extended the cleavage to Asia and opened up daunting possibilities for the West should a power axis be established between the new China and the Soviet Union. Throughout the later fifties the Cold War intensified. Stalin's death and his replacement, by Khruschev; the foreign policy of the Eisenhower Administration as interpreted by Foster Dulles; and the early graduation of the new China as a nuclear power – all had their effects on the relations of the super-powers.

In the purely economic field the influences of the Cold War were three. First, the arms race, the struggle for technical domination and the efforts of both sides to achieve a competitive edge in the cycle of missile, deterrent and counter-deterrent, constituted an immense diversion of resources to military

and defence use. Apart from the costly intricacies of rocketry and thermo-
nuclear missiles, the lesson of Korea was interpreted as being that both sides
must prepare for conventional as well as nuclear wars. By this the maximum
diversion of resources from peaceful use was attained since not only must
scientific and technological resources be harnessed to defence, but large
conventional armies be also held in readiness and nations not possessed of
nuclear weapons must contribute their quota of men and old-fashioned
military hardware.

The second economic effect of the Cold War lay in the restrictions which it
imposed upon world trade. The United States placed a veto upon trade with
the Soviet Union and its satellites and expected its example to be followed by
its supporting countries in NATO – not all of which were rigorous in doing so.
On the Eastern side bilateral trade agreements and state-trading completed
an autarky which sealed off two great regions of the world from economic
intercourse. Since the Eastern bloc relied on payments arrangements which
precluded convertibility of its currencies or their use in the West the result was
a virtually complete economic and monetary demarcation.

A third economic influence of East/West rivalry lay in the new field of
development aid. Within the large group of developing countries there were
many which were open to recruitment to either camp by offers of assistance
from the United States or the Soviet Union. While such aid was often given in
the form of 'military assistance', grants or technical defence aid, it often
overflowed into the non-defence sector. Some countries – for example Egypt –
were recipients of aid from both sides and some were quick to exploit their
position by a process of competitive bidding. Some few even remained outside
the group of aid recipients or curtailed their potential intake of assistance in
order to remain uncommitted in their support of either side. The question of
how far the distribution of aid was diverted from a Pareto-optimum by
these Cold War policies is not an answerable one. It is perhaps arguable that
aid which followed the path of political motivation was better than no aid at
all. In any event we must take it as a fact that aid in the later fifties was
politically directed, each donor country having its political preferences.[1]
Perversely it might be argued that the playing off of East and West as aid
donors by developing countries added to the amount of aid which might
otherwise have been given.

No serious attempt has been made to evaluate the economic effects of the
Cold War. It is undeniable that the continuous expenditures of the Western
countries on 'defence' contributed to high levels of employment and to
technological spin-off advantages in other industries. It is arguable that the

---

[1] Most donors concentrated their aid on groups of countries which they wished to influence.
Thus Britain and the older dominions instituted the Colombo Plan to allocate aid among
developing Commonwealth countries in Asia; France also directed aid to her remaining empire.
Israel gave aid to African countries outside the ring of her Arab neighbours. The United States
gave aid in support of her 'crusade' against Communism.

high levels of government outlay had their effects on price levels and contributed to the creeping inflation which was a feature of the whole period. In the trade field autarky transformed East and West into two distinct trading areas largely cut off from each other by non-tariff barriers.

The year 1955 presented then an international economy divided, so far as the developed countries were concerned, into two camps and, in the underdeveloped, into followers of these camps or others too poor, too uninfluential or too remote to be useful to either. For almost all countries recovery from the war was more or less complete. Physical destruction had been made good, currencies stabilised, channels of trade restored, production brought to higher levels than in 1939. The defeated and occupied countries, Germany and Japan, were well-advanced in recovery as manufacturing and trading countries. The United States no longer dominated as the only country capable of supplying its neighbour's industrial needs. With recovery came a wider range of choices in economic policies. The response now was not to the needs of survival but rather to mould long-term trends so far as they had revealed themselves in the postwar world. Moreover, the grandiose schemes of postwar reconstruction and planning were now either implemented, as in the case of the IMF and the World Bank, and had taken their place in the scheme of things or had passed into oblivion, as in the case of the Havana Charter and ITO. It was now no longer possible to build from grass roots. The best had to be made of what had been established and what had evolved.

On both sides of the Iron Curtain the years 1955 to 1970 brought significant changes in economic power and influence. Within the Communist bloc differences and ultimately distrust and enmity arose between the Soviet Union and the new Maoist China, causing the latter to emerge as a new power in Asia separate from the Soviet sphere of influence. The Marxist–Leninism of one and the blander Maoist doctrine of the other could not be contained within a single ideological and political system. At the same time the quick economic recovery of China from its civil war, its nuclear capability and its potential to dominate the whole of Asia were viewed with distrust and apprehension in the West. Only in the seventies was rapprochement between the United States and China to ease political tension in that sector of the Cold War. In the Soviet bloc in Eastern Europe the tight hold of Russia on its satellites was somewhat eased in the economic sphere, although in the political and strategic fields the sharp lessons in Soviet mastery meted out to Hungary in 1956 and Czechoslovakia in 1968, demonstrated that Soviet policy was unchanged. Nevertheless, in the sixties the economic growth of East Germany and Hungary, certain economic reforms in Poland and increasing prosperity generally in Eastern Europe had beneficial effects. There was a gradual increase in trade with the West, although on a basis of bilateral agreements. In default of an efficient institutional basis of comparative prices it was far below its potential.

In the West exciting changes were taking place. The Western European countries had staged a spectacular economic recovery, the details of which have already been examined. This recovery encompassed not only unprecedented economic growth but a realignment of economic power and influence. West Germany, from a standing start, had become the dominant industrial power with the fastest rate of growth, a surplus in its balance of payments based on a booming export trade, a strong currency nurtured by skilful monetary and fiscal policies and an industrious, productivity-conscious labour force augmented by immigration from Eastern Germany. France also had transformed itself. Swift industrial change, agricultural mechanisation, and the influence of a new technocracy all served in the Gaullist period to bring about spectacular growths in production and living standards. Italy and the smaller countries of the West participated in the general expansion. Only Spain remained to be awakened from its isolated Catholic lassitude.

The notable exception to the vitality of the West European scene was the United Kingdom, in which postwar recovery had been only partial up to the mid-fifties. Although Britain had shared in the general economic growth of the period her rate of increase in production had been almost the lowest in Western Europe and recurrent balance-of-payments crises (in 1947, 1949, 1951, 1955 and 1956) had forced upon her domestic policies inimical to sustained growth. In attempts to deal with the balance-of-payments problem and to accumulate foreign-exchange reserves recourse was made to a 'stop-go' policy,[2] by which the growth of the economy was checked when the balance-of-payments position deteriorated and the checks removed when it improved or when foreign-exchange speculation against the pound subsided. After the failure of the 1947 experiment in sterling convertibility, successive British Governments were nervous about making a further attempt. Despite pressure from the United States and the willingness of other West European countries to expose their currencies to a free market, Britain urged the continuance of a convertibility limited to OEEC countries through the European Payments Union (EPU). Not until January 1959 did dollar convertibility of sterling and the European currencies come about. Then it was not by British initiative but by the action of France, which made the franc convertible into dollars thus ending the EPU by *force majeure* and creating the convertibility of all the OEEC currencies including sterling.

[2] The theory of the 'stop–go' syndrome was that balance-of-payments deficits occurred when the economy expanded too quickly relative to other economies. Imports rose, high domestic demand drew goods from the export market, an external deficit was created. Deflation would then reduce demand for imports and by slackening home demand encourage industries to export. There were many variants of this simplistic doctrine. When, as in September 1956 and September 1958, external crisis was triggered by a speculative run on sterling the trick was to restore foreign confidence by a 'package deal' of disinflationary measures which would convince bear-speculators of the seriousness of purpose of British economic policies.

The 'stop–go' policy was the concomitant of the determination to preserve a fixed exchange rate for sterling. The result of both policies was to ensure that Britain's economic recovery and growth was determined by her external financial position as expressed through the standing and acceptance of her currency.

The primary effect of all this was to impose upon the British a sense of isolation. The Americans, in accordance with their Cold War policy of backing strong nations against the Russians, came to regard Germany as the major bulwark in the ring of European containment. British isolation from the Americans was accentuated by the Suez failure of 1956, the quarrel with the Eisenhower Administration, and the foreign policy of Foster Dulles. Meanwhile a British blunder in the economic field isolated her from the mainstream of economic events in Western Europe for a decade. In 1955 the West European powers held, at Messina, a conference to explore the way to the establishment of a customs union of West European nations. The way was open, the accent was upon haste and advance by general principles on a broad front. In this conference Britain might have participated. Had she done so, had she involved herself from the beginning in the plans which led to the Treaty of Rome, the history of Britain and of the European Community in later years would have been different. She did not involve herself. The meeting at Messina seems to have been misunderstood and underestimated by the British who did not attend.[3] They were thus excluded from the practical arrangements which were set in train to prepare the Treaty. In the spring of 1957 the British, realising their error, launched a weak counter-initiative, proposing a free-trade area in industrial products which would include Britain, the Six and certain other European countries. It was brushed aside. The Six agreed to consider it later, but were not prepared at that stage to complicate their own task by entering into negotiations with the British. The free-trade area proposal was later rejected, largely at the instigation of France: the European plans led to the signing of the Treaty of Rome in March 1957 and to the establishment of the European Economic Community.

The years following 1955 brought decline in Britain's political fortunes. A weakening of power, a failure to interpret the changes which were taking place and, although no statistics can prove it, a weariness from six years of total war and its aftermath were all inimical to British influence. Among the developed countries leadership and initiative lay along an axis between Japan, the United States and the new and vigorous Western Europe.

(iii) THE NEW EUROPE

The year 1955 was a turning-point in Western Europe. In that year a group of six[4] of the oldest and most politically sophisticated nations embarked upon a plan which was intended to lead them to economic and ultimately to political unity. It had profound influence on the period covered in the rest of this book.

---

[3] This over-simplifies the matter. The British were also repelled by the European plans for currency and political union which, although not spelled out at that early stage, nevertheless, lurked in the background.

[4] France, Germany, Holland, Italy, Belgium and Luxembourg.

In assessing the broad significance of the early plans for the EEC, it is hard to disentangle motive and effect. There had since the war been a strong intellectual movement towards European co-operation and federalism. The success, in limited fields, of organisations like the European Coal and Steel Community (ECSC) and the Benelux customs union were expressions of this. The support which Churchill and others had given to the Council for Europe and the ideas of men such as Robert Schuman and Jean Monnet had made the European movement a vocal, although not a politically powerful force. In 1954 the failure of the proposal for a European Defence Community provided the opportunity which was needed for a new European initiative in the economic field. The new plan for the Common Market was seen in several ways by its architects. It would seize the opportunity of moving towards European unity while support for the idea existed. It would embody Germany in these plans and thwart whatever nationalistic tendencies that country might still have. If the British were to remain outside that was no great matter, for was it not in the tradition of British foreign policy to avoid entanglements in Western Europe. But to economists, like Monnet, Schuman and the new breed of European technocrats, the Community meant much more. In particular, it meant size, organisation, growth and economic power to face the United States and the Soviet Union. Their arguments for the Common Market were couched in terms of its dynamic effects on its members in the short run; on a common currency and co-ordinated external and internal policies in the long run. Historical analogies of dubious authenticity were invoked to support the project. If American industrial productivity had been built on the base of a large captive consumer market, enabling standardisation and large productive units to produce at low average cost, so might European industries be nurtured by a market of 200 million consumers. It was tacitly assumed that trade creation between the members of the Community would more than compensate for such trade diversion as might be caused by its external tariff and the trade policies of other nations and groups of nations. There was a heady quality about all this thinking so long as one kept to generalities and did not submit schemes to detailed analysis. It accorded well with the speed achieved in economic recovery and the new enthusiasm for growth.

With all this went a method in the preliminary negotiation and planning. The method was simple. Avoid the disruptive issues until a firm commitment to unification had been established. Agree to agree on common principles and leave details and procedures to be settled later. In the beginning this was a highly successful tactic. It established the EEC in a very short time and set it moving in an agreed direction, but increasingly in the late fifties and in the sixties in one field after another the Community came up against the hard facts of life. The Common Agricultural Policy (CAP) was a good example. Between its broad enunciation in Article 39 of the Treaty of Rome and its practical emergence in 1962 lay a traumatic negotiating process which at times threatened the very life of the community. Another matter in which it was easy to talk in generalities but intricate and frustrating to get down to specifics was that of exchange-rate policy and a common currency for the Community. In the founding documents there was no clear commitment either to a common European currency or to a co-ordinated exchange-rate policy. Broad objectives – high levels of employment, price-level stability and external balance – were, however, soon identified and committees were established to pursue these and formulate policy. The whole intricate web of internal and external macro policies for six complex economies came up for inspection and through many committees and working groups the problem was drawn out. The old tactic was tried – an undertaking to establish a common currency by 1980, but this time and up to the time of writing it has failed. It is one thing to say, as was said in the early days: agree in principle, work out details later. This may work when enthusiasms are fresh and problems are finite. It is quite another to approach currency and exchange-rate decisions, to which nations attach the supreme test of sovereign power, in this way. To do so is only to say that something is desirable and expect all obstacles to its fulfilment to fade away.

There was a power dimension to the establishment of the European Community. Since 1945 the position of the United States among the Western nations had been paramount. Her policies and political values had prevailed. While willing to accept much of these policies the older powers, particularly France, fretted under the American matriarchy. Through the Community the old Europe would be able to meet, confer, perhaps co-operate with the United States on more equal terms. In tariff bargaining and international monetary policy there would once more be a balance of power. The days of American hegemony were over.

The motives of the individual member states in backing the Community were various and were demonstrated by the tense horse-trading which took place in the establishment negotiations between 1955 and 1957. France, perhaps more than any other major nation, has best understood the role of economic relations in power politics and here was a framework within which to operate. Moreover, there were some fine plums for the picking: the opportunity to move French agriculture into the twentieth century; a milieu within which the technocratic aspects of the Gaullist Government could flourish and bring France forward among the industrial nations; protection and wider markets for established French industries such as automobile manufacture. For France there was prospect of much gain and she bargained fiercely to harvest it. West Germany, the other senior partner, was already well advanced in growth and recovery when the plans for the Community were mooted. As an industrial power she saw their advantages and since little, if any, sacrifice was involved, she supported them. The theoretical advantages of the customs union had an appeal for a federal state only one hundred years on from the *Zollverein* which had ushered in Germany unity. The role of the

German Government in the negotiations and in the early days of the Community was in the ideological field to foster the conception of European unity and in the practical field to hold France within the group and prevent her defection, which might have occurred at any time either because advantages were being withheld or for *ad hoc* reasons, such as a willingness on the part of the other five members to admit the British.

For the other four Common Market powers the advantages of the union seemed clear. In the political field the plan gave prospect of an end to the deadly rivalry of France and Germany. For Italy it gave the prospect of a wider free market for her automobiles and light-engineering products and the hope of investment aid to develop her impoverished southern economy. For the Benelux powers the Common Market meant an extension of their existing customs union and free entry for their products to a mass market.

A fuller account of the development of the European Community is given in Chapter 9. We are here concerned only with such aspects of that record as influenced the wider political and economic ambiance of the international economy in the later fifties and sixties. Of such aspects we call attention to four. The first change wrought by the establishment of the Community was in the international balance of economic power. In such matters as international currency planning and tariff negotiations and in organisations, the IMF and the GATT, which were concerned with these matters, the six were now able to act as a concerted group. In the policy discussions within the Group of Ten[5] the Common Market countries[6] exerted considerable bargaining leverage and in tariff negotiations, particularly concerning agricultural products, covered by their own Common Agricultural Policy, they were able to face the United States on equal terms. On her side the United States was ambivalent towards the change. While loth to part with the dominating power and influence which she had enjoyed for so long in economic matters, she had at the same time pushed the Europeans since the war towards some kind of federal unity. She could hardly complain now that such a movement was proceeding apace.

A second aspect of the establishment of EEC has already been mentioned, but may be repeated in this context: the isolation of the United Kingdom in international economic affairs. The problem was now posed for that country: where, in a world in which economic and trading power had come to be concentrated into groups did the United Kingdom fit in? The ideas of the old Commonwealth as a free-trade group, or of the sterling area as a fixed-exchange-rate group based on sterling as a key currency, were clearly

---

[5] The Group of Ten consisted of the ten largest nations in the IMF, who, in accordance with the General Arrangements to Borrow (1960) undertook to lend up to $6 b. to the IMF on request. After 1960 considerable power and influence in matters of currency planning moved to the Group of Ten. It was instrumental in setting up the Special Drawing Rights arrangements within the IMF under the Rio de Janeiro Agreement of 1967.

[6] The only Common Market country not a member of the Group was Luxembourg.

obsolete. The older dominions, Canada and Australia, had gone their way – Canada to association with the United States, Australia in the direction of autonomy. India was by 1955 an independent state, with militaristic pretensions but, in economics, playing the role of a member of the Third World. The colonial empire was being quickly dismantled. The world economy by the mid-fifties seemed to have coagulated into groups – North America, the Western European Community, the Eastern Communist bloc, the Third World – to none of which the United Kingdom belonged. This isolation was calamitous for a country which, in the 1940s, had shared with the United States the economic planning of the world. It demanded a new and imaginative economic policy. Clearly a country, as relatively weak as the United Kingdom had become, had to ally herself to some of these groups. The choice was not a wide one and it was not made quickly.

A third aspect of the European experiment was that it was the culmination of the process of formal international economic planning, the vogue for which had begun in the war years, which had produced functional agencies such as the IMF and the World Bank, a commercial-policy-negotiating forum in GATT and the very habit of international co-operative effort on actions which before the war were regarded as being of national rather than international concern. Now, in this culminating effort at international control, the economic affairs of six mature nations were to be fused, co-ordinated, harmonised[7] and the whole front of such operations was to be extended to include commercial policy, transport policy, agricultural policy, fiscal arrangements, taxation, industrial location, migration and ultimately even macro-economic policy, currency and exchange rates. On some of these sectors co-operation got little further than the making of a decision to co-operate; on others action and activity penetrated far into functional minutiae and spawned committees, commissions, working parties and hordes of experts and bureaucrats.

A fourth and final result of all this was that the European approach invoked economic actions elsewhere, either in the belief that a customs union, or association with one, was a unique prescription for economic growth, in self-defence, or in mere emulation. Other customs unions appeared,[8] in Europe, in Latin America and Africa. Others, such as a North Atlantic Free Trade Area, were considered at least as serious theoretical propositions. The developing countries divided into two camps: those which anticipated advantages from an association with the European Community and those,

---

[7] The very vocabulary of Common Market planning reflects much of its overreaching vagueness. To avoid the brute fact of loss of national economic sovereignty by individual governments, economic policies were to be 'co-ordinated', social policies to be 'harmonised', agricultural policies to be pursued 'in common'. Once more what was economically desirable was assumed by a form of verbal understatement to be politically feasible.

[8] For example, LAFTA (Latin American Free Trade Area) and CACM (Central American Common Market, and in Europe, EFTA (European Free Trade Area).

like the Latin American countries, which resisted the preferential trading position which overseas territories of France and Belgium seemed destined to enjoy. For the moment commercial policy seemed a whole new game in which the rules and rewards were different from the old, plodding, bargaining approach of GATT.

(iv) CAPITAL MOVEMENTS

In any discussion of the politics of international economics attention must be paid to movements of capital. In the first period covered by this book (1945–55) capital movements did not concern us. The normal incentives to move capital were distorted; the economic process by which it moves in suspension. Money markets and their indicators, interest rates, had to be re-established. Industrial systems had to be rehabilitated. The political environment had to be understood. Flux had to give way to stability. Certainly capital moved in these reconstruction years, but it was public sector capital, flowing for political reasons in the form of stabilisation loans or recovery programmes.[9] Not until recovery was far advanced, until the prospect of another world war seemed remote, could the normal economic incentives take over. They began to do so in the later fifties from which time capital movements became an increasingly important feature of the new international economy.

As is usual in economics the theoretical model of international capital movements is tidier, more logical in its elements than is the real world. Assuming that we rule out of consideration public-sector capital flows which are usually political in motivation, and direct investment in which the capital flow is accompanied by technology, management and ultimately control from the lending country, we are left with two broad types of capital movement: long-term capital raised in the capital market of the lending country to finance activities over which it has no subsequent control in some other country and short-term capital movements which may be either the result of short commercial lending for trade transactions or of movements of semi-liquid funds from centre to centre under impulse of profit, security or the accounting arrangements of banks or corporations. Ideally the movements of both types of capital are explicable. Long-term capital moves from the rich countries, where high incomes and saved surpluses make it available, to developing countries where many profitable avenues for its investment exist; short-term capital flows to finance trade, moving to and fro in stabilising motion to adjust temporary surpluses and deficits in balances of payments. Economists, fond of demonstrating the mystic beauty of their model, will point to the developing and stabilising role played by long-term investment in

---

[9] These would include intra-government stabilisation loans, foreign aid loans, accommodation loans to governments by international agencies, loans by international banking groups such as the Basle Club, or loans for the refinancing of existing long-term debt.

Canada or Latin America before the First World War or to delicate responses of short-term capital movements to bank rate changes in the sterling world of the late Victorian era. They have learnt also, however, that perverse movements of long-term capital (i.e. from poor countries to rich) and destabilising movements of short-term capital are not infrequent problems. Between 1955 and the present we have acquired great experience of the effects of perverse capital movements, both long-term and short. If free capital flows were often a beneficent influence on the international economy of the past they have provided in the postwar period perverse influences which it has been necessary to contain.

Perverse long-term capital movements, i.e. when capital moves from poor capital-starved countries to rich capital-abundant countries, flourish under such disturbed economic and political conditions as have obtained since the war. Private capital has often left (or been frustrated from going to) developing countries to escape taxation, for fear of confiscation or because of political uncertainity. Savings of the rich in poor countries have been invested in Switzerland, New York or London. Earnings of large corporations operating in poor countries have been quickly moved to other, more stable, countries. Switzerland, with its political stability and reliable and anonymous banking system, has been the repository of capital from many countries, including often its European neighbours. In the flows of long-term capital there has been diversity. It has been difficult to observe the steady and useful tides which flowed before 1914.

Turning to short-term capital movements the picture has been even darker. From this source has come one of the greatest threats to the stability and management of the international monetary system since the war. The problem has had several facets.

The most daunting aspect of short-term capital movements has been their volume which has grown to a size such that individual central banks have often been unable to resist buying or selling pressures on their currencies when speculative movements have threatened their exchange rates. It is not possible to give precision to such magnitudes. International short-term capital is a genus which has many sub-species – trade credit instruments, short-paper such as treasury bills and short-deposit receipts, bank deposits, money held by a banking system beyond that system's capacity to absorb it, earned savings seeking safe investment. Such capital items may move in and out of the international market according to circumstance. It is impossible to aggregate the sub-totals of such items and put together figures for time comparison. It is, however, possible to judge by effects and by observing the impact of short-term capital movements upon exchange rates and money supplies it is apparent that they have come to constitute a more powerful force in international monetary movements than ever before.

Why this great increase? Several factors have been involved. The capital market is now an international market so that any given country or currency must be prepared to take overspill from any other part of the market. Thus, even if the total of short-term investible funds were no greater, sheer mobility may mean higher levels of concentration in distinct parts of the market. But they have been greater. The earnings of the oil-producing countries, themselves small and with no banking systems or national investment opportunities of a magnitude to absorb their huge surpluses, flow to the capital markets of Switzerland, London or New York for investment and re-investment. The reserve cash flows of multinational corporations move uneasily from financial centre to centre seeking security, stability or marginal advantages in interest rates. Thus from two rich sources new funds, or funds formerly invested in one centre only, became mobile within the world market. Nor was the increase in short-term mobile capital centred only in the monetary and capital sections of balances of payments. Trade items also made their contribution. With the swiftly growing volume of trade the amount of trade credit, in the form of outstanding bills of exchange or short bank loans, increased also. Moreover, it became from the fifties to the seventies, subject to new influences which gave it the same properties as shifts in liquid funds. A mass 'leads and lags' movement[10] has the same effect on the balance of payments of the country concerned as an outflow or inflow of short-term capital.

Finally, as a background to this large and mobile stock of international short-term capital there were two conditions which made its existence menacing to the international monetary system. The first of these was the atmosphere of unease and uncertainity which characterised the monetary situation of the whole period and which caused liquid funds to move from currency to currency without regard for the stability of any currency or of the system as a whole. Sterling was no longer deemed acceptable as a key currency for holding long-term balances. The U.S. dollar was new and untried in that role and as the Vietnam War and large American external deficits became its background in the sixties, doubts as to its efficiency as a long-term repository for funds were widespread.

The second condition, which after 1955 made short-term capital movements destabilising was the exchange-rate system which had been established at Bretton Woods. Under that system exchange rates of the member currencies were to be fixed in the short term but variable in response to structural changes in the balance of payments. This meant that currencies in

---

[10] A country whose exchange rate fell under suspicion of impending devaluation, which would render its exports cheaper to foreign buyers, would experience delays (lags) in payment for its exports. Since devaluation would make its imports dearer to home buyers, importers would pay for imports as quickly as possible. Thus speculation by traders in anticipation of a devaluation would have the same effect on the country's balance of payments as a withdrawal of capital. Speculation in anticipation of a revalued exchange rate would be equivalent to an inflow of capital. To a country with a large merchandise trade account such leading and lagging in payments could be a large destabilising item, particularly if added to withdrawals (or inflows) of short-term capital in the capital section of the balance of payments.

chronic deficit fell under suspicion of impending devaluation while those in chronic surplus were expected to revalue. Currency speculation thus became a one-way option, the direction of change of an exchange rate never being in doubt. A weak currency could be sold and bought back after devaluation. Alternatively it could be sold short in the forward market for future delivery when the position could be closed by the cheaper purchase. In the event that devaluation did not take place, little penalty was incurred since the currency could still be bought back at the continuing rate, only brokerage costs being involved. The result of this speculators' paradise was that large quantities of liquid funds moved from currency to currency. A weak and suspect currency had to sustain enormous selling pressure which could only be countered by the defending central bank buying its own currency on the exchange market at the cost of its foreign-exchange reserves. Time and again the British pound and other major currencies were subjected to such speculative pressure, and by the late sixties it was apparent that the menace to the Bretton Woods system from speculative capital movements was acute. Even after the general resort to managed floating in the early seventies, the problem continued, two things being apparent: that the normal procedures for the control of short-term capital flows were now ineffective in all but routine situations; and that the volume of mobile funds in the international monetary system was now so large that in a speculative confrontation no central bank, no accumulation of exchange reserves could defend an exchange rate for long if the international financial community considered it to be too high. The significance of all this was that individual countries, particularly those with leading currencies, could no longer operate independent economic policies without interference from capital movements. The normal procedures of balance-of-payments adjustment by changes in interest rates to draw appropriate capital flows were no longer effective, or were only effective with interest-rate changes of such magnitude as were damaging to domestic policy.

Institutional changes in the international capital market which took place in the later fifties also had adverse effects on the normal processes of monetary control. The Euro-dollar market, which was to become so large a feature of the international scene, had its origin in late 1958, when convertibility of Western European currencies was restored and when London was able, as a result of the dismantling of British exchange control, to resume its role as a leading financial market for international funds. The main factor, which encouraged the market and stimulated its location in London rather than New York, was the so-called Regulation Q of the Federal Reserve System. By this regulation interest paid by U.S. banks on time-deposits was fixed, while dollar deposits in foreign banks were not subject to any interest ceiling. Returns on such deposits rose in 1959 one-quarter per cent above the Regulation Q level. As a result London banks came to bid for dollar deposits which in turn they relent in the United States. Some depositors of dollars – for example, the Soviet Union – found it convenient to hold deposits outside the United States, free from the jursidiction of the Federal Reserve. Thus a group of lenders and borrowers in dollars grew up in London where lenders were prepared to lend to large borrowers at more flexible rates than those available in New York. After 1958 the market grew rapidly, greatly encouraged by the British overseas and merchant banks, whose foreign-exchange departments acted as intermediaries. The deficit of the U.S. balance of payments in the sixties ensured that dollar balances were plentiful in Europe to form a basis for the growth of the supply side of the market. Although London has been the main centre for the market, other centres than London and other currencies than dollars came to form a market for Euro-currencies, i.e. currencies traded for loans of various terms outside their domestic centres. By 1967 there were eight European countries whose bank liabilities in Euro-currencies were $14.7 bln in U.S. dollars and the equivalent of $3.6 bln in other Euro-currencies.

The markets in Euro-currencies are by now highly developed and have become a large source of short-term credit and, through the Euro-bond market, of credit for longer periods. They provide an alternative to domestic money markets and impel countries to regard their interest-rate policies in an international setting. As individual money markets have begun to fear for control of domestic rates of interest and capital flows, the Euro-dollar market has acquired a life of its own nurtured by the concurrent movement for central bank co-operation. As early as 1966 there were signs that leading central banks were taking the market in hand. From time to time increases in Euro-dollar interest rates have been forestalled or lessened by central bank consortia temporarily supplying additional dollar deposits to the market – a process which has all the earmarks of an open-market operation to adjust Euro-dollar rates and credit supply.

A market such as this – which grew swiftly and spontaneously with no official support from governments during a mere decade – must have responded to some deep-felt need in the international monetary system. Behind its complex façade and the many technical controversies which surround its operations, what are the important features which the market displays? First, it represents a form of borrowing and lending outside the regulations and limits of a national monetary system – an example of extra-territorial operations for the international business community. Second, it has provided some unknown quantity of international liquidity in that dollar balances earned by exporters to the United States have often not been exchanged for their own currencies but have been lent in the Euro-dollar market. Third, it has provided a demonstration of how capital markets develop and ramify of themselves and have between their national centres relationships which can be seen *ex post* but seldom, if ever, influenced *ex ante*. The market in both short- and long-term capital has with advances in communication become a world-wide market with which individual monetary systems have relations which are as yet very imperfectly understood.

(v) THE NEW CENTRES OF POWER

It remains, in concluding this chapter, to comment briefly on what has been its leitmotiv: that between 1955 and the present the most striking aspect of the international economic scene has been a redistribution of power. Economic power at the world level consists in the ability to influence events in three fields: access to markets and an adequate share in real trade flows; freedom to take decisions in such monetary choices as exchange rates, interest rates and capital flows, and to co-ordinate such decisions in the external field with the decisions relevant to domestic economic policies; and the ability to negotiate with other countries in all such matters from a position of strong bargaining power.

Applied to leading industrial nations these criteria indicate the redistribution of economic power which has taken place. In the case of the United States in, say 1947, her position was unassailable in all fields. In real-goods flows the world was at her door demanding her consumer and capital goods, copying her production methods and courting her life-style. In international monetary affairs she dictated her own blueprint and in the early years of the IMF was in a position to give her ideas free play. In all international bargaining she commanded such sanctions against the recalcitrant and such potential benefits for the amenable that negotiation was largely a matter of stating her wishes and point of view. The same could not be said of the American position in the early sixties. Her monopoly of supply was over. Big new producers and exporters were in the game. Her balance of payments, drained by an unnecessary colonial war, was in chronic deficit: her external accounts balanced largely by the hesitant willingness of her creditors to hold dollar balances. In monetary matters she no longer ruled through the IMF but in the Group of Ten strove to hold her own against the European group. In all international negotiations she was faced with tough opposition from nations and groups knowing what they wanted and determined to get it.

In contrast to the United States, Britain, former industrial leader, was declining rapidly. Her share of international trade, falling since the third quarter of the nineteenth century, continued its fall in the postwar period. In monetary matters, although ambitious to reinstate sterling as an international currency, she was the understudy of the United States and, unable to extricate her economy from the effects of external deficit, delayed dollar convertibility of the West European currencies until 1959. British bargaining power in economic negotiations declined. She became the European weakling, sustained by stabilisation loans and IMF assistance.

Among individual nations Japan provided a spectacular example of how the combination of economic growth and trade penetration may increase power and status. From total defeat, occupation and the not very intelligent American efforts at 'westernisation' in the immediate postwar years, Japan surged forward in the sixties to be the dominant industrial power in Asia, the possessor of the world's strongest currency and the exploiter in its burgeoning industry of new products and new techniques.

It was through groups of nations that changes in power took place in the sixties. In Western Europe the formation of the EEC gave to that group a voice to answer the United States in economic negotiations. Among the developing countries the realisation that strength lay in joint action was manifested at the United Nations' Conference on Trade and Development at Geneva in 1964 when a coalition of the leading Third World countries challenged the United States and the industrial countries as a group and found them in great disarray. Thereafter Third World operations in the GATT, the IMF and in the United Nations Assembly were conducted as a group operation.

Perhaps the greatest power switch of the period was that in which the economic power of the state, even the largest states, was challenged by multinational corporations now so large that they were surpassed in wealth only by the larger nations. The decision-making of such corporations in the trading and monetary spheres could annul or threaten contrary decisions by governments. Whole sectors of world trade, in oil, automobiles, chemicals, electronics, timber, and basic materials, are now managed by such faceless entities with loyalties and obligations to nothing save their own profit-and-loss accounts. The power of nation-states is fixed at their own frontiers; the powers of corporations have ramified and stretch beyond single states. With manufacturing in many countries, financial operations directed from one country, marketing from another and with capital derived from a wide variety of sources, such corporations may operate so as to arrange their raw-material procurement, production, distribution, profit allocation and taxation to maximum advantage. In doing so, they may possibly infringe the legal sovereignty of none of the countries in which they operate but they may also do so to the detriment of national policies and economic aims of any or all. Huge companies are not, of course, new. What is new is the dispersal of operations (and national responsibilities) which modern travel and communication now make possible. With the jet age, the telex, the long-distance telephone and modern management and computer techniques, a new and highly significant stage was reached in the postwar period. The multinational company became more than a mere amalgamation formed for overseas trading. It became a large economic entity in itself; as powerful as many governments and far more flexible in its decision-making. The problem of encompassing such corporations within a political control system assuming only the existence of nation-states is a problem which is entirely new and one in which the economic, legal and political facets have to be brought together.

Even this brief summary may be sufficient to point up the different pattern of international economic relationships which distinguished the period from 1955 to the seventies from the decade which preceded. We have stressed the differences: let us end this chapter by reminding the reader of at least one similarity. The sixties were a continuation, indeed an acceleration, of the growth and prosperity for the industrial countries which began in the fifties. The 'age of Keynes' seemed to be able to ensure high and stable levels of employment. Trade volumes expanded; very high rates of real growth were achieved, particularly in Western Europe. It seemed that the economic problems of the world economy – creeping inflation, international balance-of-payments adjustment, an orderly set of exchange rates, adequate form and quantity of international money – were growing pains and not symptoms of serious disease. Even after the currency crisis of 1967 and 1968, and with Nixon as a new President pledged to end the war in Vietnam, observers might have been excused, at least on economic grounds, for some degree of optimism. Crisis and disillusionment still lay ahead, in the seventies.

8

The Rise of the Dollar and the Decline of Sterling

(i) INTRODUCTION

This chapter will examine, through the story of the two main participants, the evolution of payments and the international monetary system between 1955 and 1964. This period must first be set in its total postwar context. The opening date, 1955, is chosen because it marks the end of what we may call the 'first dollar problem'. At, or near to, that time the American balance of payments changed from surplus to the deficit which was to increase and dominate the payments situation throughout the sixties and seventies. American accommodating finance to the rest of the industrial world ceased as it became unnecessary and the dollar became readily available either as a transactions or a reserve currency. Three years later, on 31 December 1958, the Western European currencies became convertible into dollars, thereby establishing, several years later than had been hoped,[1] the currency system agreed to at Bretton Woods. This tardiness in establishing the Bretton Woods system was, in great part, due to the delay in making sterling convertible. Our first task in this chapter then is to examine briefly the transition from the regionalised currency system of the fifties to the Bretton Woods world of the sixties.

In January 1959 began twelve years in which the main currencies (outside the Communist world) were freely convertible one to another and through the U.S. dollar, fixed in free exchange for gold at $35 per ounce, indirectly convertible into gold. This dollar–gold exchange standard ended in August 1971 when the dollar was made inconvertible into gold and when the major currencies no longer maintained fixed parities with the dollar. Thus the twelve years 1959–71 may be regarded as the high summer of the Bretton Woods payments system centred around the IMF.

Once established, the Bretton Woods system became subject to a number of problems, some of which were eventually to bring it to an end. But for a number of years up to, say, 1964 it operated satisfactorily enough and contemporary observers would not have forecast its early demise. The IMF,

[1] Originally, under the Bretton Woods Agreement of 1944, convertibility of all members' currencies was to be established after a transition period of five years from the beginning of Fund Operations. The Fund opened on 1 March 1947, thus fixing the end of the transition period as 29 February 1952.

central institution of Bretton Woods, increased in influence and became accepted as a world body in currency matters. Moreover, international finance, which had long been regarded by national governments[2] as of secondary importance in international relations, was promoted to a primary role as its influence on economic growth, bargaining power and influence came to be realised. The years 1959–71 therefore mark a distinct epoch in postwar currency history, the period of trial, failure and collapse of the Bretton Woods system. In this chapter we carry the story to 1964, up to which the problems were largely those of reassessing the Bretton Woods principles in the light of events. In Chapter 12 we deal with the many crises to which the system was subjected in the later sixties and with its eventual breakdown.

(ii) ESTABLISHING CONVERTIBILITY

An observer of the international currency scene in 1955 might have been struck by four features which carried the promise of future change.

The first was the balance-of-payments position of the United States and the changing world role of the dollar. The acute and continuous surplus in the immediate postwar years after 1952 assumed manageable proportions. The years 1952 and 1953 saw a great improvement in the international payments situation. In Europe the OEEC countries, as a group, maintained an annual current account surplus of $1.5 bln in 1953–4. The favourable balance of the United Kingdom was, at £225 m. in 1953, the highest since the war. Germany became a surplus country in 1951 but France, whose rate of growth was swift in the fifties, had recurrent balance-of-payments difficulties. Meanwhile, the export surplus of the United States shrank until, in 1953, the trade balance was in approximate equilibrium.[3] In spite of a slight recession in the United States 1954 was a year of easy payments and although the Western European trade deficit with the United States came out at $1423 m. it was more than covered by direct U.S. military expenditures in Western Europe of $1431 m. The existence of certain government grants and remittances thus enabled European dollar reserves to be augmented.

During the later fifties the trend of improvement of the balance of payments of the non-dollar world with the United States continued, despite the minor recession of 1957–8 and the emergency imports of oil from the western hemisphere during the Suez Crisis of 1956–7. The year 1958 brought a sharp reduction of American exports, the fall continuing in 1959 while, on the import side of the merchandise trade account, imports remained on a slightly rising trend from 1957 to 1960. The changes in both imports and exports,

[2] Except France.
[3] If military deliveries are excluded, the U.S. current balance changed from a surplus of $1829 m. in 1952 to a deficit of $62 m. in 1953.

which seem to have been due to changes in the trading position of the United States as postwar recovery strengthened in Europe, produced a trade balance quite insufficient to meet the external commitments of the United States on capital and military accounts. The result was the beginning of the loss of gold which the United States was to undergo throughout the sixties. In 1958 $2275 m. and in 1959 $1076 m. seemed small losses from a reserve of $19.5 bln, but they were the beginning of a rising trend.

Thus by the end of the fifties the dollar problem had reversed itself and become a balance-of-payments-deficit problem for the United States. Seen at the time as a mere interlude in the earlier problem[4] there was every reason to regard the reversal with equanimity and it was hailed as a welcome breathing-space. Now, in the perspective given by a quarter-century, the structural nature of the change is apparent. The current account surplus had become insufficient to finance capital and military outlays overseas. These were to increase and in the later sixties bear the burden of war in South-East Asia and recurrent waves of direct and indirect overseas investment.

One reason why even economists at the time welcomed the U.S. payments reversal was that it ended scarcity of the dollar as a currency. As long as strong U.S. surpluses lasted the dollar was necessarily in short supply; a currency to be hoarded, finding its way to banking reserves rather than into transactions uses. Once in deficit, dollar scarcity was replaced by foreign dollar balances which, as long as American reserves were not far short of $20 b., were of unquestionable acceptance as international money. With the rapid expansion of the New York foreign-exchange and capital markets the dollar was able quickly to move into its Bretton Woods position as the leading international currency – this at a time when increasing doubts were being felt as to the future of sterling's key currency role. Convertible into gold at a fixed price and, after 1959, convertible into all other IMF currencies at fixed exchange rates, while backed by a gold reserve of unprecedented size, it is small wonder that the dollar stepped naturally into the place formerly held by sterling and prepared for it by the Bretton Woods Agreement.

The second notable feature of the payments scene in 1955 was the growing importance of West Germany and its currency. Transformed by the currency reform of 1948 the German economy expanded rapidly. After a brief period (1949 and 1950) during which this expansion caused imports to grow without any commensurate increase in exports, the German trade balance became favourable in the spring of 1951. It has remained so ever since. This trade surplus was mainly the result of the steady expansion of exports. While imports rose from 1954 onwards they were, until 1958, outpaced by exports. During 1958, 1959 and 1960 West German trade was in surplus with every metropolitan EPU country as well as with the extra-European sterling area as a whole. With a net balance on invisibles of small dimensions the German

---

[4] Sir Donald MacDougall, in his *The World Dollar Problem* in 1957 (London: Macmillan, 1957), referred to the dollar (surplus) problem as one likely to continue in that form.

balance of payments on current account was heavily in surplus and against such surpluses only small capital exports could be offset. The result was a massive addition to German foreign-exchange reserves.

The real strength of the German surplus was the very strong competitive position secured by the Germans for themselves in export markets, a position based upon the importance conceded to the export drive by German industrialists, the competitive prices at which goods were offered, the short and well-honoured delivery dates for capital goods and the attention given to selling and marketing techniques. It was believed, particularly in the United Kingdom, that the German surplus would decline as the German economy moved towards the point of full employment; that (a) higher domestic production and income would pull in greater imports and (b) that the level of demand in the home market would pull goods away from the export market. The first of these changes occurred only slightly, the second not at all. By the spring of 1961 the German economy was the most fully employed in Europe with unemployment less than 1 per cent and with more than three vacancies for every single person unemployed. Yet this did not lead to any marked rise in prices nor to any foreign balance deterioration.

Three features of the German economy allowed expansion to continue without the expected 'heating-up' taking place: the influx of immigrant labour from Eastern Germany, the almost pathological fear of inflation by both Government and people, and the existence of certain built-in checks against inflation in the German economy, of which the high propensity to save and the low 'propensity to strike' of the German worker were the most notable.

Already in the fifties the German surplus was a structural problem in European payments and was the subject of continual criticism in the OEEC. To their credit the German Government was ready to acknowledge the existence of a surplus problem, and to take measures for its alleviation. It liberalised import policies and lent abroad in modest amount. But on the central issues – the DM exchange rate and the demand level, within the German economy – the Germans were adamant. To revalue the currency might imperil the export drive and offend a large industrial group which supported the Government. To expand the economy to the point where rising imports would eliminate the surplus would risk a rise in the German price level. Neither course was acceptable.

A third feature of the payments scene was the instability of the British balance of payments. In the immediate postwar period a large deficit was to be expected and in the circumstances the balance-of-payments performance for the five postwar years was not surprising. The country's power to export had been depleted by the war. Significant invisible items,[5] such as earnings from financial services and foreign investments normally expected to offset the

---

[5] For example, payments for shipping services, earnings from financial services and earnings from foreign investments all fell while government outlays overseas rose.

merchandise trade deficit, were now adverse and there was a high demand for imports of all kinds for capital reconstruction and consumption. But after the sterling devaluation of September 1949, with the war five years away and sterling realistically aligned with other major currencies, a more robust payments position might have been expected. In fact in the period 1950–64 what came out was a series of modest surpluses interspersed with four large deficits – the largest in 1964. Relevant to Britain's external equilibrium needs, estimated by the British Treasury in 1957 to be an annual current account surplus of £350 m., the result was poor indeed. In one year only, 1958, was this target met. Moreover, from the mid-fifties dates the long series of speculative raids on sterling which were to be such a damaging and persistent feature of the currency and a thorn in the flesh of British policy-makers throughout the sixties.

Table 8.1 summarises the British balance of payments between 1952 and 1964. At first sight the current balance, with three exceptions, seems satisfactory enough. It is only after considering certain special aspects of sterling's position that a truer picture emerges. First, among such special aspects was the fact that Britain continued into the postwar period her role as an exporter of capital but whereas in the interwar period this debit item in the capital account was offset by a large enough current surplus, in the postwar period surpluses were insufficient. The net result was one of imbalance. Second, Britain was committed under the Bretton Woods arrangements, and by her own interpretation of sterling's position as an international currency, to maintain a fixed exchange rate. This meant that rolling adjustments to the balance of payments could not be made through the exchange rate, but had to be met from foreign-exchange reserves which were perennially insufficient to meet such demands. This adjustment problem was compounded by the British Government commitment of 1944 to maintain a high level of employment after the war. This had been interpreted by both political parties to imply an unemployment rate of less than 3 per cent and in fact the rate was held well below that figure. It would be possible to extend this long list of special commitments bearing on the British balance of payments – the large military British presence abroad, the pursuit of an international role for sterling, the promise to the United States to establish and preserve convertibility of sterling – all these underscore the fact that only a rich and economically well-endowed country could pursue such roles simultaneously.

The fourth feature of the payments system in the later fifties was the proliferation of new international organisations, particularly in Europe. These were to play a role in events. In a similar category, influencing international monetary policy, was the re-emergence of central bank co-operation. The Marshall Plan, which had been launched in 1948, had led to elaborate organisation of the joint European effort for reconstruction. The Organization for European Economic Co-operation (OEEC), was responsible for co-ordinating many aspects of co-operative economic planning

TABLE 8.1

U.K. Balance of Payments, 1952–64

(£ m.)

	1952	1953	1954	1955	1956	1957	1958	1959	1960	1961	1962	1963	1964
Imports (f.o.b.)	3048	2927	2989	3386	3324	3538	3378	3640	4141	4045	4098	4370	5016
Exports and re-exports (f.o.b.)	2769	2683	2785	3073	3377	3509	3407	3522	3733	3892	3994	4287	4471
Visible balance	−279	−244	−204	−313	53	−29	29	−118	−408	−153	−104	−83	−545
Invisible balance	442	389	321	158	155	262	318	267	150	158	231	199	143
Current balance	163	145	117	−155	208	233	347	149	−258	5	127	116	−402
Balance of long-term capital	−134	−194	−191	−122	−187	−106	−196	−255	−192	68	−98	−155	−374
Balance of current and long-term capital transactions	29	−49	−74	−277	21	127	151	−106	−450	73	29	−39	−776
Errors and omissions	66	32	57	121	42	80	64	−28	292	−34	60	−71	45
Balance of monetary movements	95	−17	−17	−156	63	207	215	−134	−158	39	89	−110	−731

Source: Central Statistical Office, *United Kingdom Balance of Payments* (various years).

while functional agencies such as the European Payments Union (EPU) were responsible for technical operations each in their field. The Bank for International Settlements returned to the stage both in connection with EPU operations and as a centre for central bank meetings through the Basle Club. The fifties then, although a period during which the IMF and the Bretton Woods arrangements were in abeyance, were of great importance in the development of international economic co-operation. But they shifted the focus of co-operation to Europe and they weakened the Fund by its virtual exclusion from what became for the time being the centre of monetary affairs.[6]

We have set the international monetary scene in the fifties rather carefully because it is important to realise just what was taking place during the decade which it took to establish full convertibility between the leading currencies. In Chapter 3 we described the effects of the premature American drive to bring this convertibility about and the disastrous failure which it involved for Britain in 1947. In the next section we describe the more methodical and sure-footed approach to the same problem in the fifties.

(iii) BRETTON WOODS AT LAST

The American contribution to the attainment of convertibility in 1958 was low-key. On the European side the desirability of making currencies convertible, for at least current transactions, was acknowledged but, in the light of British experience, there was tacit agreement to 'hurry slowly'.[7] The British, despite their failure in 1947, were anxious to make sterling convertible for the increased importance this would give to the currency. From 1955 there was a loose agreement between Britain and the United States, that each by their policies would contribute to a so-called 'collective approach' to sterling convertibility. In the meantime EPU and the sterling area, linked through British participation in the former, provided a wide geographical convertibility between (a) all Western European currencies, (b) sterling, (c) all overseas sterling-area currencies, and (d) some few other currencies linked to

---

[6] This exclusion was largely due to the American decision that countries in receipt of Marshall Aid should not receive assistance from the Fund. Between 1948 and about 1955 the Fund's business with and interest in Europe was much less than it should have been.

[7] A precise definition of currency convertibility is difficult to state briefly. The convertibility sought in the immediate postwar period, and which we have so far been discussing, was a qualified one, being for non-residents only. A brief working definition which may serve is that convertibility in a currency is the power of exchanging it freely in a public exchange market for other currencies.

Not until February 1961 did sterling and the other leading Western European currencies assume full responsibilities of Article 8 of the Fund Agreement. From December 1958 until that date they operated under Article 14, which allows countries suffering from balance-of-payments difficulties to contract out of the obligation of full current-account convertibility. This distinction was largely a legal one.

sterling through 'administrative control' of the Bank of England. Between this large currency group and the dollar, however, there was no convertibility. To bridge this gap was the final task and much of the weight of it fell on the British. If full convertibility for all these countries were to be established prematurely, i.e. while the world at large had still a preference for dollars over other currencies, much of the sterling balances held by other countries would be quickly converted into dollars to the detriment of the British balance of payments and the sterling exchange rate.

Attention in the movement towards convertibility centred on sterling. As early as 1951–2 there were discussions between Britain, the United States and the IMF. The British approach was clearly to test the waters (of the exchange market) by slowly allowing limited free markets for sterling to arise. In these, as expected, sterling was initially at a discount to the dollar relative to the official rate appropriate to the IMF parities. But if, as sterling strengthened with a favourable balance of payments, the 'free' rate moved to coincide with the official rate, then full convertibility would be feasible. In December 1951 British banks were allowed to hold balances of currencies and deal in foreign exchange on a very limited basis. By 1954 in New York, Zürich and elsewhere, transferable sterling could be changed into dollars on free markets in which the rate in March 1954 was only at a discount of 1 per cent. In later 1954 and in 1955 balance-of-payments problems widened the discount to 2 and 3 per cent, but in February 1955 the Bank of England began to intervene in the free markets to support the free rate. This was a move of far-reaching consequence since the British Government was now virtually supplying dollars freely at a rate only slightly less than that on American account sterling. Convertibility seemed imminent, indeed sterling was *de facto* convertible. But *de jure* convertibility had to wait three more years. In late 1955 and in 1956 there was a renewal of the sterling area's foreign balance problem and of dollar shortage: in 1956 the external problems created by the Suez adventure and in 1957 the speculation against sterling all forced a holding action upon the Government. Not until December 1958 was sterling strong enough for a declaration of *de jure* convertibility for non-residents, bringing to an end the free markets in sterling abroad and centring exchange dealings in normal markets. The politics behind the final move towards convertibility are obscure but it is probable that, at some time in 1958, Britain promised the Americans that they would make a declaration of convertibility as soon as possible in return for American support for a revision of quotas in the IMF.[8] In the final event convertibility came upon sterling rather differently than had been expected. After years in which hopes of its achievement had ebbed and flowed with the fortunes of the British economy the final approach in 1958 was steady and gradual. Precipitated as it finally was by certain French and Western European currency reforms it came at last

---

[8] Under its new liberal lending policy begun in 1956 the IMF was by this time in need of more currencies to lend – hence the move for a revision of the original quotas.

almost as a contingent measure. It provided us for the first time with an international currency system broadly in conformity with the ideals of Bretton Woods.

(iv) GROWTH – AS NEVER BEFORE

The main features of the monetary scene in 1959 were perplexing rather than threatening but, in the main, the mood was optimistic. The salient features in the landscape of international finance were these. The United States, now a deficit country was, through its deficit, supplying dollars to a world which, for the present, was prepared to regard and use the dollar as a key currency. The British, despite recurrent balance-of-payments problems, were anxious to see sterling play an important role as a second key currency and looked forward to growing influence for the City of London now that exchange controls had been largely dismantled. Two other important currencies were emerging on the world stage – the Deutschmark and the yen – both of which, on the basis of market penetration and a huge export trade were to play an increasing role.

Apart from what we may call the 'externalities' of world finance there was the domestic condition of the IMF, which if not the leader, was at least to be the hub of the Bretton Woods system. Here, as on the wider scene, there were grounds for caution, but not for despondency. The influence of political forces upon the Fund, which Keynes had feared, was strong in its operations from the outset. The overwhelming political, economic and military dominance of the United States in the postwar years, its preponderant voting power in the Fund and the Fund's location in Washington ensured that it should be inordinately influenced in this period by the Americans. Although American dominance in the Fund diminished in the sixties, political conditions and influences continued to shape Fund policies and decisions.

Convertibility brought the Fund back to the centre of events. Since 1956 its position had been strengthened by the increase of its activities and the growing acceptance by member countries that it had a useful role to play. Now, in 1959, two technical considerations called for attention. First, it was clear that, if the Fund was to supply currencies in accordance with a reasonably flexible policy, its international liquidity holding had to be increased, either by a revision of quotas, by borrowing from richer members or by sponsoring the creation of a new international reserve unit. Second, there was evidence that the exchange-rate policies of the Fund were unsatisfactory. The exchange rate would have to be brought into play as an adjustment mechanism to aid member countries in achieving balance-of-payments equilibrium. As the Fund administered it, the exchange-rate system gave rise to currency speculation; and the Fund's arrangements with member countries for the changing of exchange rates were unsatisfactory, usually resulting in the country concerned taking unilateral action.

Finally, the Fund had, in the light of more than a decade's experience, a number of housekeeping matters to attend to. There was need to adapt its attitude towards controls, discrimination and restrictive currency practices to suit the new world of freer trade and payments which appeared to be evolving in 1959. Clearly this could not, as some Americans had thought, be its main work. Circumstances were forcing upon it the more central tasks of exchange-rate supervision and adjustment which Keynes had originally seen as central to its efforts.

Of all questions for the Fund in 1959 that which loomed largest was the provision in the world monetary system of an adequate and well-distributed supply of international money. In 1948 the ratio of gold and key currencies held by countries and international organisations to world imports was 80 per cent; by 1957 it was only 51 per cent. With the expansion of trade in the sixties it was to fall still further. This 'international liquidity problem' had several facets and it is worth while looking at these in turn. First, however, a general overview to put the various elements in perspective.

In a world of fixed exchange rates deficits and surpluses in a country's balance of payments result in additions to or diminution of its foreign-exchange reserves as its monetary authority intervenes in the exchange market to maintain the exchange rate. Under Bretton Woods principles the need for international liquidity was maximised (*a*) because exchange rates were fixed in all but the very long period, (*b*) because direct controls on balances of payments were precluded under the Fund agreement, (*c*) because leading countries were pledged to policies of full employment and (*d*) because, during the early life of the Bretton Woods system, trade had been expanding.[9] Thus the problem was, in its simplest form, to increase the total quantity of international liquidity in order to give greater freedom of manœuvre to individual countries in their balance-of-payments policies, especially to prevent them resorting to controls or disorderly currency practices which would threaten the whole system.[10]

In the real world, however, the international liquidity problem had other aspects than that of the simple aggregate. International liquidity was not a

[9] The expression $D_1 = f[\Sigma_n\{(B_1 - B_t)\}, V]$ summarises the world demand for international liquidity, where D_1 is the demand, B_1 is the balance of regular transactions, B_t the balance of settling transactions and the sum of $(B_1 - B_t)$ for the n countries of the world system is the total of residual balances requiring settlement. V is the total volume of world trade.

There is no reason to expect that imbalance tends to increase with trade volume. It is dominantly the size of fluctuations in balances of payments (i.e. $B_1 - B_t$) which determines D_1. But the disaster model is certainly one in which the volume of trade is very large and balances of payments are unstable as well.

[10] To many economists the international liquidity problem was irrelevant and could have been avoided completely by reverting to a regime of freely floating exchange rates under which balance-of-payments adjustment was achieved by a free exchange market and no reserves were necessary. Such was the view of the 'monetary school' (led by Chicago economists H. G. Johnson and Milton Friedman), which carried this politically naïve view of the perfection of market mechanisms to many conclusions in regard to economic policy throughout the sixties and seventies. It is necessary to note that a large number of economists who led the early intellectual revolt against fixed exchange rates (e.g. Meade) did not carry their arguments to the same conclusions but argued rather for a more flexible system than Bretton Woods with more effective use of exchange rates to influence balances of payments.

homogeneous element: it consisted of gold, key currencies – the U.S. dollar and the pound – three elements of varying attraction and acceptability, between which holders might switch in accordance with subjective assessments. Initially, in 1959, the switching problem was seen as one of two key currencies. The new world was to be a dual-currency world in which the dollar and sterling would be the key currencies. It was conceivable that a dual-centred currency system would result in a never-ending see-saw in which funds moved restlessly backwards and forwards between the two currencies with unstabilising effects for them and for the whole system. This proved to be a fear only partially justified in practice. Although the early sixties with its recurrent balance-of-payments problems for sterling did see that currency persistently weak relative to the dollar, it was the events which followed the sterling devaluation of November 1967 which are the keys to the breakdown of the Bretton Woods system. These events may be regarded as an aspect of the switching problem, expressing lack of confidence not in one of the key currencies but in both. The years from 1967 were to see a confidence problem of a new and more devastating kind – a propensity on the part of holders of international balances to seek security outside the key currencies altogether, either in gold or other temporarily preferred currencies. There was, indeed, a switching problem among the constituents of international liquidity, but the switch was different from what had been expected.

But these recondite aspects of the Bretton Woods system were not perceived as of great immediate concern. The simple problem of providing an adequate amount of liquidity in the light of an expanding volume of world trade claimed attention. The sixties saw a recognition of this problem and persistent efforts to solve it – by the institution in 1961 of the General Arrangements to Borrow (GAB) within the IMF, by further increases in Fund quotas in February 1966, by measures for intra-central bank co-operation and by the creation in 1967 of a new form of international liquidity through the Special Drawing Right (SDR). Efforts to expand the world stock of international liquidity were continual and widened in scope throughout the sixties. The major efforts will be dealt with each in their place. That which belongs to the very early sixties is the so-called GAB arrangements of the IMF.

The IMF existed, in part, to augment the reserve holdings of its members who might purchase from it, up to the limit of a quota, currencies which for the moment were scarce to them. Since a small group of currencies were in continual demand the resources of the Fund, in particular of these currencies, were crucial if it were to fulfil its role as a supplement to individual country reserves.[11] Means of increasing these usable resources were limited to two: by increasing the quota contributions of members or by borrowing from members. The 'increase-of-quota' route was followed but was insufficient. In

[11] This role was at best a peripheral one. Even in 1973 after the inclusion of SDRs the Fund commanded only 15.7 per cent of total world liquidity.

1959 soon after a general quota increase[12] it became apparent that, in the new convertible conditions, and with mercurial balances of payments there would be great demand for supplies of the leading currencies. The question of how to meet this demand was then a special one, apart from the general question of international liquidity. Of the methods open to it, the Fund elected to use the power to borrow from its members given to it under its founding agreement.[13] According to a staff report of April 1961 it was estimated that, over and above its normal holdings, the Fund would require about $2 bln in U.S. dollars and $3½-5 bln in currencies apart from dollars and sterling. Credit lines should therefore be sought from leading members, each for its own currency. The amounts of each currency borrowed would have to be settled by negotiation, in which account would be taken of the country's quota and the size of its reserves. After negotiations lasting four months, on 20 December 1961, the GAB were approved by the Board. These provided for loans, on demand by the Fund, by ten countries of their currencies amounting to $6 bln. Precise conditions as to the loans, their repayment, conditions and servicing were made in the agreement.[14]

The agreement of 1961 was a watershed in the Fund's development. Apart from their functional aspects certain principles were implicit in the arrangements. First, it was now acknowledged that there must always be a limit to the resources the Fund might command from quota subscriptions, [15] and that these might well be insufficient to supply liquidity in the leading currencies. Second, from a system of supplementation through borrowing to one of supplementation by credit overdrafts or drawing rights was not a great step and in this sense the GAB may be seen as a logical forerunner of the SDR scheme which was to come in 1967. Finally, with the supply of currencies by member countries went power for the suppliers. The GAB gave formal recognition to an asymmetry which existed in the Bretton Woods system, in that while there are scores of currencies in the world (and in the Fund) there is but a small number which are of real importance. The Fund, as an organisation of (at that time) seventy-one states, had entered into an agreement with a group of its richest members, to augment its resources and contribute to one of its most important functions, the supply of currencies to members. It could have been foreseen at the time – perhaps it was foreseen[16] – that the group of members concerned, not only by reason of their new role but

[12] Further quota increases were to take place in 1966 and 1970.

[13] See Article 7, Sec. 2 (i).

[14] For a more detailed account of GAB, see Scammell, *International Monetary Policy: Bretton Woods and After* (London: Macmillan, 1975) pp. 195–8.

[15] Even if it were politically feasible to raise these periodically.

[16] According to Horsefield, Mr Per Jacobsson, the Fund's managing director, had his doubts of the wisdom of group decisions within the Fund. He laid down certain principles to which any agreement which he was prepared to submit to the Board must conform. One of these was that 'the Authority of the Fund must not be impaired'. See J. K. Horsefield, *The IMF 1945–65* (Washington, D.C.: I.M.F., 1969) vol. 1, p. 511. See also Erin E. Jacobsson, *A Life for Sound Money: Per Jacobsson. His Biography* (London: Oxford University Press, 1979).

by their dominant voting power, would become the political driving force of the whole IMF. As the eventual Group of Ten they were destined to exert a formative influence on Fund developments in the later sixties.

Return now to the general picture of the new convertible system. It is possible to sum up the problems of this system as they were to be throughout the sixties in one question: how, with fixed exchange rates, were strong and weak currencies to co-exist?[17] In this respect the sides were already picked: sterling long in difficulties, the U.S. dollar now a deficit currency still enjoying world confidence as it surged to prominence as the leading key currency on the basis of a burgeoning overseas banking network, but destined for trouble as its deficit grew and became chronic; the Canadian dollar geared to its U.S. counterpart but since 1951 outside the IMF because of its free exchange rate; on the side of the strong, the Deutschmark, soon to be joined by the Japanese yen, as currencies based on apparently impregnable trade balances, the Swiss franc, secure on neutrality, conservatism and the safest of banking systems. Round these the lesser fry grouped and re-grouped according to fortune and the run of events.

Between 1959 and 1964 the vital currency was sterling. Had the pound been capable of assuming the role of key currency to which the British Government aspired, had it been backed by a stronger balance of payments, more skilful monetary policy and had it not been subject to repeated speculative attacks by lagged payments and hot money movements, then the suspicion which clouded it would probably not have been extended to the dollar later in the decade. As it was the period from 1959 to 1964 was punctuated by recurrent sterling crises which marked the end of its career as a key currency.

The British deficit on current account in 1960 was the largest since 1947, and 1961 was a year of rearguard actions to save sterling from devaluation.[18] On 4 March 1961 the German monetary authorities revalued the Deutschmark by 5 per cent. A few days later the guilder was similarly adjusted. A general realignment of currency values was now anticipated and considerable speculation resulted, much of it concentrated in selling pressure on sterling. So far as that currency was concerned British policies were simple. Their leitmotiv was to be the preservation of the external value of the pound,

---

[17] It must be stressed that the words 'strong' and 'weak' refer here to currencies within the small group of the leading dozen or so currencies of the world. Obviously strong and weak currencies can and do exist among the large number of peripheral and less-important national currencies which are not heavily traded on the foreign-exchange market and are neither key currencies nor vehicle currencies.

[18] The language here is deliberately chosen to recall the dramatic style used by writers and politicians of the sixties to dramatise exchange-rate crises. Harold Wilson spoke of 'dying in the last ditch with sterling'; an American foreign-exchange dealer at the New York Federal Reserve spoke proudly of engaging in the battle to save sterling using language adapted from Henry V's speech before Agincourt. An exchange rate was cast as a national symbol to be defended. To speak of it as a price in a market for currencies was to be prosaic if not unpatriotic.

to which overriding objective British domestic industrial and monetary policies were to be subjugated. In part this decision was due to the British desire 'to retain in London an international financial centre of the first rank and with that to maintain a fixed exchange rate';[19] in part it was the expression of an old belief that devaluation of a currency was not a weapon of policy but the final and ultimate economic disaster to be avoided at any cost.[20] Persistent British refusal to use devaluation and the persistent belief of speculators that she could not avoid it was a determinant of important events in the sixties. The Americans suffered from the same myopia, believing in fixed exchange rates and the maintenance of the sterling parity as the first bastion in defence of the dollar.

Co-operation among central banks saved sterling from devaluation in 1961. In the face of a statement by central bank governors, meeting in Basle, that no further changes in exchange rates were contemplated speculation ceased. A week later the Basle Club announced that existing rates were to be supported (*a*) by swap arrangements whereby central banks would support each other's currencies by holding balances of these currencies rather than changing them into gold or dollars and (*b*) by short-term lending to countries whose currencies were under speculative pressure. This so-called Basle Agreement of March 1961 saved sterling and with American initiative inaugurated a phase of central bank co-operation in support of weak currencies which lasted up to sterling's eventual devaluation in November 1967.

Despite this organised support sterling could not sustain its position as the second key currency. The currency was under constant scrutiny and frequent speculative attack. The balance of payments was in bare surplus (averaging £83 bln) between 1961 and 1963, but in large deficit (−£402 m.) in 1964. There was constant tinkering with domestic economic policy, largely in the hope of impressing the world at large of the British Government's determination to manage their way to stability. It was of no avail. Deficits continued in 1965 and 1966 and sterling was devalued by 14 per cent in November 1967.

It is tempting to seek explanations for the persistent weakness of sterling during the years 1960 to 1967. Certain structural weaknesses in the British balance of payments have already been discussed, and these played their part. It may well be that, come what might, these weaknesses would have been conclusive. But it is fair to say that throughout the period the British Government had to play a subservient role to the Americans, who not only directed the defence of sterling but refused to contemplate a change in the exchange rate as a viable solution. Certainly between 1964 and 1967 the

---

[19] R. E. Caves *et al.*, *Britain's Economic Prospects*, chap. IV, 'The Balance of Payments', by R. N. Cooper (Washington, D.C.: Brookings Institution, 1968) p. 153.

[20] The same belief that made Britain return to the gold standard in April 1925 with sterling over-valued at the prewar exchange rate of $4.86 = £1 rather than at some rate in accord with 1925 prices and costs.

Americans soldiered manfully on, organising both in the Basle Club and in the Fund measures for sterling's support. Between 1961 and 1964 the IMF granted three one-year stand-by arrangements for Britain and during 1964 the Fund implied by its attitude that it would go to the limit to help preserve the sterling exchange rate. The reason for this was simple. The Americans (and the Fund) believed and as it transpired, they believed correctly, that if sterling were to devalue the result would be a heavy blow not only to world confidence in sterling, but to confidence in the whole international financial structure.

Gold transactions and the gold market were a necessary part of the Bretton Woods arrangements and it is necessary at this stage to go back a little and examine the role of gold in these arrangements. To do this is but to recur to the problem of international liquidity, which involved not only the volume of such liquidity but the relative acceptability of its constituent parts, gold and the key currencies. The switching problem whereby gold, the dollar, sterling and other currencies, were to be seen as alternatives for settlement or for holding international balances, was already becoming apparent in 1960. We take up the story in March 1954 when the London gold market was reopened.

Between March 1954 and late 1960 the gold price in the London market did not move outside the prescribed Fund limits ($34.65 – $35.35 an ounce) and kept even within the narrower limits of the U.S. Treasury's buying and selling prices. In late 1960, however, the price began to move upwards under the influence of steadily rising demand and by 17 October the London price passed the U.S. Treasury price plus the cost of transatlantic freight. By 20 October the price exceeded $40 for the first time. Much of the new demand was due to the belief that the American Government would shortly increase the price at which it sold gold at the Treasury. Such a price increase had been advocated for years as a means of increasing the value of international liquidity and in spite of repeated denials by the U.S. authorities it was widely believed that sooner or later the price would be raised. Official reaction to the price rise in late 1960 was a denial, by Kennedy himself, on 6 February 1961. This, together with tight restrictions on gold dealings by American nationals and corporations, halted the price rise for the time being.

By August 1961 the price was moving upwards again and, on American initiative, it was decided to expand the supply side of the market. Hitherto the supply had come from the Bank of England augmented from time to time by the U.S. authorities. Under a new arrangement the central banks of Belgium, France, Germany, Italy, Holland, Switzerland, Britain and the United States were to share the job of price stabilisation in the market by acting as a sales syndicate. This Gold Pool operated for the first time in November 1961 and remained in operation until March 1968 although France, who had her own ideas on gold policy, left in June 1967.

The pressure of rising gold demand was incessant during the sixties. At the U.S. Treasury the attrition of reserve encashment, begun in the early fifties, continued[21] while, in the free market, movement into gold by hoarders and pressure from industrial users increased. From 1966 private demand for gold exceeded new output and the Gold Pool had continually to make use of their gold reserves to hold the price to the required $35 level. After sterling's devaluation in November 1967 the movement into gold became a stampede. By mid-March 1968 the Gold Pool had lost $2.75 bln in supporting the free market and it ceased operation.

By 1964, five years after general convertibility and the establishment of the Bretton Woods system, that system was already in some disarray. Of the two leading key currencies, one was patently declining and unequal to the role for which it cast itself; the other, while seemingly still impregnable, was nervously contemplating the prospect that soon it would have to carry the whole weight as centre currency of Bretton Woods. Already the old mystique of gold as the only acceptable form of wealth was manifesting itself as a movement away from the key currencies. But at the heart of it all was imbalance among the balances of payments of the leading industrial and trading countries. Germany, with the chronic surplus which began in 1951, to be joined in the late sixties by Japan; Britain far gone in decline now joined by the United States with its swollen capital export and public sector expenditures; France, ever ready to use international finance as a major vehicle of foreign policy – all this was the raw material of crisis and breakdown. There were more stresses than the international system could handle. With the afterknowledge of history it is hard to understand why contemporaries did not, in 1964, interpret the march of events as we do now – as a process leading to inevitable breakdown in the seventies. The reason for this myopia is simple. Trends are not easily interpreted in their beginnings, least of all in international economics. The international monetary system is a state of continuous makeshift in which views, actions and policies have frequent changes of course. In 1964 such a change of course was still seven years ahead and the world did not look bound for hell. The short term view looked difficult rather than menacing.

The Western world had weathered the war, and its aftermath. Reconstruction was now virtually complete. There had been only limited and local disasters. Unemployment, the bane of the thirties, had been banished by Keynesian controls of the macro economy and replaced by unprecedented growth in trade and output. The price pattern which had accompanied this was a mild inflation in which prices would double only in a quarter-century. If the international payments system could not easily accommodate all this it would be surprising. The new Bretton Woods procedures were having their teething troubles, but these could be met and with suitable modification all would be well. Such was the mood of 1964.

To crisis we return in Chapter 12. We end this chapter on a cheerful note

[21] Between 1950 and mid-1968 the U.S. gold stock was run down from $23 bln to $10.5 bln.

with a brief description of the economic growth of the sixties which contemporaries saw as its sparkling feature.

(v) CONCLUSION

By the late fifties the strongest expansion of output and trade in modern times was well under way. It was to continue into the seventies but interrupted by the inflation and recession which began in 1973. The early years of this expansion have been dealt with in Chapter 5. In this section it remains only to summarise (with the aid of Tables 8.2–8.5) the distinctive features of the whole period from the end of the war to 1970 as follows:

(i) The years 1945–55 can be set aside as the period of recovery from the war. Nevertheless the rates of growth of production in most countries during this period were higher than might have been expected in a period of such confusion and 1938 rates of output were reached surprisingly quickly. By 1955 recovery was virtually complete and longer-term influences were clearly at work.

(ii) The trend rate of growth of GDP for the leading industrial countries[22] over the period 1955–68 was 4.7 per cent. Around this average there was some dispersion. Significantly lower rates were recorded by the United States, the United Kingdom and Belgium; higher rates by Japan, Germany, France, Italy and the Netherlands. The Japanese rate – more than twice the average – was accounted for by the phenomenal industrial growth of that country in the later sixties. One important feature of postwar growth was the economic resurgence of Europe. The growth rate of Europe's output in total (5.5 per cent a year) and *per capita* (4.4 per cent) was far above the world average. By 1970 output per head was nearly 2½ times its level in 1950.

(iii) High rates of growth were recorded by countries which were in process of industrialisation, for example France, Italy, Portugal, Spain and Japan.

(iv) Disaggregation reveals that for the group (and for almost all individual countries) industrial output grew more rapidly than total output, while agricultural output grew less rapidly. The high rates of growth of output per employed person were in part due to shifts of workers from agriculture to higher productivity industries.

(v) Breaking the decade of the sixties into two quinquennia it is notable that, except in the cases of Japan and Italy, growth rates were slightly lower in the later years. In part this was due to the existence of some underemployment in certain industrial countries, notably the United States, in the early years, which enabled high growth rates to be achieved as the economies moved to full employment in the mid-sixties. In the later sixties action to restrain

[22] Taken here as the OECD group.

TABLE 8.2

Growth of Output of OECD Countries, 1960–70

Country	1955–68 GDP	1960–65 Output per employed person	1960–65 Total output[1]	1965–70 Output per employed person	1965–70 Total output
Canada	4.5	2.6	5.5	1.5	4.4
United States	4.0	3.1	4.8[2]	1.8	3.7[2]
United Kingdom	2.8	2.2	3.0	2.9	2.4
Japan	10.2	8.7	10.1	10.8	12.4
France	5.7	5.2	5.8	5.2	5.3
Germany	5.1	4.4	5.1[2]	4.4	4.3[2]
Italy	5.5	6.2	5.1	6.8	6.3
Belgium	3.9	4.1	5.2	3.6	4.2
Denmark	4.8	4.0	5.2	—	4.1
Netherlands	5.1	3.6	5.2	4.3	5.0
Norway	4.5	4.3	4.9	3.7	4.4
Sweden	4.5	4.3	5.3	3.2	3.7
Switzerland	4.8	3.0	5.2	3.3	3.2

[1] Gross domestic product at factor cost, 1963 prices.
[2] Gross domestic product at market prices.

Source: OECD, *The Growth of Output, 1960–1970* (Paris: OECD, 1976), compiled from tables 2 and 3, pp. 22 and 25.

TABLE 8.3
Growth of World Exports, 1960–70
Value of trade, $ m.

Year	World exports	% increase on previous year	Industrial countries	% increase on previous year	Less-developed	% increase on previous year
1960	113,100.0	–	73,168	–	28,572	–
1961	118,200.0	4.5	77,022	5.2	29,567	3.4
1962	124,400.0	5.2	82,184	6.7	29,284	–0.95
1963	135,500.0	8.9	90,581	10.2	30,649	4.7
1964	151,900.0	12.1	99,128	9.4	31,430	2.5
1965	164,700.0	8.4	107,620	8.6	33,329	6.0
1966	181,023.0	9.9	119,059	10.6	36,157	8.5
1967	190,261.0	5.1	126,188	6.0	36,767	1.7
1968	212,885.0	11.9	143,433	13.6	40,670	11.1
1969	244,059.0	14.6	171,150	19.3	49,150	20.8
1970	279,721.0	14.6	197,342	15.3	55,041	12.0

Source: OECD, *The Growth of Output, 1960–1970* (Paris: OECD, 1976).

TABLE 8.4

Trend Rates of Growth of Trade, 1955–68

Annual average rates

Country	Exports of goods and services		Imports of goods and services	
	Value	Volume	Value	Volume
Canada	8.4	6.8	7.1	5.0
United States	6.6	5.5	6.7	6.3
United Kingdom	4.8	3.2	5.2	4.1
Japan	13.9	13.7	13.0	14.3
Germany	9.9	9.0	10.5	10.9
France	9.2	7.9	10.8	10.0
Italy	13.4	14.2	11.8	12.6
Belgium	8.0	7.2	8.2	7.2
Denmark	8.1	6.9	9.0	8.7
Netherlands	7.6	7.6	8.0	8.5
Norway	7.5	8.0	7.1	7.4
Sweden	7.7	6.7	7.8	6.7
Switzerland	9.4	6.7	9.4	8.8

Source: National Accounts of OECD Countries, 1955–68 (Paris: OECD, 1970).

inflationary pressure was fairly widespread (again the United States was an example) and growth was constrained. Apart from labour availability and utilisation there is also the statistical point that high percentage growth ratios become progressively difficult to achieve as absolute levels of output rise.

(vi) Associated with the growth of output was the unprecedented expansion of international trade and investment. Over the period 1948–70 trade in manufactures consistently grew more rapidly than world manufacturing output.[23] Trade, measured by volume of world exports, grew in the sixties at annual rates never reached before. With only slight cyclical and temporary variations world trade grew steadily between 1950 and 1970 both in primary products (at 6 per cent a year) and in manufactures (9 per cent a year). However, it was trade between manufacturing countries with similar factor endowments which rose fastest. A relative shift of demand away from food and raw materials towards capital goods and manufactured products boosted the trade of the industrial and already rich countries (see Table 8.2, p. 125). Although trade for the developing countries grew, it did so more slowly, the increase being generated by the demand of the manufacturing countries for raw materials to feed their expansion.

The resources of this great expansion in international trade were to be found in: the high level of demand for manufactured goods in the leading countries; the commodity pattern of demand which enabled certain countries

---

[23] The ratio at 1.4 was fairly stable and exceeded that between 1876 and 1913, a previous period of great trade expansion, when it was less than unity.

TABLE 8.5

Percentage Distribution of World Trade, 1955–69
(based on data at constant 1963 prices)

Exports to:		Developed countries		Developing countries		World	
from:	*Commodity class*	*1955*	*1969*	*1955*	*1969*	*1955*	*1969*
Developed countries[a]	Primary products	22.0	16.9	3.6	3.1	25.6	20.0
	Manufactures	33.6	48.4	17.7	13.1	51.3	61.5
	All commodities	55.6	65.3	21.3	16.2	76.9	81.5
Developing countries	Primary products	16.7	12.3	3.2	2.2	19.9	14.5
	Manufactures	2.3	2.9	0.9	1.1	3.2	4.0
	All commodities	19.0	15.2	4.1	3.3	23.1	18.5
World	Primary products	38.7	29.2	6.8	5.3	45.5	34.5
	Manufactures	35.9	51.3	18.6	14.2	54.5	65.5
	All commodities	74.6	80.5	25.4	19.5	100.0	100.0

[a] Made up of Europe and overseas developed countries of the United Nations, *Economic Survey of Europe, 1971* (Geneva: ECE, 1972) part 1, table 2.3, p. 29.

Source: U.N., *Monthly Bulletin of Statistics* (New York).

(notably Japan) to cash-in on the manufacture of new products with wide application and mass demand in large markets; and the dismantling of barriers to trade, reduction of tariffs and the trade creation of the new customs unions – all of which took place after 1960.

One aspect of this international dimension to economic growth was a great increase in overseas direct investment, dominantly by the United States but to a lesser extent by France and the United Kingdom. The degree of penetration of certain other countries by the United States can be gauged from the fact that in 1966 investment by U.S. companies in plant and equipment as a share of the total of such investment had risen to 41 per cent in Canada, 10 per cent in the United Kingdom and 5.5 per cent in EEC. At a time when the glamour of the American economic and social image was declining abroad and when the power and influence of international corporations was giving rise to concern this penetration of industrial economies by American corporations was viewed with suspicion and given a sharp political twist in the years when Vietnam, the dollar crisis and the Nixon Administration were tarnishing the American glitter in the eyes of the rest of the world.[24]

[24] See J. Servan-Schreiber, *The American Challenge* (New York: Athenaeum, 1968); K. Levitts, *Silent Surrender* (Toronto: Macmillan of Canada, 1971); C. P. Kindleberger, *American Business Abroad* (New Haven, Conn.: Yale University Press, 1969).

9
The New Customs Unions

(i) THE FORMS

In 1957 the signing of the Treaty of Rome by six European nations[1] was probably the most important single economic event in the period spanned by this book. It marked a new stage in international co-operation. It redistributed economic power and influence, giving to the group a total industrial output matching that of the United States and exceeding that of the Soviet Union, and a foreign trade with other countries greater than any other power. It gave potential for growth to an area already registering at that time, in its constituent countries, the fastest economic growth in the world. It held remote but exciting promise of a single European super-power which would replace the national mercantilism of four centuries.

In the eternal pursuit of free trade the impossibility of complete attainment inevitably leads to settling for a 'second-best' solution. Even in the nineteenth century, a liberal era in which the theoretical superiority of free trade was at least conceded, customs unions, as areas of trade freedom, proliferated.[2] The view, borne out by the facts in the case of the German *Zollverein*, of 1834, was that regions of free trade were extendable and a stage on the way to wider freedom. The reappearance of customs unions in the mid-twentieth century owed little to such a naïve view. The motivations of the European Community were various, political as well as economic, and the Community itself, once established, impelled the creation of other groupings in self-defence or in mere emulation.

Before examining the trade groups which were formed in the postwar period we must tidy up the institutional nomenclature. There are four types of

---

[1] France, Germany, Italy, the Netherlands, Belgium and Luxembourg.

[2] An early approach to customs-union theory was to regard such unions as a step along the road to general free trade. A second-best approach is one in which free trade within country groups is at least superior to autarky but inferior to general free trade. A more modern view of customs-unions theory stresses the discrimination inherent in such an arrangement and concerns itself with the changes in economic relationships which result from discrimination, with, for example, changes in production and consumption patterns, the terms of trade, the balance of payments and the rate of growth. There are two types of discrimination in tariff theory: commodity discrimination, where different tariff rates are applied to different commodities, and country discrimination, where different tariff rates are applied to the same commodity according to its country of origin. Customs-union theory deals with problems raised by the latter type of discrimination. It is defined by Lipsey, a leading writer in the field, as 'that branch of tariff theory which deals with the effects of geographically discriminatory changes in trade barriers'. See R. G. Lipsey, 'The Theory of Customs Unions: A General Survey', *Economic Journal* (Sep 1960) pp. 498–513.

discriminatory trade and regional economic groupings: they are, in ascending order of cohesion, the free-trade area, the customs union, the common market and the economic union. The free-trade area is a loose grouping of countries between which tariffs and other barriers to trade are dismantled while each country retains its own tariff and/or trade restrictions and its own commercial policies and bargaining positions with countries outside the area. The emphasis of the group is on intra-area trade and it will probably not extend beyond this. There is no reason why the countries concerned should be contiguous. The second type of grouping, the customs union, differs from the free-trade area in at least one important respect. While eliminating intra-country tariffs and trade barriers within the union it has a concerted commerical policy and a common tariff. In trade negotiations the customs union acts as a unit and some similarity in the economic policies of members is implicit in the arrangement.

The common market carries the customs union a stage further than commercial policy into the fields of international resource allocation, tax harmonisation and labour migration. Implicit is the concept of a unified market area in which there is free movement of products, services and factors of production within what is probably also a geographically integrated country group of nation-states. In the fourth type of grouping, co-operation is pushed to the point where fusion of the constituent economies is the ultimate aim: the economic union or economic community implies a common tariff, a harmonisation of industrial and social policies, concerted monetary and exchange-rate policies, progression towards a common currency and banking system and agreed policies on transport facilities and operation. The experiments of the fifties and sixties have included all of these types but that of the European Economic Community (EEC) has been the most ambitious and the cause, or model, of the others.

(ii) THE EUROPEAN MOVEMENT

Several and varied were the plans and influences moving Europe towards unity in the postwar years. The split between East and West destroyed the potency of the Economic Commission for Europe set up in 1947, which, as a regional organisation of the United Nations, was to be concerned with the economic reconstruction and development of Europe. It declined into a debating forum in which Eastern and Western delegations debated endlessly for propaganda purposes with no prospect of action or executive power.

Within the Western European group two distinct forces, tending towards unity, soon emerged: the Organization for European Economic Co-operation (OEEC) was created in 1948 as a functional organisation to combine the reconstruction efforts of European countries in receipt of Marshall Aid; the Council for Europe, set up in 1949, was an expression of broader political federalism, attracting a diverse group of intellectuals and statesmen devoted to the ideal of relinquishing national sovereignties prior to the accomplishment of economic and political union in Europe. Thus, by alternative routes, travellers might journey to the promised land.

The OEEC can only be seen as such a route in retrospect. It was functional. It had immediate but attainable aims: European reconstruction, the efficient use of American aid, the progressive dismantling of protective barriers to trade and the eventual abolition of discrimination against the dollar as European economies strengthened. These tasks provided a proving ground which demonstrated that economic co-operation in Europe could be effective. But within the OEEC at the outset there were differences, none greater than that between Britain and France, on the role to be played by supra-national organisations in the new Europe. France, backed by the United States, wished that international administrative agencies should have power to override the sovereignties of national governments. The United States, favourably impressed and unwittingly taking the role of prophet, even suggested that the European powers should consider the creation of a customs union. But the wishes of Britain, still at that time capable of exerting considerable influence in Europe, prevailed and the OEEC convention reflected her view. Britain still wished in 1948 to retain an influence and follow a 'steering role' in Europe but to remain free of encumbrances and specific obligations.

In Strasbourg the Council of Europe was the rallying-point for all good 'Europeans', but it had only its ideals and no way to implement them. Once more the British and French clashed. The French proposal to create a European parliament in which resolutions would be passed by majority vote was not to British taste and again the British view of a unity expressing itself through government co-operation, rather than through institutions overriding national governments, prevailed. But the British victory was a pyrrhic one, for the disillusion of European federalists with the Council of Europe led them to turn their backs on Britain and move directly to European projects in the supra-national field. In the forties and fifties European unity was itself a divisive force.

Now metropolitan Europe went its own way and in 1951 the European Coal and Steel Community (ECSC) set up by what was later to be called the Six, was the first practical expression of the drive for European integration. Its immediate origin, however, was power politics. By 1950 German recovery was well under way. It was recognised as inevitable that the Allied control of the German heavy industries would soon be terminated and that the German potential to make war would be restored. This and the prospect of German rearmament oppressed the French and other Western European governments. Two plans for containment of Germany were the result. The first came from Robert Schuman in May 1950 and was to create, by the removal of tariffs and non-tariff barriers to trade in coal and steel, a common market in these products. Participants in the scheme would have equal rights of access to the products of these industries and discrimination on national grounds would be precluded. The High Authority of the Coal and Steel Community was given supra-national power (at that time so beloved of the French) and the Treaty of Paris of April 1951 signed by the Six brought the ECSC into existence as an essay in European industrial integration. For the French the arrangement gave protection against the swift rise of a German armament industry. For Germany, the ECSC meant that German industrial expansion could continue unchecked and that Germany was received as an equal partner in the European integration plan. For the 'Europeans' the ECSC was a step forward, the more so since they considered that the OEEC might well be wound up with the conclusion of Marshall Aid in 1952. Britain, invited to join the ECSC, refused on the ground that she was not prepared to allow her heavy industries to be handed over to external control.

The second move to contain any resurgence of German militarism was one to include the rearmament of that country in a European framework. France, opposed to a strong German army, proposed that all national forces in the Western group should be embodied in a European army controlled by a European Defence Community (EDC). This would have a Joint Defence Commission, a Council of Ministers, a Parliamentary Assembly and certain legal machinery. In a continent only six years from total war it seemed and was a big step to political integration. The Six moved rapidly to an EDC Treaty which was signed in May 1952. Britain, though not hostile, remained aloof.

The year 1953 saw the movement for European unity at a flood tide. Economic integration in the Coal and Steel Community, joint defence and co-ordinated foreign policy with the EDC, political union was clearly the next logical step. But idealism had outrun reality, in particular the political realities of France. In 1954 the EDC Treaty was submitted to the French Assembly for ratification. They would have none of it and, French participation in these arrangements being a *sine qua non*, they perished.[3]

The events preceding the formation of the European Economic Community have been recounted briefly because they demonstrate the development of certain forces and attitudes in the new postwar Europe. Apart from the idealistic and intellectual drive of the European movement itself, two of these were important. First was the cleavage between Britain and the

---

[3] The reasons for French rejection were many and complex. While the best of French idealism and vision propelled the European movement in such minds as those of Schuman and Monnet, deep-rooted fears and prejudices ruled the Assembly: repugnance to a German army in any form, refusal to subject the French army to outside control, a desire to see Britain in the Defence Community to augment France in the face of Germany. In fact the failure of EDC led the British to make a successful initiative for German containment when they inaugurated a series of agreements between themselves, Canada, the United States and the European powers. These created a Western European Union (WEU), terminated the occupation of Germany, guaranteed a British military presence in Europe and smoothed the entry of Germany into NATO.

European countries. For the former, old foreign policies still dictated political action: a concerned interest in Europe but no direct involvement. For the latter, an apparent identity of interest wedded them to a conception and line of action which was novel but difficult to follow: at its loftiest a progressive, practical pursuit of an ideal, at its more pervasive mundane level a sort of opportunism in which integration offered different courses and sources of advantage. This cleavage between Britain and the Six was a sort of love-hate relationship. Perfidious Albion would neither move with them, nor leave them alone. Later when she had worked out the realities of her international position she would return to them as a suppliant.

The second formative attitude in the new Europe was the swing by France away from the support of supra-national organisations.[4] In the early days of the European movement (to about 1952) the supra-national idea was supported by France but by the later fifties that support was reversing itself to give way to fervent opposition. French support of European integration in the sixties was realistic and tempered by a strong desire to reap advantages and avoid commitments.

By 1955 the European movement was recovering from the setbacks of the previous two years. A new initiative, this one in the field of trade, was brewing. The Benelux[5] countries, which had formed a customs union in 1948, brought to the Six the practical proposal that immediate plans for political union should be shelved and replaced by the more easily attainable aim of a European Economic Community evolving slowly around the establishment of a customs union. In June 1955 the foreign ministers of the Six, meeting in Messina, considered a memorandum embodying this proposal and decided that a committee, under the chairmanship of Paul-Henri Spaak, should be formed to study the practical problems and prepare the texts of the treaties necessary to establish a common market and an atomic energy pool.

The Spaak Committee began work in July 1955. The British, who had had observers at Messina, were represented, but between them and the Six fundamental differences were soon revealed. The British preference was for a loose free-trade area in industrial products worked out on a base of the OEEC countries – a wider base than the Six. The European objective was a customs union of the Six leading to increasing economic integration and ultimately to economic union. Behind these outward differences even greater cleavage lay. The British plan was flexible and capable of immediate implementation through the OEEC. It had little need of elaborate administrative machinery and little basis in theoretical doctrine. The British disliked the European plan because, in their eyes, it was elaborate and doctrinaire.

---

[4] We may define 'supra-national' powers as, at a theoretical level, giving authority to international authorities which overrides national authority by a member government; at a practical level, as giving to international assemblies the right to enactment by majority vote rather than unanimity.

[5] Belgium, the Netherlands and Luxembourg.

In November 1955 the British left the Spaak Committee, which pressed on at a smart pace. It reported to the Foreign Ministers of the Six in May 1956 and, despite some differences as to the relative importance of the atomic community and the Common Market, it went on to the drafting of the two treaties which were to create both organisations. The treaties were signed in Rome on 25 March 1957. The EEC and the European Atomic Community came into being on 1 January 1958.

In late 1955, after quitting the Spaak Committee, the British reassessed the situation. It was clear that they had underestimated the significance of the European Common Market proposal and that, if the continent, then the swiftest growing British market, was not to be closed to them, they must push their free-trade-area plan as a counter-initiative. In the summer of 1956 the plan was submitted to the OEEC and by the end of the year had received guarded approval on the grounds that Britain, the peripheral European nations and the Six (in their Community) might form a large free-trade area for industrial products. With this slight encouragement a British-sponsored committee representative of interested governments began negotiations in October 1957. But there was considerable suspicion of British motives. The FTA was seen in Europe as a mere counter-proposal impeding the Six in their tough and difficult negotiation of the Treaty of Rome. The British stressed the economic aspects of the FTA, the Six saw their proposed Community as wider and ultimately political in aim. There were also formidable technical difficulties to linking the FTA and the EEC – the role of the British overseas territories, the future of Commonwealth Preference, the British determination to exclude agriculture from the arrangements in order to maintain their own cheap sources of Commonwealth food at low prices while denying the Six access to the British food market, the problems posed under the FTA of preventing external goods from entering the Area over the lowest tariff wall for re-export within the Area. These difficulties were bound to produce hard bargaining. In the last weeks of 1958 the negotiations broke down. As on a later occasion a French veto was the final blow.

In the trade field and indeed in many other fields, Europe was now divided – the Six of the Community and the 'Other Six'[6] excluded from it. The failure of negotiation had created two trade blocs. This dichotomy was formalised when the British decided early in 1959 to form a free-trade area with the peripherals. Portugal joined the negotiations in February 1959 and the Stockholm Convention of 4 January 1960 established the European Free Trade Area (EFTA).[7]

The subsequent history of EFTA can be briefly told. It was purely a commercial arrangement, establishing free trade in industrial goods between the parties but allowing existing tariffs to stand against other countries. The group was roughly complementary in trade. Britain, the main manufacturing

---

[6] United Kingdom, Norway, Sweden, Denmark, Austria and Switzerland.
[7] Finland became an associate member in 1961.

country, occupied a dominant position in trading magnitude, contrasting in this respect with the smaller manufacturing countries, Austria and Switzerland. While four countries – Britain, Sweden, Switzerland and Austria – were all exporters of manufactures, other members – Denmark, Norway, Portugal and Finland – were exporters of food and natural resource products. The amount of pre-union trade carried on between members was lower for the EFTA than for the EEC. It is probable that, as a result of the association, the elimination of intra-country tariffs created some trade diversion, occurring in all types of goods – food, primary and industrial products.

The year 1959 was, in retrospect, a turning-point in postwar economic affairs. In the currency field it marked (1 January 1959) the beginning of convertible currencies, the end of the old dollar problem and the beginning of the Bretton Woods system in full operation. On the same day the six founder members of EEC were to make their first tariff reductions and import quota changes under the timetable prescribed by the Treaty of Rome. At the same time Britain, deprived of association with the Community, decided to go it alone. The United States now regarded the Community as the foremost economic entity in Europe, Germany as the leading power. She was even prepared to waive her long-standing objection to trade discrimination in the face of arrangements which met her repeated demand for unity in Europe. From all this Britain was excluded. She was forming, but only in default of membership of the EEC, a trade-association which was in American eyes discriminatory but carried no promise of political unity; which held little prospect of real gain and was being formed only as second best to participation in the Community. As the true nature of the British dilemma became apparent its contemplation was made no pleasanter by the sense of lost opportunity. There had been a miserable failure on her part to recognise since the early fifties the significance of what was taking place in Europe.

(iii) THE EUROPEAN ECONOMIC COMMUNITY

It is appropriate at this point to stand aside briefly from the march of events in the EEC and give a short account of the declared aims of that group and its administrative arrangements. Many elaborate and lengthy descriptions of the Community and its programmes have already been published. We give only a framework description, which will be sufficient for the purposes of this book.[8]

[8] A huge literature already exists on this subject. Readers seeking a point of entry to this literature might consult: F. B. Jensen and I. Walter, *The Common Market: Economic Integration in Europe* (Philadelphia: Lippincott, 1965); L. B. Krause (ed.), *The Common Market: Progress and Controversy* (Englewood Cliffs, N.J.: Prentice-Hall, 1964); *Treaty Establishing the European Atomic Energy Community [Euratom] and the Common Market* (Brussels: Interior Committee for the Common Market and Euratom, 1957); and Political and Economic Planning (PEP), *European Organisations* (London: Allen & Unwin, 1959). A good general and up-to-date book is Dennis Swann's *The Economics of the Common Market* (London: Penguin Books, 4th ed., 1978).

The Community was established between the Six by the Treaty of Rome on 24 March 1957. Its purpose was to integrate the economies of the member countries and ultimately, although this was not declared in the founding document, it was hoped that this would lead to political integration as well. Ten months later, on 1 January 1958, the plan for the customs union was put into effect by establishing the Community and its institutions. A year later the first reductions in internal tariffs and import quotas were made – the first steps in a twelve-year transition period.

The institutional structure was elaborate. Four bodies, the Commission, the Council of Ministers, the Court of Justice and the Parliamentary Assembly were to compose it. The Commission, consisting of nine members jointly appointed by the member governments, was to be the administrative executive, handling day-to-day business and controlling development. Only in matters of high policy was it to consult the Council of Ministers, which was to be the political executive. The Court of Justice, consisting of seven judges and a number of advocates, was to act as a court for the settlements of disputes inevitable in the integration process. Finally, the European Parliamentary Assembly with, initially, 142 delegates elected by the parliaments of member countries, was to act as a forum for discussion of integration policies and problems. It was without executive power. The main areas of Community operation were anticipated by the establishment of standing committees – the Economic and Social Committee, Economic Policy Committee, Monetary Committee and Transport Committee. The implicit aim of the whole structure, to be located in Brussels, was to make effective the transition to economic integration while preserving as much of the national sovereignty of member governments as was consistent with it.

Central to the idea of economic integration was the establishment of the customs union involving the elimination of intra-country tariffs and barriers to trade and the establishment of a single Community tariff against the rest of the world. Involving as it did the dismantling of trade barriers between large and traditionally protectionist countries and discrimination against the non-Community world, this was a formidable process. But it was at the heart of the whole conception, and to fail in it would be disaster for the entire project. Success could only come with a phased programme of abolition carried out to a schedule which was not to be departed from.

The original schedule, outlined in the Treaty itself, set a transition period of twelve years, which could be shortened if necessary but was not to be extended beyond fifteen years. Thus 31 December 1969 was the target date which might, under duress, be extended until December 1972. The twelve years was in turn divided into three four-year steps, each of which should be completed in its turn. The successive tariff and quota reductions were to be made in 10 per cent steps throughout the whole transition period, with targets to be achieved at the end of each four-year stage. There was a requirement that a unanimous vote should, in December 1961, be a condition of proceeding to the second stage but the passage to subsequent stages was to be automatic. The tariff reductions were to be 'across-the-board', applying to all goods at once as percentage reductions of the level in force at the time of the Rome Treaty.

On 1 January 1959 the first 10 per cent reduction was made and it was intended to follow this with two reductions of 10 per cent each at intervals of eighteen months, thus achieving the 30 per cent reduction, which was the target for the first four-year period. It was found, however, that adjustment difficulties were less than had been anticipated and it was decided, in May 1960, to accelerate the pace of tariff reduction. By 1 January 1962 tariffs on industrial products were down to 60 per cent of the 1957 level, thus exceeding the target-drop of 30 per cent for the first stage.

As had been anticipated, the task of making the transition to the second stage, on 31 December 1961, was herculean. Only by the symbolic device of 'stopping the clock' for negotiations which continued until 14 January 1962 was the necessary voting achieved to make the transition. Once through this barrier, however, the pace picked up. By the end of 1963, two years ahead of the target, the second-stage reductions were complete at 40 per cent of 1957 tariff level. This remaining barrier was eliminated by mid-1968, more than a year before the end of the transition period.

Quota restrictions to intra-Community trade were removed even faster than tariffs. In 1959 all import quotas of Community countries were made global, i.e. non-discriminatory with respect to other countries. The aim was to remove all quotas by 1969; in fact this was achieved by the end of 1961.

The other feature of the customs union was the common tariff protecting the area as a whole. To establish this it was necessary to make uniform the former five tariff levels of the Community countries,[9] honouring the GATT requirement that the external tariff of a customs union should be not greater than the average of the single tariffs prior to the union. For this adjustment three stages were stipulated with complete harmonisation by 1969. Here, as with the elimination of the internal tariffs the process was accelerated and was complete in mid-1968.

As internal trade barriers were removed and the common external tariff adjusted, steps were taken to replace the individual trade and commercial relations of member countries by those of the customs union. In 1962 the Council of Ministers approved a proposal for an EEC common external trade policy and by the end of the transition period individual governments no longer carried on tariff or trade negotiations, which were taken over for the Community by the EEC Commission and the Council of Ministers.

Free movement of goods within the Community was to be accompanied by free movement of labour and capital. By 1969 free movement of labour was

---

[9] Belgium and Luxemburg already had a common tariff as members of the Belgium–Luxemburg Economic Union.

not only permitted within the Community, but was encouraged by a 'clearing-house' system, portability of social-security benefits, and provisions for combating regional unemployment through incentives to labour mobility. All legal restrictions on labour movement across frontiers, such as work permits, residence time-limits and the like were removed and within any country foreign workers were deemed to have equality of opportunity in access to all jobs.[10] In the capital field free movement was already partially established before 1957 in that all Community members honoured article VIII of the IMF, which provides for freedom of movement in current payments and transfers of capital. Restrictions did persist on medium- and long-term loans, stock flotations and portfolio investment but in the hope of encouraging a European capital market these were removed between 1960 and 1966. These measures were, however, no more than permissive in that the banking systems and existing capital markets of the Community were unsuited to quick conversion to a London or New York capital-market model. It opened the way for development but much else was needed to bring development about.

With the establishment of the customs union and free mobility for capital and labour one aspect – we may call it the 'flow aspect' – of economic integration was complete. It had to be accompanied and supplemented, however, by the co-ordination, in some cases the merging, of economic policies in a number of fields – taxation, transportation, agriculture and general economic policy. Of these the two last have proved most difficult and controversial, and we shall confine discussion to them.

The Common Agricultural Policy (CAP) of the Community has been its most difficult task and has brought it often near to breakdown. Concerned as it has been with harmonising policies, prices and imports for countries in which agriculture has been different in scale and efficiency but has represented a powerful political lobby, this is not surprising. With great differences in productivity between the agricultures of the participants the removal of internal tariffs and quotas involved great differences in the distribution of benefits. The original member countries all had a tradition of protection of their agricultural sector. They went into the Community with a continuing desire to improve the living standards of their farmers, to protect them from the competition of low-cost foreign supplies and to protect them from instabilities in world primary-commodity markets. France, Italy and Germany, with large rural populations, were concerned with agriculture as a facet of social policy and were committed under the Rome Treaty to a common farm policy which would improve the living standard of rural populations.

These were the broad aims. The underlying political realities were even more compelling. For Germany and France the very *raison d'être* of the

---

[10] Except the national civil services.

Community itself lay in a reciprocal relationship of industry and agriculture. The Germans, with their huge industrial potential, wanted free access to the large French market; the French, conscious of the greater efficiency of their agriculture (particularly for grain), saw that a free Community market would be of great benefit to them. This, and the size of the agricultural sector within the Community[11] explains its inclusion in the Rome Treaty.[12] It does not, however, explain the elaborate nature of the provisions. Each country could have been left to operate its own price-support programmes protected by border duties and agricultural trade within the Community could have been carried on through bilateral agreements. Instead an elaborate system of uniform Community prices and market manipulation to maintain them was set up. There was to be free movement within the Community at these prices. We can only conclude that France was not to be satisfied with anything less than complete Community access to all markets at guaranteed prices. Her partners were apparently prepared to accept this as the high price of her participation in the Community.

The basic provisions of CAP can be quickly summarised. (1) There was to be free trade within the Community in agricultural products. (2) There was to be a uniform system of farm-income support by the establishment of common prices for a wide range of commodities. (3) These common internal prices would be protected by a set of minimum import prices for the commodities. (4) The minimum import prices would be ensured by variable import levies on agricultural products. (5) Minimum prices to Community producers would be ensured by support purchases of products. (6) Consumer and export subsidies would be paid to divert surplus products to export or into alternative domestic uses.

This set of provisions implied a stiff degree of agricultural protection and skilful intervention in domestic markets to maintain prices at desired levels without the accumulation of surpluses. The protective effect soon became apparent. Up to the primary commodity inflation, which began in 1972, EEC prices for temperate-zone farm products were between 100 and 200 per cent higher than world prices and as a result self-sufficiency in such products rose from 87 per cent in the mid-1950s to well over 90 per cent by the early seventies. Moreover, the market effects of the minimum prices for such products was to accumulate large surpluses (particularly of soft-wheat, barley, sugar, dairy products and deciduous fruits) and these were sold abroad at prices which, with the aid of export subsidies, were inimical to low-cost exporters on the world market. The signs were clear that the EEC was a considerable menace to large agricultural producers such as Canada, the United States, Australia and New Zealand, particularly if such traditional agricultural exporters as Denmark and Ireland and such a large importer as

[11] In 1958 15 m. people, i.e. a fifth of the working population of the Community, were engaged in agriculture.

[12] In contrast to EFTA, which provided only for industrial products.

Britain were to become members. During the 1950s trade and commercial policy problems in temperate-zone farm products did not loom large for the major countries. After the coming of EEC and CAP they assumed great urgency as negotiations in the Kennedy Round of tariff negotiations demonstrated.

The immediate difficulty in establishing CAP lay in the productivity differences in the agricultures of the member states, whether viewed in total or in respect of particular commodities. Two courses appeared to be open. The Community could centre its agricultural policy around the efficient producers, granting them adequate but not illiberal third-country protection and, bailing out the less efficient by region or by country, with adequate regional development and social policies. Alternatively, it could aim at a degree of protection sufficient to nurture even the weakest agricultural regions in the Community. Since the first course would require considerable tolerance by some countries and the taking of a very long-term view and the sacrifice of special advantages by others the line of least resistance in the internal negotiations was followed, with resultant protectionist bias against the world at large. Thus expediency and political desire to placate agrarian lobbies rather than real economic considerations determined the CAP structure. In the clashes which took place between member countries on prices, the length of the transition period, the commodities to come within the scope of the agreement and the autonomy to be retained by governments in respect of their agricultural industries a measure of common agreement among the Six was only achieved at the cost of a very high level of extra-Community protection. The burden of agreement among the Six was achieved only at the cost of world suppliers outside the Community. But there was also a cost to the Community itself. The determination of individual member governments to retain maximum control of their agricultural interests fragmented Community policy on many matters outside the agricultural field, for, as intra-country wrangling on agricultural matters proceeded, deals were made carrying into other fields. Thus the nationalism which the Community was intended to supersede was perpetuated within it and has been disruptive to a dangerous degree.

The CAP has, of all facets of the Community, brought it into conflict with the rest of the world, in particular with large agricultural suppliers such as the United States. One aspect of such conflict has been the inflexibility of the Community already described. Another has been the variable import levy system by which farm prices in the Community have been protected. This has been widely criticised since unlike a tariff, which has a known *ad valorem* value, the import levy varies in order to afford complete protection to the Community.

The 1960s was the trial period of CAP in which the Community was engrossed in making the machinery work and testing its effects and in which the efforts of the Community were watched obliquely by its critics abroad. By the end of the decade there was a good deal of dissatisfaction within the group at the failure of the CAP to stabilise, still less to raise, farm incomes and at the effect which it was having upon consumers' food prices. To industry and unions the policy appeared to featherbed farmers at industrial workers' expense. To monetary and financial critics the exchange rates between countries within the Community appeared to be aligned to the needs of farm prices rather than macroeconomic realities and to politicians the prospect of increasing the size of the Community by the admission of the United Kingdom appeared to raise complex issues on many fronts. The CAP certainly had proved divisive and inimical to the accomplishment of the early ideals of the Europeans. The Community buzzed with demands and suggestions for CAP amendment: for manipulation of prices, which would deal with surpluses and encourage the production of scarce commodities; for an abandonment of price policy as a means of dealing with different levels of farm income; for greater reliance on deficiency payments and regional policies; and for greater national autonomy in agricultural policy.

By comparison with these domestic dissensions criticism outside the Community was surprisingly mild. Certainly there had been, since CAP became effective, considerable trade diversion from sources outside the group and considerable trade creation within it. But the external effects were rolled off. The reductions in third-country exports to the Community increased throughout the sixties, although not impressively, the reductions in some products being more than offset by others. The fact that Community agricultural imports were in the sixties probably much below what they would have been in the absence of the policy was an accounting loss easily sustained in a period of booming world trade.

No specific references to the long-term aspects of economic integration were made in the Treaty of Rome but clearly the creation of the Community provided an opportunity for the application of a theory of economic integration to a continuing development in that direction. Only broad economic objectives were mentioned in the founding document – high employment levels, price stability, external balance – and since these were identified and since a Monetary Committee and an Economic Policy Committee had been established to pursue these objectives it was certain that community currency and exchange-rate policies would come into focus. The very diversity of the Six ensured that practical exercises in macro-policy co-ordination would not be long delayed. This uncertain state of affairs was enhanced by the fact that the founding fathers of European union had adopted from the beginning the practice of persuading member governments to accept general objectives, symbolic of unity, the detailed route to which was not defined but would, it was hoped, contribute to unity rather than disintegration. This practice of avoiding the disruptive issues until a firm, general commitment was established, is easy to criticise in retrospect but it was a highly successful tactic in the early days inasmuch as it established the

EEC in short time and set it moving in an agreed direction. In the monetary and macro-policy fields, with objectives so broadly defined, with strong mercantilist attitudes among the governments of the major participants and with the main decisions – employment and price levels, money quantity, interest rates and exchange rates – such that individual governments regarded them as strictly within their sovereignty, it seemed probable·in the early sixties that issues such as common monetary and fiscal policies and a common currency would be tactfully avoided. Events did not, however, allow this.

In the early years of the EEC no special policy existed for dealing with exchange rates. There seemed to be a tacit assumption that they would be fixed, following the conventional wisdom of that time, the requirements of the IMF and the convenience of the CAP. When, however, in 1968 macro-price-level policies in France and Germany diverged it became clear that adjustments of exchange rates were necessary and they were made. These events brought attention to exchange rates and the external/internal policies of countries in the Community and the aim of fixed exchange rates became explicit with its corollary, the harmonisation of macro policies.

If exchange rates were to be fixed and domestic policies harmonised one was more than half-way to a common currency for the participant countries. This was accentuated and the aim of a common currency made explicit by events in the international monetary field in the late sixties. The Community began to look in the direction of a common currency for political as well as economic reasons. The reasons for all this lay in Community relations with the United States. It became apparent that the U.S. dollar had become the dominant key currency and that special conditions attached to movements in the American balance of payments. That a moderate deficit might be appropriate to the balance of payments of a key currency country was conceded but not such a deficit as came with the years 1968, 1969 and 1970. Such deficits were seen by Europe as springing from the Vietnam War and as being financed by the tolerance of America's creditors to hold unwanted dollar balances. Moreover, by 1970 the U.S. deficit was feared as a carrier of inflation from the new world to the old, and Europe was looking for a realignment of European currency values in relation to the dollar. Yet how, among such a group of interdependent currencies, was such a realignment to be distributed? Germany, with its strong anti-inflationary policies and strong currency, required to revalue relative to the dollar. Of the other countries some required revaluations, some devaluations, but dimensions were in all cases in doubt. Piecemeal action would eventually lead to a new rate structure within the Community but ideally the way to handle this problem was through a common European currency unit strong enough to enable Europe to deal with the United States on equal terms. A common European currency thus became a pressing and immediate goal to be actively pursued.

There were two reactions to this problem, one in the practical field of exchange-rate management, one in the field of long-range planning. The first reaction followed a series of *ad hoc* exchange-rate changes in the late sixties and early seventies. Britain's devaluation of 14 per cent in November 1967 was followed by a devaluation of the franc in 1969 and a revaluation of the Deutschmark in the same year. Thereafter, movements of the West European currencies, either by discrete changes or by controlled floats, divided them into three broad groups: the super-strong group, headed by the Deutschmark and accompanied by the guilder; a central group with the Belgian franc; and a weak group of the French franc, the pound and the lira. The attempt to bring order into this disparate situation was to allow the Community currencies to float within a band the centre of which would move *vis-à-vis* other currencies. Thus Community countries would have the benefit of a floating rate as between their currencies and the rest of the world. In principle this was plausible enough but in practice all depended on the coefficients which determined the model, namely the width of the band and the degree of intervention required (*a*) to keep currencies within the band in reasonaßle relation to each other and (*b*) to align the band itself in satisfactory relation to non-member currencies, in particular to the dollar. What in effect persisted in the arrangement was the very thing which the system was supposed to suppress: the strong currency, the Deutschmark, stayed strong and the weak currencies remained weak. The 'snake in the tunnel' arrangement sought order among the Community exchange rates. In fact it only defined disorder in a new way. In default of very large intervention in the exchange markets, only harmonisation of macro policies could eliminate the need for intra-Community exchange margins.

The 'snake' system was only loosely organised and different West European countries have been members from time to time. When a new European monetary co-operation fund was established in April 1973 with $1.8 bln of EEC support and with the purpose of intervening in exchange markets to stabilise exchange rates within the Community, five members (Germany, France, Belgium, the Netherlands and Denmark) comprised the joint-European float. Norway and Sweden worked within the float but were not members of the EEC fund.

The second Community reaction to the exchange problem was to set up the inevitable committees and working groups to take a view of the whole situation. A committee under the chairmanship of Raymond Barre, reporting in February 1969, recognised that fundamentally any plan to order exchange rates must start one step earlier with harmonisation of domestic policies and it advocated the greatest practicable level of harmonisation, by proposing that member countries should consult on their medium-term objectives for growth and inflation rates, should examine inconsistencies and co-ordinate their financial policies so as to avoid short-term foreign imbalance. In December 1969 the Hague Summit Conference, in January 1970 a Council of Ministers and in February 1970 the EEC finance ministers, approved and recommended much of the Barre Plan.

Later, in October 1970, the Werner Committee carried on where Barre left off by putting forward a phased plan for monetary and economic union to be completed, in three stages, by 1980. The first stage, of three years, provided for full convertibility of the six currencies, a fixing of the exchange rates between the currencies, setting up of a single currency for the Community, central control of fiscal and monetary policy, a single external monetary policy, arrangements concerning capital markets, and regional policies to be determined by the Community. There was to be an authority to co-ordinate decisions on economic policy answerable to the European Parliament and a procedure for co-ordinating the central bank policies of the Community, especially their decisions on exchange-market intervention, holding of exchange reserves and manipulation of exchange rates. The margins of exchange-rate fluctuations about the parity were to be progressively narrowed and ultimately to disappear.

The Werner Plan became official policy for the Community. Moreover it was regarded as the vision of the future which aspiring new members such as Britain would have to accept as the price of admission. The acceptance of the aim of a common currency and complete monetary integration was the apogee of the Community's move towards integration. If that were achieved little would be left of the old sovereignties. But the aims set were too much. Even with determination and willingness to make national concessions, monetary integration would involve formidable problems of regional policy, employment stabilisation and monetary control. There were many who doubted, even in 1970, whether the Werner schedule could be met or the final goal achieved. France, in particular, was not of a mind to merge herself facelessly into a new European entity. As the economic troubles of the seventies accumulated and as the Community members' reactions to them were improvised, piecemeal and *sauve qui peut*, the vision faded and was accorded lip-service rather than belief. It was to be dramatically revived in 1978 when renewed currency crisis brought the Community together in negotiation with the United States at Bonn.

In the seventies the Community passed to a new stage. It had been established in so far as the basic blueprint of the Rome Treaty required. The customs union was working effectively, the common agricultural policy had been painfully established and was having effects on the agrarian structures of the participants. Many frictions of economic nationalism had been smoothed or eliminated. But on the great and ultimate ideals of economic integration the impetus had subsided and given way to plodding acceptance of the long haul. For the moment growth in terms of mere size was substituted for scope and originality. Britain, Denmark and the Republic of Ireland joined the Community in 1975, other countries were expected to follow. Ultimately the whole of Western Europe might be involved. There is always a danger that after a leap forward and during a period of consolidation such an alliance may atrophy. It is especially so when that period brings problems from outside for the organisation to meet. In retrospect it appears that the Community born in the general economic growth and optimism of the fifties, tackling its great initial problems in the still buoyant sixties was stalled when in the seventies it had to meet inflation, recession and the oil crisis, all divisive influences. These revealed the deep nationalistic instincts of members; moreover, the central decision-making machinery of the Community, never of the best, was unable to produce a single Community policy. The great central secretariat in Brussels became the target of criticism: bureaucracy, talking-shop, Eurocrat, became the current terms of abuse. Whether the pause of the seventies in the EEC is that of exhaustion and intellectual sterility, a late reassertion of their true natures by the old plotters of Talleyrand's Europe, or whether it is a breathing-space prior to further effort depends mainly on events and perhaps on the emergence of new ideas stirred by events.

10

The Multinational Corporation

'They fight by shuffling papers;
    they have bright dead alien eyes;
They look at our labour and
    laughter as a tired man looks at flies.'

G. K. CHESTERTON

(i) INTRODUCTION

In its century or so of self-conscious existence the international economy has
shrunk its distances, speeded its communications, widened the scope of its
goods and money markets and made the first halting steps towards
international decision-making. In the public sector international action has
appeared in government-negotiated financial and commercial arrangements
and in the activities of international functional agencies. In the private sector
national business has spawned international business through the operations
of multinational enterprises – large corporations with headquarters in one
country and pursuing their activities, in the manufacturing, extractive, or
service fields, in several others. Such enterprises are a result of the drive of
corporations to extend their international transactions within their own
networks of control and influence distinct from the operations of governments
in their operational areas. By nature they are large and powerful and they
touch the interests of governments and international agencies at many points.
Although large firms with diverse foreign interests are by no means new, the
postwar period, from the fifties, has seen such growth in their numbers and
influence, and they are so changing the nature of the international economy
that the multinational corporation must be regarded as the most striking
feature of institutional change in the world economy since the war. It is our
purpose in this chapter to examine the economics and some of the political
implications of this development.

(ii) THE FACTS

In establishing the facts concerning multinational corporations generalis-
ations are dangerous. In size, behaviour, effect on host countries there is

diversity. It is necessary to examine such enterprises according to a number of characteristics. This we shall do touching sequentially on country of origin, size, organisation, corporate motivation and a number of other matters.

Multinationals are the result of direct investment by enterprises in a base (or parent) country in a number of other countries. A vast expansion of direct foreign investment in the fifties and sixties has been the cause of their proliferation. In 1970 the total value of all direct foreign investment was estimated to be $250 bln with an annual rate of increase of between 10 and 20 per cent.[1] It accounted for more than 75 per cent of the capital export of the leading industrial nations as compared to less than 10 per cent in 1914. Chief among the investing countries has been the United States, which, in 1970, accounted for 55.6 per cent of the total. European firms accounted for 37.5 per cent, Canadian 3.9 per cent, Japan 2.6 per cent and Australia 0.4 per cent.[2] In fact the decades of the fifties and sixties have witnessed a great wave of American foreign direct investment, at first mainly in the extractive sector, but in the seventies dominantly in the manufacturing and service sectors. Over the whole period Canada has been the largest single recipient but after 1970 Europe went slightly ahead. The total American investment in developed countries has been 69 per cent of the total American investment as against 26 per cent in developing countries. Table 10.1 compares American direct foreign investment with exports and gives a summary geographic breakdown of such investment.

TABLE 10.1

U.S. Exports, Direct Foreign Investment, 1950–73

$ bln

	1950	1960	1970	1973
U.S. exports	10.3	20.6	43.2	70.3
U.S. direct foreign investment (book value) of which:	11.8	32.0	78.1	107.3
Total to developed areas	5.7	19.6	53.2	74.1 (69%)
Total to developing areas	4.4	10.9	21.3	27.9 (26%)
Unallocated	1.7	1.5	3.6	5.3

Source: U.S. Congress, Senate Committee on Finance, *Implications of Multinational Firms for World Trade and Investment and for U.S. Trade and Labour*, 93rd Congress, 1st Session, 1973, p. 72. Figures for 1973 were added and obtained from U.S. Department of Commerce, *Survey of Current Business* (Aug 1974) part II, pp. 18–19.

This explosion of American industry into other countries has raised fear and alarm in host countries. In Canada huge proportions of that country's

[1] These figures are quoted in S. H. Robock and K., Simmonds, *International Business and Multinational Enterprises* (Homewood: Ill., Irwin, 1973) p. 44.

[2] Ibid. p. 37.

new manufacturing industries are American-owned and controlled.[3] In Europe American infiltration came at a time when the American image, darkened by Vietnam and the crude ambition of the Nixon Administration, was already tarnished.[4] In Asia, Japanese economic expansion has caused nervous misgiving in countries anxious to develop their own industrial sectors. Thus, by small countries mindful of the threat of powerful neighbours, by countries resenting the invasion of an alien culture, by developing countries anxious to keep control of their own economic destinies, by organised labour seeing a threat to their bargaining power and by the intellectual left seeing the flowering of a resurgent capitalism, the proliferation of the multinational enterprise has been viewed with suspicion and resentment.[5]

One general effect of the size and ubiquity of the multinational corporation has been to transform many aspects of international trade itself. A considerable part of international trade is now intra-company trade, taking place at 'transfer' prices (i.e. accounting or imputed prices) which are internal to the firms themselves and not determined by market forces. Such trade is by its nature manipulated and is a function of company policies. For example, in 1968 about 25 per cent of British manufactured exports was by firms to their own subsidiaries. A second general effect on the international economy was in the changes which have been wrought in balances of payments by the wave of foreign direct investment. In the United States the value of such investment far exceeds exports and is the main tie of that country to the world economy. For other countries fundamental changes have been wrought in the structure of both current and capital sections of balances of payments, although these changes are too complex and often, at this stage, too indeterminate to analyse here.

Although multinational enterprises vary greatly in size, bigness and global extension are certainly their main attributes and judged by any acceptable criterion they include the largest corporate enterprises in existence. We must not only account for this size but also for the comparatively recent growth and proliferation of such enterprises. Before the Second World War multinational enterprises were not uncommon: after 1950 the increase in their numbers and also in their average size was phenomenal. Why was growth so great and its occurrence so clearly marked in time? There are probably several reasons.

One reason certainly was the general tendency towards increasing size of firms which has been a feature of business since at least the beginning of the century. Economies of scale had for long been increasing the marketing, technical, financial and managerial optimal size of operation. Take-overs,

---

[3] For a Canadian cry of alam and warning see K. Levitt, *Silent Surrender: The American Economic Empire in Canada* (Toronto: Macmillan, 1971).
[4] See J.-J. Servan-Schreiber, *The American Challenge* (New York: Atheneum House, 1968) and Edward A. McCreary, *The Americanization of Europe* (New York: Doubleday, Garden City, 1964).
[5] For a balanced American view of the phenomenon see R. Vernon, *Storm Over the Multinationals. The Real Issues* (Cambridge, Mass.: Harvard University Press, 1977).

mergers, groupings and consortia became prevalent. With technical innovation the technical optimum size of many operations was necessarily raised, and finance, management and marketing had to follow suit. But this tendency towards increasing corporate size does not in itself explain the extent to which size increased. It would have been likely that, in the absence of other factors, the tendency towards growth would have spent itself, checked by normal diseconomies of scale. Outside the multinational field comparatively small firms were able to make profits and often hold their own in competition with firms of greater size.

But other factors were operative and they coalesced in the postwar period. The first was the growing divorce of ownership and management in larger firms which ensured that management became a *corps d'élite* with its own criteria of corporate success and motivations somewhat different in emphasis and ranking from the entrepreneur of classical firm theory. Profits, although still important, became secondary to growth of the enterprise and to corporate power to manipulate shareholders, consumers and government. A second factor making for growth lay in the common practice whereby governments in their taxation policies favoured retention of profits as compared with their distribution. A large pool of reserves was therefore typically available for expansion. But over and above these two factors there were three influences which in the late fifties enormously favoured the international expansion of corporations and pushed far out the point at which diseconomies of scale would normally have become operative. These were the revolution in communications and transport which made world wide operations swift, easy and comparable to intra-regional operations a generation earlier; the advent of computerisation and business-machine accounting which provided for wider coverage of salient information and more elaborate planning of corporate operation; and the revolution in business education and management science which caused a far more technically efficient generation of managers and planners to be produced. If all this is accepted it provides an explanation of why in a decade the private sectors of the great industrial powers were able to grow and ramify and had incentive to do so, in a way not possible until that time.

With the great size of multinational enterprises has come a redistribution of power in the international economy but, before examining the redistribution, it is necessary to distinguish the types of organisation of the multinationals themselves for this is one determinant of power. With a multiplicity of corporate organisational forces three broad classes of multinationals seem to emerge. First is that where a large corporation in a parent country, say the United States, exercises control, by majority holding, over subsidiaries in various host countries. The subsidiaries are regarded as subservient to the parent company, existing primarily to enhance that company's power in its own country. Management and intra-subsidiary relations are international only in the sense that they cross national boundaries. The reality is likely to be that the strength of the parent company and its country transcends the welfare and interests of the subsidiary and its host country. The multinational company in this form can be seen as an expression of economic nationalism, even of neo-imperialism. It was thus that critics such as Servan-Schreiber, Levitt and others saw the influx of American enterprises to their countries.

A second type of multinational organisation is that where subsidiaries of a holding company are allowed to act with a high degree of autonomy. The connection between parent and subsidiary remains in the field of ownership and does not extend to management or control. There is little sense of corporate entity or of a headquarters to be obeyed. There is equally much less cause for friction between host country and parent country.

The third type, and it applies to some of the largest multinationals, is that where the parent country and subsidiary relationship is soft-pedalled and replaced by the concept of an integrated international enterprise claiming international objectives and an international corporate identity and image. The scope for clashes of subsidiaries with host-country and regional governments is great, but now it is not a clash with another country or culture so much as with a faceless international colossus in which it is difficult to identify the motivations and locate the sources of power and control. Such an organisation is more truly international than either of the others in that integration takes place in production between many locations, marketing strategy is aimed at many markets and seen as an overall world operation, capital is obtained in many capital markets and working capital in several banking systems. National governmental authority is not so much aggrandised for a parent country as avoided so far as possible. What emerges is a global enterprise organised to avoid national or regional pressures or at least to subordinate them to the corporate plan.

These three categories oversimplify the diversity of multinational firms. Within each group there are many variants. There are hybrids which partake of elements of all the groups. It is true also that the third group is never so divorced from a national identity as we have pictured it. General Motors, in many ways distinctive of this group, is still seen, however it may see itself, as an American corporation. Nevertheless, it is tempting to argue that, if growth of corporations continues at the headlong speed of the past two decades, it may be towards the third group that multinational enterprises, existing and to come, are tending.

We have sketched how in the fifties and sixties a number of influences allowed multinationals to grow and proliferate swiftly. These influences were, however, largely permissive. It is necessary also to ask: What motivates growth, other than economies of scale? What leads domestic firms to become multinational? What leads those already multinational to expand their activities?

Extractive industries have always shown a tendency towards multinational organisation, particularly for materials existing in short-supply deposits and requiring continual augmentation from new sources. The law of diminishing returns drives inexorably towards exploration and the forestalling of discovery or exploitation by competitors. It is no accident that oil, nickel, uranium, bauxite and ores are the stock in trade of many companies on the Fortune list.

In the field of manufacturing the motives for international expansion are many and familiar. Most are economically rational, some are highly irrational. We list a few. Firms already with foreign markets invest in subsidiaries in those markets in order to lower production costs, eliminate transport costs, facilitate after-sales service, give the product the spurious appearance of native production, pre-empt local or other competition, or obtain a production footing within a trade barrier. Firms may follow peers. One American bank in a European centre in the sixties brought the others. One oil company in a developing country brings the rest, drawn by emulation rather than hope of immediate profit. Despite the allegations of many host countries of foreign penetration and take-over, subsidiaries of multinationals were often planted there at host-country request or went in response to the baits of tax holiday, subsidy, free accommodation or other tangible or intangible benefit. Even Canada, whose nationalists are loud in condemning the American industrial pressure, has been a beneficent host on many occasions. There are few countries which have not, for purposes of employment or regional policies, sought the establishment of plants controlled from abroad. Finally, although it may seem a truism, manufacturing firms pursue profit by planting subsidiaries in fast-growing markets. There can be little doubt that the attractions of prosperous Europe and the burgeoning of the European Community was a major cause of the wave of American direct investment there during the sixties.

In the service field direct investment, coming as it did rather later than in manufacturing, has reflected a determination by firms to provide multinational services for multinational business. Thus is explained the proliferation of American overseas banking in the sixties, the spread of multinational hotel chains, management consultancy, accountancy, advertising and the like.

(iii) THE IMPACT OF MULTINATIONAL BUSINESS

When we come to consider the impact of the great increase in multinational business we may do so in two stages: the influence on the single nation-state and the influence on the international economy as a whole. First the nation-state, which, in this context, we may distinguish as host or parent country. In some cases, of course, it may be both.

Attitudes in the host country towards establishment of foreign subsidiaries is varied, ranging in spirit from the welcome-mat to legal control or virtual exclusion. The attitude may differ over time. The country which welcomes the establishment of a multinational plant in a regional unemployment blackspot may in five years be deploring its presence because the region has become dependent upon it. A country at a certain stage of industrial growth may be encouraging direct foreign investment within its boundaries: at a later stage it may be deploring the foreign ownership of its main industries. Interest groups, industries, policy-makers and governments may have different views at one time and another to foreign industrial penetration. The argument is disorganised, the balance of view uncertain. We can but report some of the main concerns.

There is a long tradition of hostility towards foreign corporations in extractive industries. These are often in developing countries[6] and in remote areas where the company town and the foreign enclave become features. The management and atmosphere is foreign, the product is mainly exported, the benefits, save that of employment, accrue elsewhere. Thus natural resource exploitation by the foreign corporation has become to critics the archetype of economic imperialism. The latter-day sensitivity to pollution and rural spoliation has tarnished the image yet further. Perhaps this stereotype is somewhat overdrawn, but it has been drawn from life.

The manufacturing multinational is more complex. As such it integrates itself more into the host economy. There may be a native presence in its management: the product may be for local consumption. The unit is likely to be large, a good employer with a good community image. It exists not in isolation but more often as a part of the general industrial structure with competitors which are a check on its activities and suppliers who value its demands.

The tangible benefits of a foreign enterprise to a host country are several; why else are they accepted and often courted? It is worth listing such benefits. First, foreign direct investment represents an infusion of development capital which may accelerate growth and, whether profits are reinvested or not, generates income. Moreover, since the project has presumably been vetted for profitability by the foreign investor, its marginal efficiency may be high. Even if the host country is itself capital-rich the foreign enterprise frees capital to be used elsewhere. Advanced industrial countries, alive to the hostility often invoked by foreign enterprises, have been quick to accept them only on one special term, locating them in depressed areas and welding them into regional development policies. American investment in Western Europe has frequently been directed to development areas – in Scotland, South Wales, the less-prosperous regions of Belgium and Germany.

The second advantage of direct investment to the host country is then employment creation. U.S. industry in Britain has been accepted, albeit grudgingly, by the more insular elements of the Labour Party and trade

---

[6] A leading exception to this is Canada, where resource industries – nickel, uranium, pulp and paper, oil – are mainly owned and operated by the U.S. multinationals.

union movement, because of its employment benefits.[7] In Western Europe and Latin America the employment effects have also been high. The secondary and tertiary effects of these injections are not known, but have probably been considerable.

Third, we may cite certain probable balance-of-payments benefits accruing to countries hosting foreign firms.[8] The goods they produce may compete with imports and reduce these: they are likely to export at least part of their output; to the extent of these effects the merchandise trade balance is likely to be improved. There are the favourable balance-of-payments effects of the initial investment outlays, the establishment costs and possible ongoing outlays for subsequent expansion. Against this capital account influx must, however, be set the debits of outflow of repatriated dividends and profits, royalties payments and fees for patents, industrial knowledge and management services. Such credits and debits in the balance of payments, but not their net effect, are anticipatable. Other secondary effects are possible: local firms may be stimulated to greater export and import-competing effort by the competition of the multinational; a larger industrial base and hence more foreign trade may be encouraged by the subcontracting and factor needs of the multinational; there may be increased dissemination of knowledge and industrial know-how stimulated by its very presence.

One thing is certain in regard to balance-of-payments effects: the task of quantifying them, for either host or parent country, has only just begun and, aside from a few gallant estimates by individuals and groups, we have no reliable data, and have to fall back on mere impressions. We may, as we have done above, identify the main debit and credit flows in the balance-of-payments accounts but we cannot separate elements in the flows which are our concern from other flows. Almost complete disaggregation of many standard balance-of-payments items would be required. As to the indirect and long-term effects they are probably unknowable in any precise sense. The impression – it is little more – exists that the balance of payments is advantaged for the host country by direct investment. Professor John Dunning has estimated that U.S. direct investment in the United Kingdom caused a net gain on current account of the balance of payments in 1965 of $33.6 m.

---

[7] The Economists Advisory Group, a private research organisation, has estimated that one-third of U.S. direct investment in Britain has been in official development areas and has provided some 150,000 jobs. Cf. 'United States Industry in Britain', by J. H. Dunning and R. Pearce (London: The Financial Times, 1974) p. 4. For a good discussion of why host countries welcome multinationals see J. N. Behrman, *National Interests and the Multinational Enterprise* (Englewood Cliffs, N.J.: Prentice-Hall, 1970) chap. 2.

[8] The total impact of foreign direct investment on partner and host countries' balances of payments is imponderable and the subject of controversy. Since we cannot describe the whole of this debate we are content to list, in their places, the probable balance-of-payments advantages and disadvantages. The net effect cannot be stated in general terms, but might be researched for individual case studies.

and inward capital flows in that year of $204.0 m.[9] To the extent that the estimate is reliable it points to impressive balance-of-payments effects on a host country at the height of the U.S. direct investment wave.

A fourth benefit to the host country may lie (though this is often disputed) in the acquisition of technological and managerial skills. The products, methods and processes of the multinational may be disbursed through its subsidiary.[10] Mere observation of its method of operations may be beneficial to native industry. At the least there is a 'production demonstration effect', at the best there is dissemination of knowledge, training programmes, lessons in capital intensity. There may be a general upgrading of industrial activity from receiving talented, knowledgeable and ingenious immigrants of this sort.[11]

Last among benefits must be listed the significant contributions to tax revenue which come from large multinationals wherever they are located. It has been estimated that, in 1970, foreign subsidiaries of American multi-nationals paid $8.4 bln in income taxes to host governments, while taxes, other than those on income, probably amounted to $10 bln.[12] The revenue of major governments from the oil companies in recent years, especially since the establishment of the Organisation of Petroleum Exporting Countries (OPEC), must have been immense.

So much for the benefits of hosting multinational enterprises; what of the disadvantages?

Probably the greatest claimed disadvantage of receiving a multinational subsidiary is the submission to corporate power. The multinational parent may be so great as to challenge the Government of the host country. We are treated to many sensational indicators of the size and hence the power and influence of the largest multinationals.[13] These are crude but startling comparisons, unscientific but worth while for their shock effect, for certainly there should be no complacency about the potential challenge of corporate giants. One aspect other than the mere size of multinational corporations is their pervasiveness and the uncertainty as to where within them are the power points upon which, in negotiation or quarrel, one must act. If this is true of the large-power governments how much more is it true of developing countries

[9] Quoted in *The Growth and Spread of Multinational Companies*, Economist Intelligence Unit, OER Special No. 5 (Oct 1969) p. 22.

[10] To the extent that the return on superior technology and/or managerial skill is absorbed by the foreign company, prices of commodities and of native factors remaining unchanged, there is no direct benefit to the host country.

[11] Great importance is attached to the dissemination of knowledge, technology and skill in the host country by Harry Johnson. For an examination of the welfare effects of direct investment through this and other channels see 'The Efficiency and Welfare Implications of the International Corporation', in C. P. Kindleberger (ed.), *The International Corporation* (Cambridge, Mass.: MIT Press, 1970) pp. 17–35.

[12] See Senate Committee on Finance, *Implications of Multinational Firms* (1973) p. 444.

[13] For example we are told that the sales figures, profits, cash flow, whatever may be chosen for the comparison, exceed the GNP of Belgium or the Netherlands, *a fortiori* that of Somalia.

which often are perforce host to multinationals in pursuit of industrial development. Certainly and in the last resort the size and power of multinational corporations is a new survival kit for' capitalism. In the nineteenth century (up to say 1914) firms were national and typically small but their survival and interests were protected by identity of interest with Government and ruling class. In this age when Government, as like as not, is collectivist in sympathy, size and power will enable the corporate sector to survive and, so far, prosper.

A second concern of host governments is that it is usually in the most profitable, technologically advanced and growth-potential industries that multinational subsidiaries appear, thus moving control of the best of the industrial sector to foreigners. From this it is but a step to argue that diffusion of technology between countries is at the mercy of decisions made by multinational corporations. The multinational corporation is therefore seen as symbolic of the technology gap long apparent between the developing and developed countries.[14] From the mid-1960s this became an anxiety also for mature industrial countries. Not only was the United States' technological dominance a source of apprehension, but it was expressed in great part through the vast expenditures of American multinationals on research and development and was a special manifestation of the new 'technology gap'. In industry after industry the technological sophistication of the United States appeared to spring from the large sums deployed to research and development by American-based multinational firms.[15] The fact is that all governments wish to have tight supervision over technology, seeing it as a dynamic mainspring of their industry. They wish to nurture it for themselves, feeling threatened if it is disbursed from abroad and still more menaced if it is withheld by foreign corporations. Technology nurture has become a desired aspect of national sovereignty.

Supporters of multinationals claim beneficial effects from them in technology transfer.[16] Not only is their technology and expertise exported to host countries where it has beneficial effects, but multinationals by reason of their wealth and power are the natural exponents of research and innovation. It is argued that multinational subsidiaries spend more heavily on research in

---

[14] For example in 1968 payments for imports of technology by thirteen developing countries, embodying 65 per cent of population and 56 per cent of GNP of developing countries was estimated at $1.5 b. – over one-half of the flow of direct foreign investment to all developing countries during the same year. See U.N., *Multinational Corporations in World Development* (New York, 1973) p. 50. For an interesting assessment of the cost of acquisition of new technology to developing countries, see *Transfer of Technology*, Report by the Secretariat of UNCTAD (Geneva: Nov 1971) pp. 17–18.

[15] For some American firms, e.g. IBM and Kodak, the resources applied to research were equal to or greater than the gross sales of their European competitors. See K. Waltz, 'The Myth of National Interdependence', in C. P. Kindleberger (ed.), *The International Corporation* (Cambridge, Mass.: MIT Press, 1970) p. 217; and J. Dunning, 'Technology, United States Investment and European Economic Growth', p. 165 of the same book.

[16] See reference to H. Johnson's view in note 11 on p. 155.

their host countries than do domestically-owned industries. While economists of the right see multinationals as the natural dispensers of technology among countries, governments, economists of the left and a good many middle-of-the-road analysts see them as contributors to the technology gap. Certainly there is no sign that technology passes according to any sense of mission on the part of corporations. It is a function of profit and the corporate interest. Governments have little influence over the nature of technology transfer, its timing or its influence on domestic as distinct from foreign-owned industry.

A special aspect of technology transfer which has been much discussed has been the growth of royalties, fees and patent rights flowing to firms for the use of their techniques abroad. Payments of such fees approximately doubled between 1965 and 1973.[17] The location of patents and the flow of royalties have been cited as evidence that developing countries tend to become consumers of technology and that this is particularly so in certain newer industries.[18] A picture is drawn of backward countries whose growth is not only stunted but whose malformation is the source of rich revenues to multinationals.

A third concern, or group of concerns, springs from the new-nationalism of the sixties, concern with subordination of one's economy and country to a particular foreign country which because of its foreign policies or other characteristics is in disrepute. This is the aversion to American corporate domination, exemplified in French abhorrence of American influence in any form; it is the national aversion to American industrial penetration in Canada, nervous ever of its large, unpredictable and unruly southern neighbour. It is anti-Americanism (and repugnance for the Japanese) manifesting itself in a particular field. It is a disquiet which has many facets, some of which must be mentioned. There is the fear of political penetration following the economic. The American Government, it is alleged, has control over corporate policies of parent companies in the United States. These policies are passed on to subsidiaries abroad regardless of whether they are acceptable to host governments. American anti-trust laws come to influence mergers in the host country; export policies of subsidiaries become subject to American influence. Business decisions, it seems, are taken abroad and are subject to the coercion of a foreign government. Canada and Latin America have been sensitive to such influences. Then there is the apparent threat to national identity and culture. Foreign standards and economic values are imposed. Through advertising the pattern of life is threatened by foreign behaviour which is the prerequisite of the mass market. *Per capita* income may be increased but it is at the price of a 'candy-floss' society which is its unwelcome accompaniment.

[17] The estimate is that of R. Vernon and was compiled by him from IMF sources. See *Storm Over the Multinationals* (New Haven, Conn.: Harvard University Press, 1977) p. 7.

[18] See, for example, C. V. Vaitsos, 'Patents Revisited', *Journal of Development Studies*, vol. IX (1973).

A fourth host concern is that decisions of the multinational enterprise, taken elsewhere, will be detrimental to the host economy. The very flexibility of multinational management makes it possible to eliminate plants here and replace them elsewhere. Employment policies can be threatened by sudden shut-downs or labour layoffs.[19] Such actions may be justifiable in terms of the economic plans for the multinational corporation but be inimical to the interests of one or more host countries. In the extreme case a multinational may shut down its operations in a country entirely if it considers the economic climate unfavourable.[20] There is a degree of flexibility and mobility in multinational corporate operations which states do not command in their economic (and regional) policies.

A fifth concern of the host country may be with what we may call the micro effects of foreign investment; that is, the effect which multinational enterprises may have in the host country upon groups, particular markets and interests. Labour comes at once to mind and the sense of impotence which trades unions often experience in negotiating with foreign-owned firms is well known. But there are other groups. Skilled labour and, in particular, specialised management and research personnel are likely to be attracted to the large enterprise by larger salaries, better working conditions and the prospect of personal career advancement in an international milieu. Smaller domestic firms will object to the withering competition of the international giant. Equally they may be inhibited by not being able to obtain locally the money capital which the foreign-controlled enterprise can obtain easily from many sources abroad. In factor buying, product design, marketing and finance the multinational is likely to have the competitive edge on the domestic firm.

It would be difficult to exhaust the list of criticisms and doubts which are generated in the host country by foreign investment. It follows a spectrum which runs all the way from reasoned economic argument to blind prejudice and xenophobia, but in the last resort it reduces to three points of conflict. First, the multinational corporation is seen as the agent of a foreign power which, through the subsidiary, can exercise its influence in the host country. Second, the foreign-controlled company is suspect simply because it is foreign; and third, the multinational corporation is able to evade the checks and controls of the host-country Government while not being subject to regulation by any international agency, as governments may be.

Before leaving national country concerns with the multinational corporation it is necessary to touch briefly on the matter as it may appear to parent

---

[19] In 1977 the International Nickel Corporation laid off 3000 workers from its plant in Sudbury, Ontario – a company town with little alternative employment. Simultaneously its operations at a plant in Guatemala were expanded.

[20] On several occasions between 1974 and 1976 Henry Ford threatened to close Ford operations in the United Kingdom because of the unfavourable industrial-relations climate; in 1977, in an improved industrial and economic climate, the location of a Ford plant, estimated to cost £250 m., in Britain was the subject of high debate and was courted by the British Government for location in one of a number of areas of high unemployment.

states. This is less discussed and until the end of the sixties there was a tendency for critics of multinationals to assume that they are always an asset to their parent countries. In the late sixties the criticism of the New Left and after 1971 of the American AFL–CIO was brought to bear on several aspects of American multinational operations which were held to be detrimental to the economy of the United States. In Europe, British and Swedish labour began to voice similar concerns. At the same time a number of revealed scandals of Nixon-Administration collusion with American multinationals abroad tarnished the corporate image. Much of the criticism was anecdotal and poorly documented, but it was powerfully argued and must be summarised here.

The labour movement was concerned about the export of American jobs. It was alleged that, with high American labour costs, exporting plants in the United States were being replaced by manufacture in countries to which the goods had hitherto been exported. Sometimes the products were imported back to the United States. The American balance of payments thus lost on four counts: the original foreign investment, the loss of export sales, additional imports and the investment of profits in the host country rather than through repatriation to the United States. Moreover, there was, it was alleged, a transfer of technology to the foreign country which, thus equipped, soon would emerge as a competitor to the United States.

Two other sources of parent-country displeasure have been identified by U.S. critics. The first lay in the tax advantages enjoyed by American multinationals. Since U.S. tax codes enable corporations to retain earnings abroad incurring tax liability only when profits are repatriated, such profits are reinvested abroad, a double loss to the United States, which loses the revenue and the benefit of the investment.[21]

A second cause of concern lies in the identification of American multi-nationals with the foreign policies of the United States. The foreign connections of large American firms leads them to seek 'friends' in Washington. Such friendships may be cultivated for mutual advantage, firms expecting U.S. Government support in their foreign operations in return for information or assistance in foreign countries penetrated by the firms. Not only is this inimical to the detachment with which foreign policy should ideally be conducted, but it implants in foreigners an image of the United States in which private firms are identified with official policy.

We may summarise these parent country concerns about the effects of multinationals under one broad reaction: fear that the firms operate beyond the control and without thought for the interests of the parent government.

---

[21] The Nixon Government in 1973 and 1974 tried to reduce tax advantages accruing to multinational firms. Cf. R. Vernon, 'Does Society Also Profit?', *Foreign Policy*, no. 13 (1973–4) p. 110.

(iv) TRADE

The effects of direct investment on the balances of payments of host and parent countries has already been touched upon. There are, however, wider implications, especially those for the international monetary system and world economy as a whole, which must be mentioned. Here again, meaningful statistical measurement is often not possible, but the existence of broad flows and their implications can be seen. Two such flows are relevant here.

First of these is the huge volume of intra-firm trading which now takes place within the general flows of exports and imports recorded by countries. These exports and imports are internal transactions to international corporations, either finished goods for direct resale abroad or 'further manufacture' goods – components, sub-assemblies and the like. The dimensions of these flows are hard to determine but certain general magnitudes are accepted. In 1975 32 per cent of all U.S. imports were from U.S. affiliates in which the United States had a 50 per cent or greater interest. If the criterion were expanded to include U.S. affiliates in which the U.S. interest was 5 per cent or more the comparable figure was 42 per cent. This figure does not include non-U.S-affiliate sales of which British, Swedish and others must have been considerable. It seems that, according to the definitions one adopts, a third to a half of American imports in 1975 were in the form of intra-firm sales.[22] Apart from merchandise trade there certainly is a considerable amount of intra-firm invisible trade. Putting all together one economist has estimated that 50 per cent of world trade should now be regarded as being on an intra-firm basis.[23] Disaggregating, one finds that for certain commodities, both in food, primary materials and manufactures, the percentage (by value) of intra-firm trade as part of total trade is often in excess of 50 per cent.

The significance of such trade is great, but cannot be explored here. We must be content to list the fields in which recognition of its importance has become essential. The first and most general is in the field of international trade theory itself. Accustomed as international economists are to regard trade flows as being impelled by relative factor endowments of trading countries and adjusted by changes in relative prices, they must now see them, at least in part, as the product of a command system within firms and at prices which often bear little relation to costs of production. Second implication is that the effects of devaluation for the adjustment of a trade balance must be reassessed in the light of these new facts. Large parts of trade flows it would seem, are beyond the reach of such adjustment. Nor is the list yet complete.

---

[22] The source for these estimates is W. K. Chung, 'Sales by Majority-Owned Foreign Affiliates of U.S. Companies, 1975', *Survey of Current Business*, vol. 57, no. 2 (Feb 1977) p. 35.

[23] A useful survey of intra-firm trade was made by G. K. Helleiner in a paper 'Intra-firm Trade and the Developing Countries: Patterns, Trends and Data Problems' given by the author at a seminar at the University of Sussex, 7–11 November 1977.

Customs-union theory, tariff policy, foreign-exchange controls and corporate fiscal procedures must also be reassessed.

The second effect of multinational corporations upon balances of payments concerns leads and lags in international payments and hedging against exchange rate fluctuations. Here we have no statistical evidence. It is impossible to separate multinational leading and lagging in payments for traded goods from the aggregate flows of the balance of payments. Neither is it possible to distinguish inflows and outflows of hot money which originate in precautionary transfers of funds by accountants anxious to avoid risks in holding this or that currency. Nevertheless, from the mere proliferation of multinational enterprises and from their size it is evident that the redistribution of their financial flows must be large. How far such redistribution extends from the role of risk-averter to risk-taker it is also impossible to say. To protect the organisation from uncertainties is one thing; how far fund movements are used to exploit currency uncertainties is another. The Rubicon must often be crossed. In particular the one-way-option speculation of the Bretton Woods adjustable peg system before 1971 must often have offered large pickings. It was certainly observable during the heavy speculative attacks on the pound and dollar between 1964 and 1971 that a new force was at work in that the sheer volume of withdrawals from a currency were now so great that official monetary authorities were unable to counter them with the reserves at their command. A new situation had arisen, in that if it was widely considered that a currency would be devalued, then adverse speculation decreed it so. That situation has continued, even under floating exchange rates, into the seventies.

(v) POLICY

This chapter has been concerned not with events but with changes in the economic environment, changes which are clearly discernible but not easily measurable. From such a situation inevitable differences of interpretation arise. There is scope for prejudice and irrationality. In particular there is cleavage between political desirability, however that may be interpreted, and economic welfare. In the rich countries the political left and the nationalist right form uneasy alliances against what they present as a capitalist rogue elephant. In the developing countries the contribution, past and potential, of the multinational firm to development is either only grudgingly acknowledged or is presented as a form of neo-colonialism. The value of its contribution is hotly debated.[24] The economist, faced with the inevitable weighing of a balance of advantage, has his own problems of interpretation

---

[24] This is demonstrated by the many reports of international agencies, particularly UNCTAD, upon the relation of multinationals to the development problem.

and of presenting his findings to an audience which has usually prejudged the issue.

As this writer sees it we face three issues if national policies towards multinationals are to evolve.

The first task is for national governments to face the conflicts which arise between the immediate material benefits usually arising as a result of investments by multinationals and economic nationalism. It must be accepted by national governments that to pursue policies of discouragement to foreign firms implies a probable lower rate of economic growth in the long term. Not only will such policies diminish the industrial sector of the country concerned by forgoing the location of foreign-controlled plants, but it may invoke negative reactions by firms already there. The power of multinationals is more likely to grow than not. What is required is a policy seeking for an optimal degree of foreign penetration, sufficient to stimulate, augment and diversify the host economy while avoiding the threat of foreign economic manipulation and cultural submersion. The measures which express such an optimal policy require to be subtle, flexible and many-faceted. This is an age of resurgent nationalism, difficult to endure because it is often mistaken for patriotism and difficult to combat because it is irrational. But economic horizons grow larger and cannot be contained and the multinational is a creature of world economics towards the encroachment of which economic nationalism is a defence mechanism.

The second task is to recognise one aspect of national hostility to the multinational firm, the fact that it appears to operate beyond host-country control; and establish international obligations under which it must operate. As a former age attempted to control firm size and potential for exploitation by anti-trust legislation this age must by international agreement define the limits of corporate power. A case has been made earlier in this chapter that certain aspects of multinational behaviour may fall outside host jurisdiction or indeed any jurisdiction. A series of international agreements covering specific areas or a code of corporate behaviour to which countries might be invited to subscribe would be a first step in the direction of international surveillance.

The third task is, at this stage, indefinable but concerns the actions of multinationals in the world financial field, in their relations to national monetary policies, currency stabilisation, international capital markets and flows of investment funds. At many points in this sector the monetary policies of national governments and the transactions of multinational corporations cross and become entagled. It is necessary to know the areas of conflict and in turn move to eliminate them.

Part Three

The Years of Crisis, 1964–78

I I

Confrontation with the Third World

'What else have you got in your pocket?'

The Dodo to *Alice in Wonderland*

(i) A CONSCIOUS UNITY

In early 1964 the first session of the United Nations Conference on Trade and Development (UNCTAD) was held in Geneva[1] signalising the emergence of a view among the developing countries that the time had come for changes in the trade policies of the developed countries. At the three-months-long conference the objectives of these policies and the institutional arrangements which must give expression to them were subjected to severe and continuous criticism by the delegates of developing countries.

The thrust of the developing countries' criticism can be summarised as follows. Two distinct and successive approaches to development planning became discernible. The first played down the role of trade and aimed at industrialisation and the production of import substitutes. Investment was, so far as possible, to be channelled to domestic industry. While tariffs protected the home market from industrial imports, exports were to be treated with varying degrees of tolerance and the balance of payments was to be handled by direct import and payments controls and by multiple exchange rates. The difficulties of such a policy were soon apparent. Import substitution meant higher costs and as the range of domestic production was extended to cover more products for the production of which the country was less well-endowed, the cost discrepancy between home-produced goods and imports became progressively greater. Moreover, protection shielded domestic industries from the competition which they required in order to induce efficiency.

A second and slightly later approach to trade by developing countries was a partial reversion to the classical view of trade as an agent of growth. In part this was the result of disillusionment with the policies of autarky already described; in part it was the growing realisation that the amount of aid flowing, or likely to flow, from the mature to the developing countries was

---

[1] A second session was held in 1968 and UNCTAD was made a permanent agency of the United Nations, located in Geneva. Sessions are held at four-year intervals.

166 The Years of Crisis, 1964-78

insufficient in itself to produce the rate of growth which the developing countries required; and in part it was the result of a demonstration effect, of the spectacle of accelerating growth for the developed countries (since the Second World War) under the stimulus of the greatest upsurge in trade the world had ever seen. The practical effect was that the developing countries began to rally to a view summarised in the slogan 'aid through trade'. This impelled a keen criticism by them of all commercial policies which inhibited trade, especially the commercial policies of the developed countries and, by inference, of the whole GATT system.[2]

The developing countries' case against the GATT system and for a revision of commercial policy in their favour rested upon several arguments. First, the GATT system was a 'rich man's club', its trade policies being relevant only to trade between the developed countries while it worked to the detriment of the exports, particularly the manufactured exports, of the developing countries.

Secondly, about 80 per cent of developing countries' exports consisted of primary products. Upon such exports, import quotas were often imposed by industrial countries. Many were subject to tariffs or non-tariff barriers and others, not obtainable in the importing country, were subject to consumption taxes.

Third, in the imposition of tariffs by the industrial countries against primary-product imports, the principle of the effective rate of protection was invoked by the critics to explain that nominal tariff rates understated the actual degree of protection.[3] Most primary products used by the importing country as raw material inputs were allowed to enter with low or zero tariffs. But if such products were embodied in processed intermediate goods they were subject to higher tariffs and as the value added increased so did the tariff. The protective effect of the tariff was therefore increased and the

---

[2] An excellent account of the best thought on trade policy for the developing countries in the late fifties was given by Raul Prébisch in his *Towards a New Trade Policy for Development* (New York: U.N., 1964), a report which organised for the UNCTAD conference of 1964 the main issues as Prébisch saw them at the time. Against the background of an interesting historical analysis the author distinguished the immediate problem as being one of dealing with the developing countries 'persistent trend towards external imbalance'. Against this trend, which he regarded as inherent in development, Prébisch developed his arguments. These centred on two problems: the relative stagnation of earnings from exports of primary products and the necessity for developing countries to develop an export trade in manufactures. For the first problem the advocated solution was that of international commodity agreements; for the second, tariff preferences by the industrial countries in favour of imports from developing countries. For both of these solutions GATT was regarded as unsuitable and changes in its procedures were called for. The Prébisch Report came opportunely, for it summarised with great cogency the theoretical arguments current at the time among politicians and economists in the developing countries. It was to be the basis of the case for an alternative to the GATT system. A good critique of the Prébisch Report is to be found in H. G. Johnson, *Economic Policies Towards Developed Countries* (London: Allen & Unwin, 1967) pp. 25-33.

[3] The concept of the effective rate of protection is well-known and the reader may refresh his memory of its intricacies from any international trade manual. See, for example, the author's *International Trade and Payments* (London: Macmillan, 1974) pp. 139-141.

exporting primary producer was forced to export the product in its rawest form, thereby forgoing export advantages which might accrue from processing the material domestically to an intermediate or final stage.

Fourth, one result of the successive rounds of the GATT negotiations which had taken place by the late fifties was that tariff rates on the types of manufactures exported by developing countries[4] were higher, on average, than tariff rates on sophisticated manufactures exported by mature countries. Again effective rates of protection were considerably higher than nominal tariff rates.

The solution to the barriers imposed against the exports of the developing countries might have appeared to be the negotiation in the GATT of removal of all such barriers. To this there were two obstacles. First, the GATT provided for reciprocity and non-discrimination so that the developing countries had to offer trade advantages to the mature countries in return; moreover, advantages so yielded would be generalised under GATT's most-favoured-nation procedures. Second, the developing countries demanded more than tariff concessions from the mature countries. They demanded complete removal and a period during which their nascent industries might grow. This involved unilateral tariff concessions by the mature countries – an 'infant-industry argument' in reverse. What was demanded were preferences by the developed countries in favour of the goods of the developing countries.

We may summarise the commercial policy of the developing countries as it emerged in the early sixties as having four main elements. First, there was insistence on the necessity for schemes to promote stability and an upward trend in primary-commodity prices. Second, developing countries wanted preferences in the developed world for imports of their manufactured goods while being free to close their own markets to the exports of the developed countries. Third, they attempted to follow current fashion by establishing among themselves a number of customs-unions and free-trade areas. Finally, realising that GATT and reciprocal bargaining might still have tangible benefits to offer, they did not withdraw from that system but remained within it, holding a watching brief.

The reception given to such arguments by the developed countries, in particular by the United States, was aloof and non-committal. The group defence, so far as any was clearly enunciated, was lame. Preferences, it was argued, are discriminatory and therefore undesirable. True, preferences existed in the British Commonwealth system and in the EEC but GATT had proscribed preferences and discrimination, the Commonwealth preference system was on the way out and the EEC was a customs union which was giving free trade to six countries. To embark on a world-wide system of preferences, arbitrarily determined, would be a retrograde step. Equity would be impossible and there would be endless wheeling and dealing to establish the

---

[4] For example, labour-intensive products of light industries.

preferences. Apologists for the developed countries argued that their tariffs were not high and that, if industries in the developing countries were efficient, these products would not be excluded. This argument was not very convincing. In 1965 Bela Balassa told us[5] that in 1962 while the average nominal tariff on consumer goods for the EEC was 17.8 per cent the average effective rate was 30.9 per cent. For Britain the equivalent figures were 23.8 and 40.4 per cent; for the United States 17.5 and 25.9. For intermediate products commonly exported by developing countries the average nominal and effective rates in 1962 were as follows: the EEC 13.3 and 28.3 per cent; Britain 17.2 and 34.3 and the United States 15.2 and 28.6 per cent.

Apart from plain tariffs the developing countries increasingly complained of non-tariff barriers operated against them. The growing wish of temperate-zone countries to protect their agriculture, the United States' quotas on meat, petroleum, sugar and cotton textiles, the agricultural policy of the EEC, the Canadian quotas on textiles – all these were objects of criticism. The developing countries had grounds for the assertion that there was discrimination against them.

For the six years after the establishment of UNCTAD little was done by the developed countries to expand the trade of the developing countries. The United States was firmly opposed to the granting of preferences and within the rich countries imports of manufactured goods were vigorously opposed by strong industrial lobbies which argued that free admission of low-cost foreign manufactures would drive domestic producers out of business, create unemployment and intensify regional economic disparities within their countries. The plain fact is that the developing countries and their sponsors were asking too much. To permit tariffs in poor countries to exclude developed-country products, to eliminate their own tariffs against manufactures from the developing countries and to cap all by stabilising (or helping to stabilise) the prices of primary products, thereby worsening their own terms of trade, was to attribute to politicians and business a degree of altruism and idealism they have never possessed. To preach such doctrines to backwoods senators from the Mid-West, French-Canadian textile manufacturers in Quebec or their counterparts in Britain, France or Germany was an exercise in futility.

At the UNCTAD meeting in New Delhi in 1968 the developed countries felt obliged to offer an olive branch. It was agreed that a system of non-reciprocal preferences for the import of manufactured and semi-manufactured goods from developing countries should be worked out and applied. What appeared in 1971 was only a shadow. Preferences were to be extended, but certain products were excluded – these usually including the products which were most important to the developing countries.

---

[5] See 'Tariff Protection in Industrial Countries', *Journal of Political Economy* (Dec 1965).

(ii) TRADE NEGOTIATIONS AMONG THE DEVELOPED COUNTRIES

It is time to place the confrontation of developed and developing countries in a wider setting and give a brief account of general trade negotiations in the sixties.

By the end of the fifties tariffs and barriers to trade were being reduced by the industrial countries through the GATT and to a lesser extent the IMF.[6] Four objectives underlay this drive for liberation: non-discrimination, trade expansion, the establishment of a stable world trading system, and reciprocity in negotiation. The first of these was an American ideal, pushed by that country since the negotiations, which had taken place even during the war, for the setting up of the Bretton Woods arrangements and immediately after for the establishment of ITO. In the American view non-discrimination in trade was an attainable ideal, fully consistent with the values of a protectionist country. The power and influence of the United States must be used with a crusading zeal for its establishment. Trade expansion was not only an objective but by the early fifties was taking place. Some part of this expansion was claimed as the result of reduced trade barriers – the elimination of bilateralism, the progressive removal of exchange controls and, by the end of the decade, a widening measure of multilateral trade. By the later fifties it was observable that the western nations were experiencing a trade-powered boom. Further freedom of trade might be expected to accelerate this.

The establishment of a stable world trading system was implicit in the aims of the GATT, which was now a world forum for commercial-policy negotiation of which the aims[7] were mainly negative, and aimed at prevention of those elements which had disturbed and constrained the trade of the interwar years. Finally, reciprocity, the principle of concession for concession, had been built into the machinery of the GATT negotiation since its inception. It was insisted on by the United States, which made it the basis of all tariff bargaining and was emulated by other countries because it provided a favourable general climate for tariff reduction.

The Dillon Round of trade negotiations, between 1960 and 1962, was the fifth of the GATT series and was mooted as early as 1958 when Douglas Dillon, Under-Secretary of State in the United States, toured West European capitals to muster support for a new round of tariff negotiations. Renewal of the Reciprocal Trade Agreements Act in 1958 had empowered the President to reduce the American tariff by 20 per cent, the object being to negotiate

---

[6] It will be remembered that GATT deals with tariff bargaining, the IMF with direct controls, either monetary or in the form of import quotas, embargoes or the like.

[7] 'Buried deep' as two writers put it 'in GATT's Gothic syntax'. See G. and V. Curzon, 'The Management of Trade Relations in GATT', *International Economic Relations of the Western World*, part II, vol. 1, ed. Andrew Shonfield (London: Oxford University Press for the Royal Institute of International Affairs, 1976) p. 150.

with the new EEC before it established itself as a customs union and a discriminatory trade area among the leading countries. The fact was that the United States had reached a parting of the ways in her postwar commercial policy. The path so far pursued by the GATT had suited her well. Discrimination, the American *bête noire*, had been curtailed and if this had been done at the price of some mild tariff concessions under the Trade Agreements Act 1934, and its extensions then the price was small. But now there was the EEC and its tariff, excluding American goods from one of the richest markets in the world. The United States had welcomed the Treaty of Rome on political and on some economic grounds. Now she was not so sure. She had to accommodate herself to the high common tariff of the Community and to the Common Agricultural Policy. To do this it appeared necessary, in 1960, to negotiate major reciprocal tariff concessions.

Initial response to the American initiative by Britain and powers outside the Rome Treaty was not encouraging. Such powers were intent upon their own responses to the Treaty. In particular, Britain was absorbed with her proposal for a free-trade area for the whole of the OEEC and regarded a general tariff discussion as out of place until that proposal was adopted. When, however, the French Government announced in November that it would not participate in such a free-trade area the political climate changed. Britain and her future partners in EFTA were forced to re-examine their options, particularly as to how they might mitigate the discriminatory effects of the new customs union. Within the EEC itself, there was a group – Germany and the Benelux – which favoured multilateral negotiations. These were countries whose pre-union tariff lay below the projected common external tariff (CET) and which faced increases in the prices of intermediate goods imported when CET was imposed. France, under a cloud for its intransigence, consented to enter multilateral discussions, if only to keep the situation under surveillance. On 17 November 1958 ministers accepted a programme for a new GATT round. Procedures were agreed upon during 1959 and negotiations opened on 1 September 1960.

The first phase of the negotiations – until May 1961 – was concerned with compensations in the rates of individual EEC countries when CET was struck. For example, CET rates might bring reductions in equivalent Italian rates and rises in German rates. Suppliers of goods concerned would then be advantaged if they wished to expand their exports to the Italian market, but be injured if they at present supplied the German market. How were third parties to be compensated for loss of markets? A serious difference here arose between the EEC members and the rest. The former argued that, except for a list (list G) of sensitive items and the changes which would be wrought by the Common Agricultural Policy, the compensations provided a zero sum game. The latter argued that this was irrelevant: what really mattered was the situation of every external country before and after CET. To tell the British that in a given commodity they lost the German market but gained the Italian was a dubious palliative. After lengthy in-fighting in which the externals, hotly resisted by the Community countries, tried to force item-by-item bilateral talks, the EEC agreed to discuss the severe-loss cases. Finally CET duty was reduced on about two hundred products of interest to twenty-one countries.

The second and main phase of the negotiations was concerned with the settling of tariff concessions on a reciprocal basis. These were conducted on a product-by-product basis in accordance with lists of products on which concessions were asked. The Secretariat circulated the request lists to all participating parties. In accordance with these, offer lists were drawn up and negotiations went forward on a bilateral basis. One feature which quickly emerged was that request lists for concessions greatly exceeded offer lists. For example, the EEC list of requests to the United States was five times as long as the U.S. list of requests to the EEC. Some countries, such as Australia, which were large importers of manufactures, received from the EEC multi-page lists of requests for tariff concessions but themselves submitted very short request lists. This feature of the negotiations placed a severe constraint on reciprocity at the outset. Some countries, in order to improve their negotiating position, brought forward supplementary lists of items on which they could afford to offer concessions, either items in which they had minimal trade or for which tariff cuts carried little domestic industrial risk.

By 1962 the Dillon Round was over. Its achievement was small. Gardner Patterson estimated that 'the unweighted average tariff on manufactures may have been cut by about one percentage point'.[8] The only positive outcome of the Round was a promise by the EEC to apply a 20 per cent across-the-board reduction in its tariff if and when the United States would engage in a further round of reciprocal negotiations. Even this promise was broken when at a later stage a dispute with the United States on agricultural policy raised the commercial temperature. But the real cause of failure of the Dillon Round lay not so much in the difficulty of negotiating tariff reductions but in the changes which had taken place in the political background. In the United States Kennedy had recognised the weakness of the U.S. bargaining position and was moving towards a new trade bill in Congress which would empower a new liberalising initiative by the Administration. In Britain membership of EFTA was regarded as a temporary expedient pending success of the British application to join the Community. It was clear that, once that took place, a complete realignment of commercial policies would follow. From most national viewpoints the appropriate course seemed to be to bury the Dillon Round with appropriate decorum and await events.

In retrospect it is fairly clear that by 1962 the GATT type of item-by-item negotiation had run its course. It had had some success. The high tariffs in the forties had been fairly easy to reduce, simply because they were so high and

---

[8] See G. Patterson, *Discrimination in International Trade: the Policy Issues* (Princeton: Princeton University Press, 1966) p. 174.

the results had then been generalised among countries by the *most-favoured-nation* procedure. But by the Dillon Round most countries were getting down to a core of tariffs which were inviolable because they impaired the interests of key industries with vocal and powerful political lobbies. Moreover, by 1960–2 trade liberalisation in the West had gone some way. Not only had tariffs been reduced but balance-of-payments controls had been removed. Further tariff cuts must hurt some industries. Those which were to make the sacrifice could hardly be blamed for looking critically at those which were to benefit or to be left untouched. The GATT method of item-by-item reduction only concentrated industrial attention on this inequality of sacrifice. The time was clearly ripe for a new general approach whereby tariff reductions might be negotiated in a linear fashion which would dispense with intra-industry or (in the EEC) intra-country comparisons of burden.

1962, the year of Kennedy's Trade Expansion Act was a key year for U.S. commercial policy. The new Administration was anxious for a new look in trade relations. The new Act, which was enacted for a five-year period, was a serious attempt to come to terms with changing trade conditions, in particular with the changing economic relations between the United States and Europe. It also breathed new life into GATT, under whose auspices the tariff negotiations were held and which needed resuscitation after the poor results of the Dillon Round. The Kennedy Round provided the GATT with five years of hard bargaining, new aims to pursue and a measure of success at the end.

In May 1967 bargaining ended in an agreement which produced tariff cuts averaging 35 per cent on some 60,000 internationally traded products. This was supplemented by an anti-dumping agreement and by an arrangement whereby the developed countries (especially the United States and the EEC) were to provide the developing countries with wheat and food-grains over a period of years. Not all, however, was sweetness and light. The Kennedy Round's greatest success was in cutting tariffs on industrial goods, but it revealed also the great obstacles to trade which existed in the form of non-tariff barriers[9] and it made only a minimal contribution to expanding the trade of the developing countries. For the United States the great disappointment of the Kennedy Round was its failure to gain access for its farm products to the markets of the EEC.

All in all the conclusion of the Kennedy Round marked the high-water mark of the movement for trade liberation in the twentieth century. Like the Cobden Treaty of 1860 it seemed to bring the western world to the threshold of free trade. Even the United States, traditionally protectionist, saw in trade expansion in freer markets a solution to her growing balance-of-payments problem and through trade agreement with the EEC a base for a world trading community. But it was only a threshold. The years which were to follow saw a shutting of the door and an apparent retreat to new policies often

---

[9] For example, restrictive government buying policies, special export finance, or, in the United States, the Buy-American legislation.

in contravention of the GATT. Since 1967 it has been downhill all the way.

For the resurgence of trade barriers in the seventies there are probably several reasons. One may be that, in the immediate postwar period, the leading nations were anxious to expand world trade as an employment and growth-creating vehicle. By the seventies, by when trade had been expanding for over twenty years, countries had become used to such expansion and were anxious to experiment with policies not of a general nature, but designed rather to increase their share of further expansion. A second and immediately imperative reason, however, lay in the balance-of-payments problems which increased and ramified during the sixties – in the growing U.S. deficit and confidence problem, the British attempt to maintain sterling as a key currency, the surpluses of Germany and Japan, and the external problems of a host of other developed and developing nations. The United States led the way with capital controls from 1963, the British experimented with import surcharges and import deposit schemes, the EEC closed the door on temperate-zone agricultural products; exchange controls, non-tariff barriers and deficit suppression policies became commonplace. The new trend was not of a dimension to compare with the neo-Mercantilism of the thirties, but it was a retreat into self-interest which boded ill for the future. The new attitudes were reflected in the new customs unions in which the trade-creating attributes of theory were secondary to the trade diversions of expediency.

The Kennedy Round was the last great effort to liberalise trade through the GATT which falls within the time-span of this book.[10] In the years which followed – well into the seventies – economic attention was focussed elsewhere in the international economy, on the collapse of the Bretton Woods system and the plans for international monetary reform and in a world swept by external events – the Vietnam War, dollar crises, inflation and OPEC – trade liberalisation was set aside, almost forgotten. We are not able at this time to say whether this has been a mere intermission in the pursuit of freer trade or the beginning of a new period of trade restriction. Certainly this period has been a difficult one for GATT as an international co-operative agency. Concerned as it is with the process of trade liberalisation and the preservation of certain trading conditions, its success must always be judged by its progress towards the goal of free trade. To stand still for lack of initiative, worse still to regress, is failure. It was able to survive because the course of world events and the steady expansion of world trade provided it up to 1967 with an environment in which it could demonstrate moderate results. The initial negotiations of 1948–58 and the adaptation of the Agreement, the accommodation within the agreement of EEC, the tough bargaining of the Dillon and Kennedy Rounds and the setting-up of the Tokyo Round of 1978 in a growing atmosphere of import restraint by the leading powers – these have

[10] At the time of writing, mid-1979, a further round of GATT negotiations is concluding in Geneva.

been the stages of the GATT's development. An intermission of a decade has revealed basic problems which threaten the GATT system.

The first of such problems is that there is an apparent *de facto* retreat from the principles of GATT. The problems which have already been touched upon have forced the leading countries and groups of countries to adopt new policies which are often in contravention. Such devices, it may be argued, demonstrate unilateral commercial policies which, if not checked, may mean an end to non-discrimination, reciprocity and the aim of a negotiated approach to freer trade. The United States has been stalled in advancing further along the path she has followed since 1934 by the relative failure of the Kennedy Round to secure her agricultural products entry to the markets of Western Europe. Britain, as ever pragmatic in her commercial policy, has been absorbed by the EEC, while to the developing countries the GATT is supported only in the hope that some benefit may one day be derived from it.

The second problem is that there appears to be no way within the GATT in which the divergent commercial policies of countries and groups can be reconciled and fused together into a general liberalising advance. At the worst, one might foresee a number of trading groups emerging, each dominated by a great economic power; the EEC covering Western Europe and the Mediterranean basin; the United States with Latin America and possibly Canada; and possibly a zone in Asia with Japan as its centre. Such grouping might be workable; it is unlikely that it would be optimal. Escaping from this dismal view there are those who argue that the GATT system may yet be saved. They base their argument on the claim that the main deviations from the GATT principles have been in specific industrial sectors particularly agriculture and that deviationist policies have been *ad hoc* rather than demonstrative of fundamental changes of commercial policy. GATT, it is argued, can adjust to the new features which seem to threaten its existence.

Third, it is possible to take a much more disturbing view of the present commercial relations of the great powers. It is this. The United States emerged from the nineteenth century as the greatest industrial power, her strength based on wealth of materials, high capital–output ratio, the existence of a captive mass market, a deployment of large resources to research and development, a nice balance between population and economic resources. In the fifties and sixties it became apparent that some of these forces operated now only partially, that other countries, particularly Western Europe and Japan, were catching up and the American industrial lead dwindling. With this came the formation of the EEC and other trading blocs such as that of the developing countries. These are having, and will continue to have, a profound effect, perhaps an eroding effect, upon the trading position of the United States, with, in turn, great effects upon her commercial policy. It is possible to argue that we are now passing through a crucial formative period in which the GATT and the system it represents may not survive. The test lies in the success or failure of the Tokyo Round of tariff negotiations.

(iii) THE NEW INTERNATIONAL ORDER

An account must be given of the sharpening confrontation between the developed and developing worlds in the seventies. Since we deal here with recent events we pass from history to contemporary politics, in which analysis, where made, must be tentative. We will not attempt a consecutive narrative of events but try to summarise the growing intensity of north–south confrontation[11] in the main fields in which it lies.

Events sharpened confrontation to three points: in the areas of monetary relations, commercial policy and primary-commodity-price stabilisation. In each of these areas the developing countries sought to wring concessions from the developed. Changing in strength of thrust and emphasis, and accompanied always by a general demand for aid and for debt remission, the media, ever vigilant for a cliché, spoke of a demand for a 'new international order'. Carrying moral overtones this term suggested emancipation from inequality, exploitation and injustice. It also polarised discussion: who was not entirely for was against such an order.

Economic events in the seventies contributed to the confrontation. The decade began with crisis in the international monetary system, the breakdown of the Bretton Woods system in 1971 and difficulties in implementing the Smithsonian Agreement in 1972. In 1973 the oil-export embargo by the Arab suppliers and the fourfold increase in the price of oil created very large deficits in the balances of payments of the developed countries, triggered a recession of greater depth than any since the Second World War which, with a severe worsening of the terms of trade of these countries, produced the unprecedented combination of recession and price inflation. The economic climate of the seventies became sombre and threatening, a contrast to the stimulating economic weather of the fifties and sixties. Encouraged by the success of the oil-producing countries other primary-producing countries began to examine the potential advantages of forming cartels to withhold supplies and manipulate the prices of their products.

In the monetary field ambitions of the developing countries to make use of international arrangements went back at least as far as 1967 and the Rio Agreement to set up Special Drawing Rights (SDRs) to be administered by the IMF. The purpose of the Agreement was to establish the SDR as a fiduciary-reserve asset for central banks, capable of expansion *pro rata* with the growth of international trade. The developing countries were quick to see their chance. How were the new units to be distributed among IMF member countries. Further, which countries were to be beneficiaries from the seigniorage which would result from the costless creation of a fiduciary reserve asset? There was here, it was argued, a once-in-a-lifetime opportunity for

[11] In the ever-changing jargon of international political economy the relations of developed and developing countries in the later seventies was named for the relations of the hemispheres in which each group of countries lies.

improvement in the distribution of world income. In the controversy which followed, technical arguments and value judgements clashed. The technical argument was that, to launch the SDR, complete confidence in it as a money form was essential. To institute the link[12] as even a partial vehicle of aid disbursement would be to undermine such confidence by flooding the new unit into the reserves of a group of chronic-deficit countries. Moreover, if held by these countries for long, would the interest charges on the SDRs be met? The technical arguments were powerful, the value judgements appealing. The result was the stalemate so familiar in international negotiation as the link proposal wended its way from committee to committee, ultimately to become irrelevant as SDR allocations ceased in the new world of fluctuating exchange rates after 1973.

Although the voting power of the developing countries in the IMF is considerable, their attitude towards that body is somewhat similar to that towards the GATT – that it is a rich-country game in which the dice are loaded against them. There is some reason for this view. Since the early sixties much of the key negotiation and decision-making within the IMF has been done in the Group of Ten or in committees in which the leading Western countries have had a dominant voice. While there have been Fund measures directed specially to benefit poor countries,[13] on the big issues the rich countries have made the going.

In the area of commercial policy the thrust of the developing countries was, as we have seen,[14] towards a lowering of developed countries' protection against their products. In this they failed. The seventies have been a period of increasing barriers to trade. Liberalism came to its flood tide in the Kennedy Round and then retreated.

In 1976, three years after the OPEC price rise when recovery from the shock of its effects was giving confidence to the developed countries but the necessity for a *modus vivendi* with the developing countries was apparent, a Conference on International Economic Co-operation (CIEC), or North–South Conference, met in Paris for eighteen months. It was attended by twenty-seven countries[15] and it met outside the jurisdiction of the United Nations or its functional agencies – its declared purpose, to establish the 'new international order'.

Even with a limited number of participants CIEC included country groups

---

[12] The 'link' was of course between the creation of SDRs and the distribution of a lion's share of the new units to the developing countries to deal with their perennial balance-of-payments deficits.

[13] For example the setting up in 1974 of an oil facility to help members of the IMF most injured by the increase in oil prices.

[14] See pp. 166–8 above.

[15] All the major economic powers except China, the Soviet Union and East Germany were represented. Inevitably many smaller developing countries were excluded – a fact which enabled the developing countries to refrain from agreeing on certain matters on the ground that they could not speak for the entire Third World.

with disparate interests, forced into the experiment by extraordinary economic circumstances even what was to be discussed was in doubt. Moreover, the fact that the Conference was to be held outside the U.N. umbrella changed relative negotiating strengths. The 'northern' countries (i.e. the major economic powers) felt uneasy away from the GATT and the IMF where they play the economic game according to accepted rules and conventions; the southern (developing) countries were happier outside the functional agencies but lacked the numerical force which they command in the U.N. Assembly. Most groups hoped for a successful conference although 'success' might have been differently defined. For the developing countries it might well lead towards a new order; at least it was a step forward from UNCTAD, now twelve years old and bogged down in its own problems. For the major powers it held a chance of establishing a new *status quo* to replace that which had been destroyed by the oil crisis. The OPEC countries expected that the Conference might establish the conditions under which the cartel would operate in future.

Few international conferences achieve their aims entirely. CIEC, with its aims defined in such grandiose terms, was conventional in this. During its long sitting not only were many matters discussed – the energy crisis, commodities, trade, aid, debt remission – but economic circumstances were themselves changing. The Conference had to adapt to such changes. Elections took place, attitudes of governments changed, rates of inflation slowed, unemployment persisted. Problems appeared in new perspectives.

CIEC had some achievements. A $1 bln package of special action for the poorest countries was put together by the northern countries. There was some remission of debts of the poorest countries. Support was given, in principle, by industrial countries for a common fund for commodity-price stabilisation. Some developed countries made commitments on future levels of aid and assistance. Energy problems were discussed and an attempt was made to arrive at a formal programme of energy co-operation. Enough was done, or promised, to keep the dialogue going and prevent total breakdown, but the hard, practical achievement was small. The most grandiose item – the common fund – was only outlined; its real structure remained to be negotiated and still remains as we write.

The failures of the Conference were all too clear.[16] The developed countries had failed to bring the OPEC countries into the wider setting of long-term energy-policy co-operation. Perhaps they feared to press the issue too hard when further oil price increases were possible. OPEC on its side wished to avoid firm commitments because it wished to retain its oil bargaining power for use in the wider North–South debate. Among the developing countries

---

[16] The best lengthy analysis of the new international economic order is to be found in *The New International Economic Order: The North–South Debate*, ed. J. N. Bhagwati (Cambridge, Mass.: MIT Press, 1977).

there was reluctance to push OPEC in any direction for fear of offending a future benefactor.

One major failure was the lack of frank and constructive discussion on the huge debt accumulations of middle-income developing countries. Such debt accumulation acquired a dangerous new twist in that such countries, wishing to avoid the stringencies of IMF borrowing, turned to borrowing from commercial banks, which, assessing loans on a case-by-case basis, became heavily committed but did not impose conditions on economic policies as a functional agency would have done. The result was, and increasingly is,[17] that major defaults could have disastrous consequences for international banking and the northern countries.

Another failure was that of trade. The developed countries looked forward to a new round of multilateral trade negotiations in Geneva. With unemployment, recession and aggressive producers' lobbies there was no prospect of tariff remission for the products of the developing countries.

The best that can be said for CIEC is that in a situation of dichotomy and confrontation it at least did not break down. It kept the dialogue going. Something was done to educate the northern countries. The southern countries achieved minor gains but were not content. Surely they could not have expected that a new international order could be achieved in eighteen months. Advances of this sort are only made when political realities and economic necessities come into unique alignments. That was not the situation in Paris.

[17] At the 1978 Annual Meeting of the IMF and World Bank in Washington, Mr Robert McNamara hailed private-sector lending as useful, providing it was to 'middle-income' developing countries. The IBRD forecast that commercial bank debt of the Third World would rise from $84 bln in 1975 to $350 bln in 1985.

12

The Breakup of the Dollar-Exchange System

(i) INTRODUCTION

The international monetary crisis, associated with the seventies, began much earlier. The devaluation of sterling in 1967 is a convenient date from which to trace its derivation. Prior to that date the world monetary system operated with two key currencies, the pound and dollar – the latter the more important because of its increasing liquidity role and its link with gold. During the sixties certain basic weaknesses in the Bretton Woods system revealed themselves: the difficulty of adjusting balances of payments under a system of virtually fixed exchange rates, the problem of providing a world stock of international liquidity appropriate to fixed exchange rates and, most destabilising of all, the problem of preserving international confidence in key currencies when the economies of the key currency countries themselves were in difficulties and when large amounts of international money were free to move from centre to centre in an international capital market. These problems were countered, as we have seen,[1] by extending the world liquidity base, first by the GAB arrangements of the IMF and in 1969 by the Agreement to set up the Special Drawing Rights (SDRs) scheme for the systematic creation and issue by the IMF of a new international reserve unit.

These measures were not sufficient. The devaluation of sterling, which the British, aided by the Americans, had for years tried to prevent, had destroyed confidence not only in that currency but in the dollar as well. For four years, from November 1967 to August 1971, the U.S. currency was subject to a crisis of confidence which had to be met ultimately by measures which ended the Bretton Woods system itself and ushered in conditions in world payments which have not yet (1979) been stabilised. In this chapter we shall examine: the circumstances which led to the American decision to opt out of its key-currency role in Bretton Woods; the defence of the dollar as a deficit currency; the new conditions created by flexible exchange rates for the leading currencies after 1973; and the impact upon these new currency arrangements of strains, some exogenous like the oil crisis of 1973–4, some endogenous like the great inflation of the mid-seventies and the accompanying recession in the industrial countries.

[1] See pp. 117–20 above.

(ii) THE DEFENCE OF THE DOLLAR: THE NIXON MEASURES AND THEIR AFTERMATH

In the sixties a basic feature of the world payments system was becoming apparent, its asymmetry. Satisfying and convenient as it might be to regard this system as composed of many more or less homogeneous national units, each with its currency of which the external value was reflected in a network of equally significant exchange rates, the facts dictated differently. National units are of very different sizes and trading and monetary significance and only a small number of exchange rates are important. Even within the group of about twenty important currencies the majority are 'vehicle' currencies used for commercial purposes. A few, the 'key' currencies, stand out and claim attention. Their problems and characteristics are crucial and the leading key currency has special problems, unique to the main reserve and intervention currency. These problems dominated the period between the mid-sixties and the present.

Under the Bretton Woods system the dollar was the central currency. All IMF currencies had fixed parities in relation to it. Through its convertibility into gold (at $35 per ounce) it linked the whole IMF system to that metal and related all exchange rates to the price of gold. It was the reserve and intervention currency. In a world of n countries, as long as one currency acts as *numéraire*, only $(n-1)$ exchange rates can be independently determined, the nth is implicit in the others. $(n-1)$ countries hold the nth currency as reserve and intervene with it in foreign-exchange markets to stabilise their own exchange rates. It is the role of the nth country to remain passive, to refrain from intervention and allow the $(n-1)$ countries to control their exchange rates, either moving them within narrow limits[2] or changing them by discrete devaluations or revaluations from time to time as balance-of-payments policies require. The exchange value of the nth currency cannot change. Its role as *numéraire* makes stability essential. Thus a key-currency country is denied use of the exchange-rate weapon to influence its own balance of payments.

Supplies of a key currency to the world at large must be adequate for countries to hold reserve and intervention balances of the currency, but not so large as to create surplus balances and impair confidence in the key currency. The balance of payments of the key currency must therefore be in easy balance or slight deficit to create this optimum. To state the requirement in terms of the dollar: the American balance of payments had to be sufficiently in deficit to supply the world with dollar balances, not so much in deficit as to impair confidence in the dollar's future value or its link with gold. Moreover, in so far as the U.S. Government wished to adjust its balance of payments by changes in relative prices it could not do so by devaluing the dollar exchange

---

[2] Plus or minus 1 per cent during most of the Bretton Woods period.

rate, but had to resort either to changes in its domestic price level or induce changes in the exchange rates of other trading countries.

Devaluation of sterling in November 1967 turned suspicion upon the dollar. In the spring of 1968 the price of gold on the free London market rose to more than $40 per ounce. The establishment of the two-tier market in March did little to stem the outflow of American gold reserves, which had once seemed impregnable. In 1969 forty-six countries converted dollars to gold, in 1970 sixty countries converted $630 m. and by early 1971 the gold reserve ($17.8 bln in 1960) stood at $11.0 bln. At this rate of attrition and allowing for speculative acceleration of withdrawal there was a bare five years' supply available in 1971.

All this was but the outward manifestation of a disequilibrium in the U.S. balance of payments almost continous since 1957. Thus the so-called 'dollar problem', charted and analysed by numerous commentators,[3] was initially a dollar scarcity, caused by an American surplus from 1945 to 1955, and latterly a dollar glut caused by a growing deficit from 1959 to the present.

To analyse the determinants of the deficit from 1965 to 1975[4] would be a major statistical exercise. We must content ourselves with identifying the main strands in the pattern. Between 1964 and 1973 the annual average export surplus on goods and services was $2.8 bln,[5] but the overall balance-of-payments deficit requiring to be financed by reserves was, on average − $5.7 bln, with very large deficits of − 9.8, − 29.8, and − 10.2 bln in 1970, 71 and 72. Clearly the source of the deficit lay in capital items too large to be offset by moderate surpluses. These capital items consisted (with different weights at different times) of external government grants, overseas direct investment and U.S. military expenses abroad. In plain terms, Vietnam, American political commitments abroad and the great surge of American direct overseas investment were too large to be financed by U.S. earnings on current account. The result was deficit, decline of the gold reserve, the piling up of surplus dollar holdings abroad and, from 1968, a problem of confidence in the dollar's future.

American domestic economic policy added its influence. The true

---

[3] For a major study of the dollar shortage of the period 1945–7 see Sir Donald MacDougall, *The World Dollar Problem* (London: Macmillan, 1957), and *The Dollar Problem: a Reappraisal*, Princeton University, *Essays in International Finance*, no. 35 (Nov 1960). See also F. H. Klopstock, *The International Status of the Dollar*, Princeton University, *Essays in International Finance*, no. 28 (May 1957); C. P. Kindleberger, *Balance of Payments Deficits and the International Market for Liquidity*, Princeton University, *Essays in International Finance*, no. 46 (1965); B. Tew, *The Evolution of the International Monetary System, 1945–77* (especially chap. 9 on 'The dollar in the sixties') (London: Hutchinson, 1977). On the wider issues of international monetary reform, before and after 1971, see G. M. Meier, *Problems of a World Monetary Order* (London and New York: Oxford University Press, 1974); W. M. Scammell, *International Monetary Policy: Bretton Woods and After* (London: Macmillan, 1975), and John Williamson, *The Failure of World Monetary Reform, 1971–74* (London: Nelson, 1977).

[4] From 1973 a new element appears in the U.S. (and other countries') balance of payments – the effects of the rise in oil prices.

[5] There were trade deficits in only two years, 1971 and 1972.

weakness of the American balance of payments between 1968 and 1970 was obscured by high interest rates and contractionary policies so that some capital inflows and smaller capital outflows actually produced small liquidity-balance surpluses in 1968 and 1969. But these were replaced in late 1970 and in 1971 by higher interest rates as the Administration primed the economy for Nixon's second-term election in 1972. This resulted in massive capital outflows and the expansion allowed prices to rise sharply. The balance of payments in 1970 had an unprecedented deficit of $9.8 bln. In 1971 it was three times that.

In a world payments system every deficit has a surplus elsewhere to offset it. The offsetting surplus of the U.S. deficit was shared by West Germany, Japan and a few lesser countries. A pattern had emerged which was to dominate the seventies: on the one side the U.S. deficit, on the surplus side a hard core of West Germany and Japan. How was the burden of adjusting this disequilibrium to be shared? Each side protested the other's responsibility.

In the dispute of adjustment one powerful argument was on the American side. As the centre country of Bretton Woods, its currency tied to gold and convertible to it, the United States could not use the conventional de-valuation weapon. The alternative policies to adjust the deficit were: (*a*) revaluation of the currencies of the surplus countries, (*b*) deflation in the United States itself, (*c*) expansion of the economies of the surplus countries, or (*d*) direct suppression measures on the U.S. deficit by tariffs or controls on imports.[6] Of these options, (*a*) was the preferred one for the United States, but rejected on several grounds by the export lobbies and governments of the surplus countries; (*b*) was politically non-feasible for Nixon, going into election for his second term; (*c*) was rejected by the inflation-fearing Germans, and (*d*) contravened the tenets of trade liberalism subscribed to by Bretton Woods. The American choice was for (*a*) on economic grounds. Nixon's problem was to create political pressure to force this choice on Germany, Japan and the other surplus countries. To do so he was prepared, in the event, to sever the U.S. link with gold and to break up Bretton Woods.

In the first half of 1971 the U.S. balance of payments deteriorated sharply and Nixon decided on dramatic action to bring to heel these fractious and unco-operative Europeans and Canadians whose aims appeared so inimical to American interests. In August 1971 a package deal, the so-called Nixon Measures, was announced, the most important being three in number: the American gold price was raised, devaluing the dollar in gold terms by 8 per cent; convertibility of the dollar through the sale of gold at the U.S. Treasury was ended; and an import surcharge of 10 per cent was imposed on U.S. imports. Apart from these specifically monetary measures there was a general attack on aid disbursements to the developing countries which was, in a narrow sense, an attempt to reduce pressure on the U.S. capital deficit but, in

[6] Some controls on U.S. capital movements had already been introduced during the sixties; for example, the Interest Equalisation Tax of 1963.

a broader sense, gave recognition to the so-called 'crisis of aid' and reflected the disillusionment of aid-granting countries with development attainments. American aid was immediately reduced by 10 per cent and in October 1971 the U.S. Senate went further by rejecting the whole American foreign-aid programme. In both Third World and industrial-country relationships the Nixon Measures were a turning-point.

The measures carried a request and a threat: a request to certain countries to permit a realignment of exchange rates conducive to improvement of the U.S. deficit, and a threat of American protection and trade war if the request were ignored. As an earnest of the threat, Canada who claimed special relationship with the United States to exempt herself from the surcharge, was told that the only special thing about her position was her trade surplus with the United States. It became apparent that the changes of 1971 were not merely weather changes, but changes in climate, changes in American policies which had been constant since the war, changes in relations with the Soviet Union and China, a determination to withdraw from entanglements in South-East Asia. In Europe Britain was entering the EEC; China was joining the United Nations. The old and familiar world of the Western Alliance, the Marshall Plan and Bretton Woods was being exchanged for a nebulous world with new rules of the game in every sphere, political and economic.

The Nixon Measures achieved their immediate aim of bringing the leading powers opposite the United States at the bargaining table. In return for lifting the 10 per cent surcharge and as a result of negotiations within the Group of Ten, exchange rates were adjusted on a multilateral basis and the results embodied in the Smithsonian agreement of 18 December 1971. Revaluation of currencies ranging from 7.5 to 17 per cent relative to the dollar were achieved[7] and greater flexibility was given to the exchange system by a widening of the Bretton Woods margins to ±2.25 per cent of parity. The U.S. price of gold was raised from \$35 to \$38 per ounce[8] – a change in the international *numéraire* but little else.

Entering 1972 it seemed that a satisfactory adjustment of the world payments system had been made. Bretton Woods seemed to be still intact but a little more flexible. The United States had dealt with her deficit by a considerable depreciation of the dollar and the gold exchange standard of the 1960s had become a dollar standard with that currency as the reserve and intervention currency. Perhaps all this was a mere rolling adjustment of the system, now set for the new conditions of the seventies. It was not to be.

Throughout 1972 and to March 1973 the Smithsonian system was eroded by a series of changes which transformed world monetary relations. For this there were several reasons. The first was continuing lack of confidence in the dollar. No one believed that the Smithsonian depreciation would correct the

---

[7] West Germany 13.6, Japan 16.9, France and the United Kingdom 8.6 per cent.

[8] This had little significance in that the dollar was still inconvertible into gold, but it did raise the dollar value of that part of reserve assets of countries held in gold.

U.S. deficit. The parities established in December 1971 were the result of hard bargaining, brittle and ripe for change. Moreover, it was known that key personalities in the United States regarded them as provisional, perhaps even a prelude to a floating dollar. In these circumstances foreign central banks were loath to hold dollars. Nevertheless, the Japanese and German central banks accumulated dollars at such a rate that their banking systems were threatened with over-liquidity. At the bottom of it all was the American balance of payments which, despite the depreciation, produced large deficits in 1971 and 1972. The whole situation was classically ripe for a speculative run on the dollar which was to make the Smithsonian arrangements intolerable.

Throughout 1972 dollars accumulated at an alarming rate in the surplus countries and the dollar was supported continually by the Japanese and West German central banks. The guilder and the Belgian and Swiss francs were at the upper limit of their range and despite capital movement controls and interest-rate manipulation imbalance continued. Rumours of exchange-rate changes were rife and were intensified by the British float of 23 June and the EEC manipulations to create the 'snake in the tunnel' system. During the second part of 1972 the United States operated in the foreign-exchange market to ease downward pressure on the dollar and upward pressure on the Deutschmark. On 19 July a Federal Reserve programme of Deutschmark sales for dollars was inaugurated. American intervention in the exchange market continued into 1973 but to no avail. The Smithsonian parities were now beyond help. Announcements in early 1973 of a further increase in the U.S. trade deficit for 1972 were a final blow to confidence. Between 1 and 9 February the Bundesbank spent almost $6 bln to resist a revaluation of the Deutschmark. On 10 February 1973 the Japanese authorities ceased their support and closed the exchange market. The pound, Canadian dollar and Swiss franc were already floating well outside the Smithsonian band. On 12 February the United States announced 10 per cent devaluation of the dollar under the so-called Volcker Agreement, the first of a whirlwind series of negotiations conducted by Paul Volcker, the U.S. Under-Secretary to the Treasury.[9] The devaluation of the dollar was achieved by raising the dollar price of gold from $38 to $42.2 an ounce, leaving the gold value of other currencies unchanged. The lira and yen went to floating rates.

The Volcker Agreement was in fact a second international exercise in negotiating exchange parities,[10] but even after its completion in February 1973 there was little confidence in its durability. By then two things were apparent: first, there was a fundamental disequilibrium in world payments, with chronic weak currencies and chronic strong currencies, so that, in a

---

[9] For a good account of these and subsequent negotiations from both the personal and technical angles see G. M. Meier, *Problems of a World Monetary Order* (Oxford: 1974) pp. 183–206.
[10] The first was the pattern agreed at the Smithsonian – the result of bargaining among the Group of Ten.

world of mercurial capital movements, it was doubtful whether any set of fixed parities could be held for long; second, it was becoming apparent that a series of *ad hoc* adjustments had by 1972 destroyed the Bretton Woods system and that a complete reform of the monetary system was overdue. The first of these problems was met by the Paris Agreement of March 1973, the second and more fundamental one by the inauguration of a theoretical and academic debate.

The Paris Agreement established the international payments system much as it now is. It ended the Bretton Woods system of the adjustable peg and established floating exchange rates for the leading currencies covering 70 per cent of total world trade. When fourteen countries[11] met on 9 and 16 March, the pound, the yen, the lira and the Canadian dollar were already floating. Now the EEC countries of the snake (West Germany, France, Benelux and Denmark) agreed to a joint float against the dollar, Germany revaluing by 3 per cent *vis-à-vis* the other snake members. Sweden and Norway joined the snake; other European countries floated separately. Thus the fourteen largest countries in the world system ended the dollar standard, a nineteen-month experiment, and left the dollar itself to float. Other members of the IMF (more than 100 countries) went their own ways. Some pegged to the dollar, a few pegged on sterling, some pegged on baskets of selected currencies.[12] What had been advocated by a few academics as early as 1951 had come into being in 1973, a world of flexible exchange rates.It was no longer a dollar standard for the dollar was no longer the *n*th currency and *numéraire*, nor was the dollar so important as intervention and reserve currency but it retained its central position of wide acceptability and international unit of account, although the latter role was weakened in July 1974 by the use of the SDR (defined in relation to a basket of currencies) as statistical unit of measurement and record.

(iii) THE DEBATE ON INTERNATIONAL MONETARY REFORM

The debate on international monetary reform which began in 1971 was the most wide-ranging and fundamental which had taken place since the preparations for the Bretton Woods Conference in 1944. There was, however, an important difference. That earlier debate had contemplated a clean start, the establishment of a new monetary system in the vacuum left by the war. The debate of 1971 took place to amend a monetary system already in being and on which countries had views and vested interests. Reform, involving many countries, was much more difficult than reconstruction by two countries thinking along similar lines. Moreover, international finance, once

[11] The Group of Ten plus Switzerland, Denmark, Luxemburg and Ireland.
[12] The exchange-rate pattern at March 1973 is well summarised in the *IMF Annual Report* (1975) table 16, p. 24.

the purview of the specialist, had become hot politics, the concern of the media and a significant weapon of foreign policy.

It is convenient to discuss this debate not through a seriatim record of events, since the net achievement of committees, groups and negotiations was zero, but by identifying the issues around which the debate moved and on which agreement was essential if progress was to be made. These issues were:

(a) On what base or according to what *numéraire* were currencies to be linked;
(b) what were to be the reserve assets and the intervention currency;
(c) what forces for correction of balance of payments imbalance were to be built into the system; and
(d) what was to co-ordinate policies within the system and what sanctions would apply against recalcitrant members?

These have been the criteria for criticism of international monetary policy since economists turned their attention to the gold standard in the early years of this century. The setting was different, the jargon changed. The fundamental problems remained.

The debate opened with proposals by Mr Anthony Barber, British Chancellor of the Exchequer, to the Annual IMF meeting in September 1971, a month after the Nixon Measures. Barber advocated (a) a system in which parities would be expressed in terms of SDRs; (b) in which the SDR should be the main reserve asset; (c) international liquidity would consist of SDRs so that further IMF creations of the unit would determine the volume of international liquidity; and (d) multicurrency intervention would support parities, weak currencies being bought by strong currencies, residual balances being kept by a clearing union and settled periodically in SDRs.

The Barber Plan served to focus attention on main issues but received little support. The United States supported what it called a 'Grand Design' but was notably vague on key issues; the IMF appointed a committee which reported in August 1972[13] and held close to the American line and to earlier Fund views on the exchange-rate system. The most important executive action by the IMF Board was to set up a Committee of Twenty (under Jeremy Morse of the Bank of England) to examine the whole question of reform. Supplied for its guidance with a memorandum from the U.S. Government it fell to work in November 1972.[14] Described in Morse's own words its objectives were ambitious. Its task was 'to build, as at Bretton Woods, a complete design for

[13] *Reforming the International Monetary System: A Report by the Executive Directors to the Board of Governors* (Washington, D.C.: IMF, Aug 1972).

[14] Changes at the U.S. Treasury in 1972 accounted for growing interest (but not commitment) to general reform. Shultz, the new Secretary, was of broader view and discernment than either Connally or Volcker, staunch adherents of bargaining, horse-trading and *ad hoccery*.

an international monetary system that would last for twenty-five years'.[15]

During 1971 and 1972 the broad issues of reform were discussed widely and in the Morse Committee. The Barber Plan, involving as it did a recognition of the SDR as the international reserve asset, provided a convenient agenda, although one controversial issue, the question of how flexible exchange rates should be, had been avoided by it but became a focus of controversy in 1973. One issue which received early attention was that of settling the *numéraire*; that is, in what terms should currency values be defined – a key currency, gold or some independent accounting unit such as the SDR?[16] There was anxiety here to avoid using a currency as an international unit, thus creating adjustment problems for the country of that currency. Gold, as a unit, had little support, except in France, and the weight of opinion favoured its eventual demonetisation. The SDR, already in being and under Fund control, seemed to be the acceptable choice.

Two other immediate problems are worthy of note. The first was the old question of which country (or group), the surplus or the deficit country, was to bear the burden of adjustment and what sanctions could be brought to bear upon countries to adjust. This question, recognised by the founding fathers of Bretton Woods and thought to have been solved by the Scarce Currency Clause[17] had recurred throughout the postwar period. It had been a quarrel between the surplus West Germany and the other deficit Europeans in OEEC throughout the fifties and sixties, it had precipitated the Nixon Measures, it is central to the dollar problem now, as we write, in 1979. In the Morse Committee the U.S.A – as a deficit country anxious to throw some responsibility on surplus countries such as Germany and Japan to expand their economies and reduce their surpluses – advocated that statistical indicators[18] should be kept and sanctions such as fines or charges, applied, progressively against surplus countries.

A second pressing problem, the solution of which was a precondition of reform, was that of the 'dollar overhang'. During the long period of U.S. deficit large dollar balances had accumulated in the central banks of surplus countries. What arrangements could be made to substitute SDRs for these balances if the SDR were to be made the reserve unit? Should such substitution be compulsory or optional? What effect might such substitution have upon the general acceptability of the SDR? These were tough questions and were debated at length both within the Morse Committee and elsewhere.[19]

---

[15] See *Finance and Development* (Washington, D.C.: IMF, Sep 1974).

[16] Later, in July 1974, the SDR was established as such an accounting unit, it being defined in terms of the values of stated quantities of a collection of sixteen national currencies.

[17] Articles of Agreement of the IMF, 22 July 1944, Article 7.

[18] Based on reserve levels.

[19] The same problem existed, but in lesser magnitude, with the sterling balances, held by many countries which were, or had been, members of the sterling area.

This was the high summer of approval for SDRs. It was widely agreed that the new reserve unit was to replace the key currencies and that further periodic issues of the unit, similar to those of 1970 and 1971, would be made by the IMF. By these the world stock of international liquidity would be augmented while the conversion of currency 'overhangs' would establish the homogeneity of the stock in terms of one unit controlled by the Fund.

Such were the problems facing the Committee of Twenty.[20] Its failure to resolve them was due to two sets of forces: failure to reach a consensus on the issues and the growing realisation that national differences were non-negotiable; and the impact of events which subjected the international monetary system to new strains – in particular the exchange crisis of February/March 1973 and the huge rise in oil prices and world inflation of 1974. By January 1974 the Committee, realising that a new situation had been created, willy-nilly, by events, resolved to shelve the intractable problems of reform and turn to immediate problems. In doing so they merely recognised a change in the climate of opinion. The switch to floating exchange rates was clearly regarded by many, including the monetary authorities of the United States and Britain, as likely to be prolonged. In the whirling tides created by the oil crisis, maintenance of any fixed set of exchange parities seemed impossible. Moreover, a solution to the 'overhang' problem by the substitution of SDRs for currencies was not acceptable. The conception of the 'Grand Design' with which the Committee of Twenty had ambitiously set out in 1972 was formally abandoned in June 1974 in favour of 'Immediate Steps',[21] directed at the short-term situation. These short-term proposals were in themselves important. They were:

(i) To establish an Interim Committee at Ministerial level as a new IMF working group. This was set up in October 1974 and superseded the former, much narrower, Group of Ten.[22]

(ii) To value the SDR in terms of the average value of a collection of sixteen national currencies. This was done in July 1974.

(iii) To study the Fund arrangements for gold. This led to steps towards the demonetisation of that metal after a meeting in Jamaica in January 1976.

[20] For business purposes the Committee of Twenty consisted of: one member and two associates for each of the twenty countries choosing an Executive Director of the IMF; a Committee of Deputies to identify proposals for approval; an inner group (with Morse as chairman) to act as secretariat and steering committee. The task of reform was expected to take two years, the first year to identify and resolve main issues, the second to negotiate, codify and embody solutions in legal form.

[21] These were set out in Part II of the Committee's *Outline of Reform* of 14 July 1974. See *International Monetary Reform: Documents of the Committee of Twenty* (Washington, IMF, 1974).

[22] Students of the techniques of international negotiation will be interested in the emergence, as from the IMF Annual Meeting of September 1973, of a new international planning group, the Group of Five (G5), consisting of the finance ministers of the leading countries, United States, Japan, France, Germany and the United Kingdom. This came to be a very important group, meeting at IMF meetings or at any larger forum in which the ministers were in attendance.

(iv) To adapt the Fund Agreement to a world of floating rates, and.

(v) To examine the position of the developing countries in the new conditions created by the oil crisis, inflation and the shift to floating exchange rates.

The fourth and fifth tasks were the most difficult and controversial. They have been the subject of IMF studies and meetings of the Interim Committee. Some progress has been made. Much remains to be done.

(iv) A WORLD OF FLOATING EXCHANGE RATES

Between 1970 and 1973 the leading currencies abandoned the IMF system of the adjustable peg and allowed the exchange rates of their currencies to float at market rates or at rates in the market influenced by the intervention of their national exchange funds. Canada led the way in June 1970, sterling abandoned a fixed parity in June 1972, the Japanese yen and Italian lira went free in February 1973, and the U.S. dollar and the leading West European currencies floated in March 1973. In June 1974 the IMF issued guidelines for the management of floating exchange rates and in January 1976 the Interim Committee recommended that the Fund articles be amended to take account of the new conditions. Thus in three years the main prop of the Bretton Woods system was kicked away, adjustment of balances of payments was thrown on the exchange rate and the international liquidity problem was transformed.

The mass movement to floating rates was only partially the result of intellectual conviction. Canada had long been an exponent of floating rates,[23] but the other countries floated largely because it was the residual policy choice. Other exchange patterns (the gold standard, the adjustable peg) had been tried and found wanting. The remaining alternative of free rates, carrying a rather unsavoury, confused and ill-interpreted record from the later thirties, remained. Bankers, most politicians, business and the financial establishment were sceptical, but a large body of reputable academic opinion had long advocated flexible exchange rates and now served to rationalise their adoption.[24]

As between the leading economies, attitudes towards floating rates varied considerably. The United States, long a sceptic, was won over by the first two years' experience of a floating dollar. The instabilities and uncertainties

[23] Canada, for trade and other reasons, likes to regulate her trade with the United States (her leading market) through the exchange rate. Thus destabilising changes in macro policy to tune her economy to fluctuations in the U.S. economy are avoided. Canada was on a floating rate from 1950 to 1962.

[24] A good and fairly complete list of academic economists favouring floating exchange rates is given in F. Machlup, *International Payments, Debts and Gold* (New York: Scribner's, 1964) p. 357. From 1964 on, support for floating rates grew in academic circles and by 1970 there were few economists of high standing who still supported the adjustable-peg system. Perhaps the greatest single book on the controversy is E. Sohmen's *Flexible Exchange Rates*, rev. ed. (Chicago: Chicago University Press, 1969).

anticipated by the American financial establishment did not arise. International liquidity was initially increased. The exchange market was orderly and the crisis brought on by the rise in oil prices in late 1973 and in 1974 proved less disastrous than had first appeared, especially since the dollar overhang was virtually eliminated by the high demand for dollars to settle oil deficits. But behind all this was the beneficent influence of an improving balance of payments, which swung from an average quarterly deficit on goods and services in 1972 of $-$\$1482.75 m. to an average quarterly surplus 1973–5 of \$2401.83 m.[25] This improvement was, in great part, the result of the continuous depreciation of the dollar which had taken place since 1970. By mid-1973 the dollar stood 19 per cent below its external value in mid-1970.[26]

The U.K. abandonment of a fixed parity on 23 June 1972 marked the end of a twenty-five-year struggle to hold stable the exchange rate for sterling. Although devalued only twice during this period the policies pursued to support a fixed exchange rate, in particular the 'stop–go' policy of the fifties and sixties and the recognition of the primacy of payments, had left their marks on the British economy, the slow rate of growth and poor performance of which have persisted in the whole postwar period. One may view the decision of June 1972 as a fresh start, one of those disconcerting, swift and belated changes of policy to which the British are subject. Assuming, as must have been the case, that the decision implied a formal ending of the responsibilities of a key-currency country it was a blessed relief and an opportunity. Economic aims and policies could be reassessed particularly in the light of pending structural changes in the U.K. balance of payments due to her dwindling oil imports.

If ever there was a time for a new start for Britain it was June 1972. Instead, after a promising start in early 1973, sterling declined *vis-à-vis* its trading partners by 19 per cent between December 1972 and December 1975. In part this was due to the higher rate of inflation in Britain in 1974–5 and in part to high public sector expenditures and a decision to 'go for growth', ignoring the balance-of-payments constraint. In fact the depreciation of sterling would probably have been greater but for heavy official British intervention in the forward market which served somewhat to lull foreign expectations as to sterling's future. In mid-1975 a series of new depreciations of sterling took place, triggered off by foreign reaction to British failure to control the trade unions and their rampant demands for wage increases. Between December 1975 and April 1976 the weighted average depreciation of the pound was 8.5 per cent – much greater than would have been appropriate to the relative rise in the British price-level.

In Western Europe exchange rates in the post-1971 period were dominated by the arrangements known as the 'snake in the tunnel'. The

[25] See *Survey of Current Business* (various dates).

[26] Measured relative to a collection of fifteen major currencies. See *World Financial Markets* (New York: Morgan Guaranty Trust Co., Aug 1976) pp. 6 and 7.

countries of the EEC were moving quickly in the early seventies in pursuit of monetary union. Such a condition postulated ultimately a single currency and, in preparation for this, fixed relations between national monetary units and harmonisation of domestic monetary and fiscal policies.

When the Smithsonian Agreement (December 1971) enlarged the band within which Bretton Woods currencies might fluctuate from ± 1 per cent to ± 2.25 per cent this increased flexibility was not to the liking of EEC planners. Under the new arrangement an EEC currency moving from floor to ceiling (or vice versa) would fluctuate 4.5 per cent relative to the dollar but, for two European currencies changing from floor to ceiling and ceiling to floor, the fluctuation would be 9 per cent, a degree of fluctuation which did not accord with the process proposed in the Werner Report of October 1970. Under Werner recommendations EEC central banks should, from January 1971, have restricted the relative movements of their parities to a band narrower than the band of their fluctuations *vis-à-vis* the dollar. Thus Community countries would have the benefit of a constrained floating rate as between their currencies and a floating rate as between Community currencies and the rest of the world. This arrangement sounded plausible but, in practice, all depended on the coefficients which determined the model, namely the width of the band and the degree of intervention required (*a*) to keep currencies within the band in reasonable alignment and (*b*) to align the band itself in satisfactory relation to non-member currencies and in particular to the dollar. The process of intervention and the aim to eliminate inter-EEC margins are too complex to examine here[27] but what has in effect persisted in the arrangement was the very thing which the system was supposed to suppress: the strong currency, the Deutschmark, stayed strong and the weak currencies remained weak. The 'snake in the tunnel' arrangement sought to impose exchange-rate order within the Community. The fact was that, in default of very large intervention in the exchange markets, only harmonisation of national growth, employment and price policies could eliminate the need for intra-Community exchange margins. Not until June 1978, at a meeting of the leading European finance ministers in Bremen, was new meaning given to the snake arrangements by a renewal of the EEC drive for monetary union.

The snake in the tunnel has been only loosely organised. Different West European countries have been members from time to time. When a new European Monetary Co-operation Fund was set up in April 1973 with $1.8 bln of EEC monetary support and with the purpose of intervening to stabilise exchange markets within the Community, five members (France, West Germany, Belgium, Holland and Denmark) were in the joint-European float. Since then countries have come and gone, the greatest consistencies being the membership of West Germany and the absence of the United Kingdom.

[27] See B. Tew, *The Evolution of the International Monetary System, 1945–77*. (London: Hutchinson, 1977) pp. 175–7.

We have had only five years' experience of floating exchange rates. They have been years of crisis and swift change. Nevertheless it is appropriate to take stock, however prematurely.

One striking feature of the floating exchange-rate system has been the patterns of strengths and weaknesses of currencies which have emerged. Most consistent has been the Deutschmark, strongest currency of the West reflecting a record of balance-of-payments surplus going back to 1951. In contrast the U.S. dollar, weak throughout the sixties and source of the crisis which broke up Bretton Woods, improved in the period 1973–5 but relapsed from 1975 to the present. Chronic weakness of the dollar and persistent strength of the Deutschmark and yen has been the recurrent problem of the monetary system of the seventies. Depreciation of the dollar and appreciation of the surplus currencies has done nothing as yet to adjust the fundamental disequilibrium.

One question, long asked by critics of floating exchange rates, troubled the practical working of the system: what would be the degree of official intervention in the market for a currency? Conventional wisdom had always interpreted 'floating' exchange rates as allowing at least such intervention as to iron out short-term fluctuations and provide an orderly market. The question remained, however, as to how such a general directive might be interpreted. Three views seem to be reflected in the behaviour of the major countries. Britain, with the longest experience in managed floating, took an essentially *ad hoc* view. The Exchange Equalisation Account often supported the pound for long periods, as it did in 1973 and 1974, but allowed depreciation to take place, either when support intervention would have been too costly (as in 1975) or when general economic policy seemed to require a lower value for sterling as in 1976. This practice of making the rate conform to the wider conditions and aims of macro policy, of minimising the exchange-rate constraint, was appealing but it would have required much larger reserves than the Bank of England had at its command.

The United States favoured only light intervention in the market and indeed left the rate between the dollar and the snake countries entirely free for months in the spring and early summer of 1973. Thereafter (from July 1973 to early 1975) only light smoothing intervention was used and the term 'benign neglect' was coined to describe the American policy.[28] In November 1975, in the so-called Rambouillet Agreement, six leading countries agreed to work jointly for greater stability in economic and monetary conditions which was interpreted by some participants as binding the United States to deal with her

---

[28] This policy had critics in the United States. Alfred Hayes of the Federal Reserve Bank of New York (see *Emerging Arrangements in International Payments*, 12th Per Jacobsson Foundation Lecture, 31 Aug 1975) argued that in a free market the dollar-exchange rate oscillated too violently on either side of equilibria levels. This was due to lack of confidence and knowledge in default of an official directive, large speculative capital movements and thin markets in which professional operators avoided taking positions.

fluctuating exchange rate. But the Americans still insisted that there should be no return to controlled exchange rates and that exchange market intervention should be minimal. The United States, once the great opponent of free exchange rates, had executed a complete *volte face*.

The European countries of the snake were the leading exponents of market intervention of which the snake itself was an expression. They argued that the U.S. currency was still a key currency and its holders had the right to expect that the United States would support its value. As things were, it was on the European central banks that the heaviest burden of dollar support fell and they were entitled to protection of the world value of their dollar balances. The United States was unmoved. Even in the heavy decline of the dollar in late 1977 and 1978 they allowed the rate to sink, despite continuing European protests, to which were added those of the OPEC countries seeing their oil-earned dollar balances eroded not only by inflation but by a decline in the dollar's value in terms of other currencies.

The argument of forceful versus minimal management of exchange rates was at bottom a continuation of the old argument of fixed versus free rates. The advocates of forceful intervention believed that by holding rates stable for periods of time the uncertainties of a free system could be avoided. Experience seems to have shown, however, that strong and persistent intervention poses technical problems which are hard to solve. How to distinguish between short-term changes, cyclical fluctuations and the beginning of longer-term trends has been a baffling diagnosis which has sometimes driven the United Kingdom, Japan, Italy and France close to a resumption of pegged exchange rates. Whether to defend particular levels of a flexible currency rate or to allow it to move freely and often wildly in pursuit of equilibrium is but a new variant of an old problem.

One feature which has emerged progressively during the period of floating rates has been greatly increased speculative pressure bearing on a rate which the authorities wish to maintain. The pound in 1976, the lira in the same year, the Canadian dollar in 1978 and the U.S. dollar in the same period have all been demonstrations of the impossibility of the monetary authority to hold an exchange rate which the international financial community suspects cannot be held. In the face of this evidence the lightly managed versus the tightly managed currency argument becomes academic. So too does any question of returning in the near future to a régime of fixed rates.

(v) THE OIL CRISIS

So far in this chapter we have been concerned with international monetary problems and policies but beyond passing references we have not examined the great changes in the international economic environment which were a feature of the years from 1973. The great inflation, the oil crisis and the world recession which followed produced a more complex economic environment than any since the war.

The year 1971 marked the first break in the long growth-trend of the industrial economies. In six[29] of the seven leading OECD countries there was slight recession in 1971–2. The real GNP of OECD countries which had 5.4 per cent growth rate per annum from 1959/60 to 1971/2, dipped to 3.8 per cent in 1971. With the Smithsonian Agreement in December of that year and despite dollar difficulties in early 1972 forces making for expansion were still strong. There was a marked upturn in 1972 and expansion in 1973, the real growth rates of OECD countries rising to 5.7 and 6.3 per cent respectively. One reason for this sharp recovery was the conjuncture of expansionary forces in all the main industrial countries with considerable spin-off effects for world trade. Moreover, countries were anxious for expansion and allowed the general rise in world liquidity, reflected in their reserves to pass on to the domestic money supply. Weighted averages of national money growth rates in terms of domestic currency rose sharply in 1971–2. Combined with this was a pattern of expansionary monetary and fiscal policies by most countries in 1972. Once an expansionary movement was under way the easy international reserve position enabled countries to take a tolerant attitude if balances of payments went into deficit. To sum up, there was in 1972–3 a unique concomitance of expansionary forces at work. The result was the sharpest increase in economic growth of the postwar period.

A boom such as that of 1973 might have been expected to generate a significant rate of inflation and such was the case – consumer prices in the OECD countries rising, on average, by 7.9 per cent from 1972 to 1973 as compared with an average increase of 3.9 per cent in the 1962–72 decade. This was the expected concomitant of industrial expansion, but the most significant influence was the rise in primary-commodity prices which had begun in 1972. Tables 12.1 and 12.2 show the pattern of this increase. Whatever indicators are used to describe the primary-commodity inflation the features are clear. There was from 1971 a wave of price increases, slightly differently phased for different commodity groups, but all peaking and subsiding in 1974, when the influence of the oil-price inflation was at its height. Since the effect of primary-commodity prices on finished goods is lagged the rise in oil prices, which was more immediate in effect, came just in time to coincide and reinforce the price influence from other commodities. Thus the inflation of 1974 was the combined effect of these factors: domestic pressure on prices from expansionary monetary and fiscal policies in the industrial countries; rises in primary-commodity prices (other than oil) of almost 8 per cent; and the effect of the oil embargo and oil-price rise in the last weeks of 1973. Any one of these influences would have been sufficient to

[29] United States, Germany, United Kingdom, Italy, Japan and Canada.

TABLE 12.1

Spot Price Index of World Commodities (excluding fuels)

(1970 = 100)

	1971	1972	1973	1974	1973–4 low	high
All items	92	111	164	208	135	217
Food	97	121	173	239	146	281
Industrial materials	86	97	153	168	122	204
Fibres	99	135	236	214	205	278
Metals	80	78	113	145	81	195

Source: OECD, *Economic Outlook* (various issues).

TABLE 12.2

Consumer Prices 1972–7

(1970 = 100)

	1972	1973	1974	1975	1976	1977 (May)
Canada	108	116	129	143	153	164
United States	108	114	128	139	147	155
Japan	111	124	154	172	188	203[1]
Australia	112	123	142	163	185	201[2]
New Zealand	118	128	142	163	190	204[2]
Austria	111	120	131	142	153	160
Belgium	110	118	133	150	163	174
Denmark	113	123	142	156	170	186
France	112	120	136	152	167	181
Germany	111	119	127	135	141	147
Greece	108	124	158	179	203	226
Ireland	118	132	155	186	220	241[2]
Italy	111	123	146	171	200	231[1]
Netherlands	116	125	137	151	165	176
Norway	114	122	131	150	163	177
Sweden	114	121	134	147	162	177
Switzerland	114	124	136	145	147	148
United Kingdom	117	128	148	184	215	249
OECD (total)	n.a.	119	135	150	163	175[1]
OECD (Europe)	n.a.	123	140	160	178	198
EEC	n.a.	n.a.	n.a.	157	175	194

[1] April 1977.
[2] February 1977.

Source: OECD, *Main Economic Indicators* (various issues).

generate a strong fillip to world inflation. Together they produced the greatest and most widespread inflation of modern times.

The commodity-price inflation was a phenomenon in itself demonstrating to the industrial countries that sudden turns in their terms of trade were still a factor to be reckoned with. On the supply side of the market poor harvests in a number of countries reduced supplies while output from primary-product processing industries was curtailed in the early seventies by the inhibiting effect of price controls on capacity. On the demand side sharp increases in consumer incomes had their effect on final demand while the general industrial expansion generated a rise in demand for industrial materials. As excess demand caused primary-product prices to rise the inevitable specu- lative element entered the market. Stocks were held against further price increases and the quickening rate of price inflation led to switches from monetary forms of asset to claims on real assets such as primary-commodity futures. This served to prolong the commodities boom, particularly after the upward revision of inflationary expectations in late 1973. Nevertheless, by 1975 the prices of all commodities were past their peak.

In October 1973 the Israeli victory in the war with the Arab states brought an embargo by the Arab oil states on supplies of crude oil to industrial countries. This brought swift restriction in oil-based energy supply and great increase in its cost. The embargo was soon replaced by cartelised supply arrangements for oil under the Organisation of Petroleum Exporting Countries (OPEC) and by December 1973 the price of crude oil was about 150 per cent above that of October. Eventually by early 1974 the American price of imported crude had risen from $3 to $10 a barrel in one year. Thus the independently generated rise in oil prices was congruent with the peak of the primary-commodity inflation.

The international economic conditions created by these events are best dealt with not by a consecutive narrative but by distinguishing the main economic problems involved and looking briefly at how they were handled. Two such problems can be distinguished: the inflation problem manifesting itself in the sharpest, greatest and most widespread price increase of the century, and the recession which this generated; and the adjustment problem for balances of payments transformed by the oil crisis. These problems we consider in turn.

In a world in which prices were already, in 1973, rising at approximately 8 per cent the impact of the oil-price inflation was catastrophic. Table 12.2 shows the course of consumer prices in the leading countries. The pattern was uniform, although dimensions varied. 1974–5 was the peak year in which all countries experienced unprecedented inflation rates, compounded of, at first, buoyant demand, rising food, raw material and energy prices and in- flationary expectations. As soon as the inflation gathered way changes occurred in the pattern of final demand and the rate of growth of demand declined. Falling real disposable incomes, automatic tax increases on nominal incomes and a sharp check to private investment as prime costs rose and demand declined all served as brakes on the industrial economies. As early as the end of 1973 inventories were rising and in the first half of 1974 industrial recession was under way. In the United States there was a 13 per cent drop in output spread over seven consecutive quarters; for the OECD countries over a similar period 11 per cent. For the first time since the Second World War unemployment rose above the acceptable full-employment datum of 3 per cent. In 1975 the United States registered an unemployment rate of 9 per cent, more than double the 1962–73 average. In all the major countries high and persistent unemployment and industrial recession was the accompaniment of the price inflation. Although slow and fitful recovery began in 1975 and the rate of price increase declined, the coupling of recession and price inflation persisted.

It is impossible here to analyse the policy reactions of individual countries to these events.[30] The great dilemma was how to deal with sagging output and employment without intensifying inflation. To the extent that countries met this dilemma differently, much of the difference in rates of recovery is attributable. The trouble was that the normal macro-economic precepts explained the breakdown but they could not solve it. Directly the rise in oil and energy prices took place there was a great diversion in the income flow to purchase the same quantity of energy. This diversion drew down the demand for other categories of output with the inevitable contractionary result. It was impossible in the short term and hazardous in the longer term to increase government outlay by fiscal policy to compensate. Moreover, with money markets disturbed and interest rates soaring it was difficult to meet government borrowing requirements without increasing money supply. Every government had before it the nightmare of turning the already high inflation-rate into that of a hyper-inflation.

The second problem created by the oil crisis was in the field of international payments: how to deal with the enormous deficits of the oil-importing countries and surpluses of the exporting countries. In 1974 the OPEC export surplus was $55 bln: in 1975 it was $32 bln. The import deficits of the oil importers of course corresponded. Exchange rates could do little to adjust such a deficit. No exchange rate existed between the OPEC countries' currencies and the U.S. dollar, the accounting unit of the international oil market. Moreover, even if such an exchange rate had existed its depreciation would have been ineffectual to adjust the deficit. The demand elasticities of the oil-importing countries for oil and of the OPEC countries for manufactured imports are both likely to be very low, and relative price changes would do little to adjust such a deficit. Exchange rates had some influence on the distribution of the total oil deficit among the various deficit countries, but this may be ignored in this discussion.

Reaction to the balance-of-payments problem was prompt. In January

---

[30] A good brief summary of the policy reactions of the leading countries is Stanley Black's *Floating Exchange Rates and National Economic Policy* (New Haven, Conn.: and London: Yale University Press, 1977).

1974 guidelines were issued by the IMF[31] which recommended that deficit countries should not (a) attempt to adjust the deficits in their current accounts by deflation or other normal adjustment methods, but should (b) finance the deficits by external borrowing preferably from the OPEC countries. This directive reflected a purposive decision not to allow the deficits to increase domestic deflation and to avoid paying the higher oil costs by transfers of official reserves to OPEC which would result in maldistribution of international liquidity.[32] The decision to finance the oil deficit by borrowing from the OPEC countries was possible because these countries were accumulating U.S. dollars which, in default of capital markets in the oil-producing countries, could only be invested in the oil-importing countries.

Table 12.3 shows how capital offsets to the OPEC current account surpluses of 1974 and 1975 were distributed. 42 per cent of the surplus (in

TABLE 12.3

The OPEC Surplus (1974 and 1975) and How it Was Financed
($ bln)

	1974	1975
Financial surplus[1]	55.0	31.7
Investments in the United States (dominantly bank deposits and Treasury bills)	12.0	10.0
Investments in the United Kingdom	7.2	0.2
Eurocurrency bank deposits plus domestic currency deposits in countries other than United States and United Kingdom	22.7	9.1
International organisations	4.0	2.9
Grants and loans to developing countries	2.5	4.0
Direct loans to developed countries (other than United States and United Kingdom)	4.5	2.0
Other net capital flows	2.1	3.5
	−55.0	−31.7

[1] The financial surplus for 1974 was revised downward. It was originally estimated at $65 bln.

Source: Summarised from *World Financial Markets* (New York: Morgan Guaranty Trust Co., Sep 1976).

1974) went into the Euro-currency markets, 35 per cent were invested in liquid assets in the United States and United Kingdom. 12 per cent were met by IMF and World Bank loans and other miscellaneous capital flows accounted for the remainder. Much of the funds lent by OPEC to the Euromarket and to the United States were re-lent. For example, the United Kingdom, Italy and France met a total current deficit of $23 bln by official private borrowing in the Eurocurrency market and the international bond market and actually increased their official reserves over 1974. It should be remembered that, like a private banking system, Eurocurrency bankers can

[31] See IMF, *Annual Report of IMF for 1974* (Washington, D.C.: IMF, 1975).
[32] Despite this the OPEC countries did accumulate very large reserves.

create Eurocurrencies on an increased deposit base. What happened in 1974 and after was that Eurocurrency creation took place on the basis of Eurodollars held by OPEC and that these new deposits were then acquired by oil importers, to meet their deficit or to hold as reserves.

Apart from the capital financing of the 1974 deficit by the means described forces were expected to reduce the OPEC surplus in subsequent years. One such force was the increase in imports of the OPEC countries generated by the rise in incomes in those countries. The oil-importing countries might be expected to reduce their demands for oil in the long run by shifting to other forms of fuel and energy and by curbing what had, at lower prices, been a profligate demand for oil. There were hopes, too, that the OPEC countries might be induced to spend some part of their surplus in the form of aid to the poorest countries of the Third World. Nevertheless, in spite of these influences, the OPEC surplus was regarded as a feature of world payments which at best might extend over a period of a decade and at worst might be intensified by further rises in the oil price or by some new twist of fortune in power politics.

Look more closely at the basic forces involved in adjustment of the OPEC surplus. In essence, of course, adjustment was inevitable. Given that OPEC was paid in dollars for its oil it could only divide the proceeds between spending on imports and saving, investing the savings in foreign money markets. Thus the OPEC surplus on current account was certain to be offset by its lending on capital account. Given that this condition was fulfilled, two other conditions were necessary: first, the surplus had to be lent among the deficit countries in a distribution appropriate to the size of their deficits, and second, switches of assets between deficit countries had to be such as could be handled smoothly by financial institutions and markets. These two latter conditions came to be known as the 'recycling' problem and the 'switching' problem.

For recycling to work optimally each deficit country required loans on capital account of dollars equal to the oil deficit it was incurring. From the OPEC point of view this was not their concern. Two main capital markets existed for the investment of their surplus dollars, the British and American, and in these in 1974 35 per cent of their dollars were invested. Changes in this amount and its distribution might be expected at any time in accordance with changing OPEC expectations. For distributing dollars among the deficit countries in proportion to their deficits either such countries had to earn dollars by surpluses with non-OPEC countries or they had to borrow dollars from the supply available at large in OEDC capital markets. Both these things happened. Swings in balances of payments among oil-deficit countries did serve to redistribute dollars and in these swings changes in exchange rates, under the now floating market, may have played some role.[33] But the main

---

[33] It is impossible to quantify the categories involved here. For example, there is no way of knowing what part of an exchange-rate change might be attributable to an oil deficit and what part to changes in relative inflation rates with other countries.

recycling took place through relending. In 1974 and 1975 $32 bln was lent by the oil countries as deposits in Eurocurrencies. This formed a base for new lending of Eurocurrencies to non-OPEC countries. It is certain that a large part of this went to oil-deficit countries, either in the developed or developing world. Finally there was some planned recycling through the IMF and the World Bank.

The striking aspect of the recycling process was the role played by the private institutions of the capital market. In part this was due to the greatly increased scale and scope of the international capital market, in particular the Eurocurrency market, of which the capacity was tested for the first time. But it was also due to the changing preferences of national monetary authorities. Whereas, in times past, a deficit not coverable by reserves was met by an appeal to the IMF for stand-by credit or currency exchange, this was now short-circuited by borrowing in the private market abroad. Although such loans had a higher interest cost they freed the monetary authority from the policy constraints which the IMF was likely to impose as a condition of such facilities and left the IMF and public-sector arrangements either for developing countries or to act as lender-of-last-resort in the event of strain on the private institutions. Strain did appear in 1975. Credit ratings on some countries were revised and some banks became alarmed at the sheer size of their balance-sheets. The weaker brethren, the United Kingdom and Italy, had recourse in 1976 to the IMF and the United Kingdom in 1977 borrowed $3 bln from a consortium of eleven countries. Canada, on the other hand, was able to underpin a sagging Canadian dollar in 1977 and early 1978 by loans from banks and by bond issues raised on the New York market.

The 'switching' problem raised by the oil deficit did not in the event raise anxiety. It was initially thought that large amounts of oil-surplus money deposited in London[34] might be switched without warning to other financial centres and that the size and uneasiness of international capital movements would become unmanageable. Such did not prove to be the case. Certainly, as has already been argued, the volume and mobility of international capital is now immense, but there has, thus far, been no major crisis attributable to the switching problem in itself.

We close this section by drawing attention to an important monetary feature of the years 1970–5, the great increase in international liquidity which took place during that period. Table 12.4 shows that, with the exception of gold, all categories of international reserves rose throughout the period. For this the prime reason was that, throughout the whole period of dollar crisis and the breakup of Bretton Woods, the dollar deficit had resulted in the pile-

---

[34] In 1974 there was Arab fear that oil money invested in the United States might be seized by the U.S. Government as a bargaining counter to prevent further rises in the price of oil. London, although at that time not attractive financially, seemed more reliable. As time passed (and particularly once Kissinger was replaced as Secretary of State) confidence in U.S. financial probity increased.

TABLE 12.4

Changes in Official Reserves, 1968, 1970–4

(billions of SDRs)

	1968	1970	1971	1972	1973	1974
Gold	38.9	37.2	36.1	35.8	35.8	35.7
SDRs	–	3.1	5.9	8.7	8.8	8.9
IMF position	6.5	7.7	6.4	6.3	6.2	8.9
Foreign exchange	32.0	44.5	73.9	94.9	100.7	124.7
Total	77.4	92.5	122.2	145.6	151.4	178.2
Change in total, of which			29.7	23.5	5.8	26.7
Claim on United States			27.4	10.0	4.6	8.2
Eurodollars			0.8	7.5	4.9	12.5
Other Eurocurrencies			0.7	2.0	1.6	0.2
Other			0.8	4.0	– 5.3	5.8

Source: IMF, *Annual Report of IMF for 1975* (Washington, D.C.: IMF, 1976).

up of dollar balances outside the United States. These had accrued to central banks attempting to stabilise their currencies in relation to the dollar and to banks abroad in the form of Eurodollars. If to this pile-up of the main reserve currency we add the creations on a reserve base of further Eurodollars, the IMF lending and SDRs, a threefold growth of official reserves took place between 1970 and 1974. Moreover, this was only official reserves. In addition a great augmentation of liquidity in the form of private-sector borrowing was available. The rise in international liquidity, official and second-line, was unprecedented. At the same time it should be remembered that while international liquidity increased, almost the whole of the increase went to the OPEC countries. Indeed, if one takes account of the large increase in prices in 1974, the real reserves of the non-OPEC countries declined. It is in these circumstances remarkable that, in 1974, the greatest year of balance-of-payments disequilibrium since the war, the world obtained the reserves it required. That it did so is due to the recycling process described above, the flexibility of the world-capital market, the removal by the United States in 1974 of controls on capital outflow and the considerable faith in the dollar as a currency despite its long decline since the mid-sixties. The swift manufacture of the necessary liquidity to meet the oil crisis enabled the non-OPEC countries to survive that crisis with only slight effect on their real living standards. The creation of 'second-line' liquidity in large amount prevented the alternative means of meeting balance-of-payments disequilibria – the reduction of real income in the deficit countries.

13

Imbalance among the
Leading Currencies

'In the imperceptible but eternal march of the world,
we regard events as motionless in a moment of vision,
too short for us to perceive the motion that is sweeping
them on.'   PROUST, *Remembrance of Things Past*.

(i) THE NEW ECONOMIC CLIMATE

By the end of 1975 the first oil crisis was over. It seemed that shortage and the
price of oil was not to bring capitalism to its knees. OPEC, after its initial
successes, was following the behaviour pattern of any other cartel. The
ambitions of other primary producers to cartelise their products to the
detriment of the industrial countries were seen to be vain. Inflation, although
still high, was declining and a slow, fitful recovery from the recession was
under way. Doomsday, although still to be thought of, had perhaps been
postponed. But there was to be no early return to the heady days of growth
and rising real income. A harsher, squally, less predictable climate set in.
There was to be, it seemed, a period of uncomfortable adaptation.

What are the characteristics of this climate? First, there has been in the
seventies a clearly marked check to the pace of economic growth, particularly
in the industrial countries. Manufacturing production in those countries
between 1973 and 1977 grew at only a fifth of the rate which had obtained in
the years 1955–73. In the developing countries, however, there was only slight
decline in the rate of advance. It is now apparent that this relative industrial
decline began in the second half of the sixties, first in the United States, the
United Kingdom and France, later in Germany and Japan. With this relative
industrial decline there occurred a decline in the rate of growth of trade.
Between 1973 and 1977 a rate of growth of world industrial production of 16
per cent was matched by the same growth in the volume of world trade. This
1:1 ratio was in contrast to a ratio of 1:1.6 in the period 1948–73. Moreover,
in the recent period the share of industrial countries in total trade fell from 68
per cent to 63 per cent and their intra-trade from 51 to 44 per cent. Thus some
argue that we have been witnessing in the seventies not only a check to the
halcyon growth of the previous quarter-century but a process of 'de-
industrialisation' which may mark the beginning of a 'post-industrial era'.

Second, in the monetary field, two important institutional changes have taken place: the abandonment of gold and a gold exchange standard and the general adoption of floating exchange rates. Within this system basic imbalance persists. Strong countries – Germany, Japan and others – and weak countries – the United States, the United Kingdom, Italy and changing lesser fry – polarise the payments system and tax the exchange-rate pattern to adjust their relative strengths. At the same time the industrial countries have (since the early seventies) become on balance net importers of capital and their former role as providers of money capital to the rest of the world has passed to the OPEC countries whose surplus on current account between 1973 and 1979 amounted to £230 bln. This surplus has been disbursed through foreign-placed bank deposits which, in turn, are re-lent in the form of bank loans of short and medium term.

Third, price inflation still runs strongly in almost all countries, with modal rates of 6–20 per cent per annum in the industrial countries and much higher rates in the developing world. Are we to regard such rates as tolerable for the next decade, as we did 3–4 per cent in the fifties, or are we to persevere with disinflationary policies to reduce them, even at the cost of lower growth and some underemployment?

Fourth, in the domestic economies of the West unemployment has returned, but in a different form from that of the thirties, its cure not amenable to Keynesian strategies. A labour force, swollen by the baby-boom of the post-war years and by the invasion of work-hungry women, faces a labour-demand curtailed and redistributed by capital substitution, technological change and sectoral regrouping. The concentration of unemployment in the lower age-groups and the slow realisation that old concepts of labour hiring, job security and career prospects must be revised, present a formidable challenge in economic and social management.

Fifth, in the political field there is still the cold war, warmed a little by détente but still generating astronomic arms expenditure, perverted trade patterns and struggles for political spheres of influence euphemised by flows of aid and technical advice. But on the western side of the divide the scenery is different. The United States, which, until the sixties, led and decided policies, is no longer supreme. The European Community claims parity in leadership while non-aligned countries and groups skirmish for advantage. The old American hegemony had much to admire, much to dislike and deplore, but it was simple and workable. It has been succeeded by a diversity of aim and method which has made international political economy intricate and dangerous.

Sixth, in the trade field there has as yet been no widespread reversion to protection and autarky. The world, it seemed, learned the lesson of the thirties and despite some symptoms of reversion even the oil crisis has not brought disaster. But if there has been no general lapse, the way ahead is far from clear. GATT, at the time of writing, claims that in its most recent round in Geneva there has been a widening of reciprocal free trade, but it is clear that two familiar issues persist – free trade in food and free entry to the mature economies of the burgeoning industrial output of the developing countries. Moreover, outside GATT there has been a steady drift towards protection. Voluntary export restraints, anti-dumping measures, non-tariff barriers and state trading have proliferated and as long as the payments problem remains there is always the chance that deficits may be met by exchange controls and trade-restraining measures.

Finally, but on a more cheerful note, the international economy and its institutional machinery has stood up well to its first major test since the war. There have been strains but no breakdown. While power politics in a nuclear age concerns itself with very simple issues and warfare can no longer be seen as a natural extension of diplomacy, economic and particularly currency issues have become focuses of negotiation. While such negotiations, even at summit level, are no less materialistic than before, it appears, at least to this writer, that the pitfalls are more clearly seen. Keynes argued at Bretton Woods and Savannah that currency matters were for the technician and the expert, an arcane pursuit for modern alchemists. Perhaps in this he was mistaken. Perhaps it was the French, who from Talleyrand's time have regarded high finance as a fit study for the statesman, who were right.

In the twelve preceding chapters it should be possible to discern much of what is shaping the international economy as we enter the last decades of the twentieth century. Two tasks remain: to look briefly at the present state of the international monetary system, and to identify the central problem of imbalance which faces that system at present.

(ii)   MONETARY AFFAIRS: ON FROM BRETTON WOODS

It has become fashionable to regard the events of 1971–5 as marking the end of the Bretton Woods system. Since then, five years have elapsed in which monetary events have been differently ordered. Whether this constitutes a fundamental change of pattern or a discontinuity, a change of direction or a change in method and aims is, however, a question we must face at this stage. We shall attempt to form a view by doing two things: first, recalling briefly the essence of Bretton Woods and comparing it with any order which may be seen in the present system; and second, by glancing at the institutional arrangements which have replaced the Bretton Woods framework.

The original conception of Bretton Woods was that of a system of multilateral payments in which national currencies were linked by a network of exchange rates, fixed in the short term but variable in the long. The short term was seen as a period in which variations in a country's balance of payments could be dealt with by transfers of reserve media – gold or acceptable foreign exchange – which, if insufficient, could be augmented by drawings on the central pool of the IMF. The long term might well bring structural changes in balances of payments which would require changes in exchange rates. Adjustment of the balance of payments was thus seen as a long-term process achieved by changes of exchange rates over which the Fund would have some influence. This was the central doctrine; it was supplemented by other assumptions. The IMF would act as a central agency through which monetary co-operation would operate. Disequilibrium in balances of payments was a two-sided phenomenon and onus for adjustment rested equally on the deficit and the surplus countries. Finally, member currencies were of similar importance since for each country a balance-of-payments disequilibrium had to be corrected when it occurred and each country contributed a quota of its currency to the Fund's pool. The entire conception was symmetrical and an advance on the gold standard which preceded it but which, in its later days, it came to resemble.[1]

In its quarter-century of life the Bretton Woods system was modified in several ways. The equality of currencies gave way to a recognition of the importance of key currencies and ultimately the system centred around the U.S. dollar which acted as reserve and intervention currency and linked all other currencies indirectly to the value of gold. The importance of reserve media and the relation of the world stock of international liquidity to the volume of world trade was increasingly recognised and the SDR was added in 1970 as a Fund-created reserve unit. The Fund evolved in unanticipated ways, but kept its position at the centre, while the main features – multilateralism, fixed exchange rates, gold, key currencies – remained to the end, and it is with them that the system is identified.

The system which remained after the events of 1971–5 was vestigial of several of these features. Multilateralism was unimpaired, the co-operative element was still active, expressed in the continuance of the Fund and in the activities of many committees and working groups, the key currency approach was increasingly stressed but two aspects of the old system were radically changed: the role of gold and the function of exchange rates as a medium of balance-of-payments adjustment. In the original conception of Bretton Woods gold had been an international *numéraire* in terms of which, through the gold-convertible dollar, all other currencies were expressed and their interrelating exchange rates fixed. In its latter days the system came near to being a gold exchange standard. After 1971, when the dollar was no longer convertible, all that was changed. Steps taken since have sought to remove gold as a unit of account and a reserve medium.

The new role of exchange rates after 1971 was a piecemeal effort to provide – what Bretton Woods had never provided – a working system of

---

[1] Readers who find this account of the Bretton Woods system truncated may refer to chap. 5, 'The Bretton Woods Model: the Principles of the System', in my *International Monetary Policy: Bretton Woods and After* (London: Macmillan, 1975) pp. 108–122.

balance-of-payments adjustment. The unsatisfactory performance of the adjustable-peg system, the growth over a decade of academic support for free exchange rates and the conviction by politicians that, in the racing economic tides of the seventies, no fixed exchange rate could be held for long, all served to establish floating exchanges for a long period of time. If we admit, going back to fundamentals, that any international monetary system must have three characteristics: international money, an adjustment mechanism and co-ordination from the centre, then the first two of these had been radically altered from 1971 and the third had to fall into line to allow any sort of system to continue.

The institutional changes were made by the IMF. It was a case of recognising realities. At a conference in Jamaica in January 1976 the existing conditions concerning gold and exchange rates as they had developed since 1971 were legalised.

So far as gold was concerned two aspects were important: its role as international *numéraire* and its function as a medium for holding central-bank reserves. The first of these settled itself as one country after another abandoned fixed parities between 1971 and 1973. It was assumed that if parities were ever fixed again they would be defined in terms of the SDR, which was rapidly establishing itself as the international unit of account. In its role of international reserve medium, held and dealt in by central banks, the situation of gold was more controversial. Gold, originally exchanged between central banks at an official price of $35 per ounce had seen two increases in the official price[2] while in the free market the price was much higher. Central banks were, therefore, faced with the attractive alternative of selling gold in the free market at a high price, which was in contravention of Bretton Woods arrangements, or of selling in the central-bank market at the low official price. Not surprisingly, official gold transactions virtually ceased and there was an uneasy lull in the controversy of how and at which price gold should be exchanged. The French, following their gold standard predilections of the Gaullist years, wanted free central-bank dealing at whatever price a free gold market might determine. The United States at first supported the *status quo*, but later yielded somewhat to the French view. Ultimately, after negotiations in 1974 the IMF Interim Committee proposed arrangements to the Jamaica meeting which were adopted and which lay somewhere between the United States' and French extremes but leant strongly in the direction of demonetising gold. The official price of gold was to be abolished, the obligations of IMF members to make certain transactions in gold with the Fund were to cease, the Fund was to return one-sixth of its gold to members in proportion to their quota and auction off another sixth using the profits[3] for the benefit of

[2] One from $35 to $38 per ounce in December 1971 and another from $38 to $42.2 in February 1973.

[3] Profit per ounce being the difference between the former official price and the price at the auction sale.

developing countries. There was to be no increase in the gold stock of the IMF and no attempt to support the price in the free market. After the Jamaica Conference the IMF implemented, between 1976 and 1979, the active aspects of this policy. However the free market price of gold, reflecting as it did the frequent desire of people and institutions to hold gold as an asset-hedge against inflation, rose steadily. By early 1980 the price was just below $600 per ounce. While the edicts of the IMF might deprive gold of its *de jure* monetary status, commodity arbitraging of the metal continued and gave it a unique 'quasi-monetary' status.

The response of the IMF to the reality of a world of fluctuating exchange rates was slight. Being concerned with following rather than leading world opinion, the Fund's initial reaction was to await events and see whether the move to free rates was to be transitory or long-lasting. Among the leading countries opinion was polarised between the Americans who increasingly warmed to the new condition and the French who led a European group of varying convictions, who felt that the par value system should soon be restored. By 1975 the French had moved some way towards accepting the American view of free rates. Temporary improvement in the U.S. balance of payments, the standing of the dollar and the climate of the foreign-exchange market played some part in this and by November 1975 when a summit meeting of the Group of Five (plus Italy) met at Rambouillet the French and their supporters were prepared to concede to the American view. This allowed a move forward and in January 1976 in Jamaica the IMF Interim Committee settled new IMF rules to supersede the par value system in the Articles of the Fund. The agreement was in fact a considerable concession by the last supporter of the adjustable-peg system, in that any restoration of it would require an 85 per cent vote in the IMF.[4]

The Jamaica meeting agreed on changes in the IMF Articles, which gave sanction to the new look on gold and exchange rates. In addition other Article amendments gave authority for a general increase in quotas. All in all the Jamaica meeting was a considerable 'house-tidying' operation. With its amendments to the Articles and the earlier 'IMF Guidelines for the Management of Floating Exchange Rates' the Fund was set to play a central role in the monetary system.[5] It is far more flexible. Perhaps the lesson has at last been learnt that it must not entrench itself in impossible positions from which there is no retreat, as it did in its obstinate opposition to free exchange rates in the fifties and sixties.

---

[4] A majority which, on IMF voting procedures, would require the support of the United States.

[5] For interesting glimpses of the Fund's inner workings in the late fifties and early sixties, see Erin E. Jacobsson, *A Life for Sound Money. Per Jacobsson: His Biography* (London: Oxford University Press, 1979).

(iii) IMBALANCE AMONG THE MAJOR CURRENCIES: AN OLD PROBLEM, A NEW SETTING

During 1977–9 instability has prevailed in international payments. A familiar pattern has reappeared – that of imbalance between groups of leading countries. In the present case instability is polarised between the United States on the one hand and Germany and Japan on the other. Groups of other countries adhere to each side but may be set aside in this discussion, their strengths and weaknesses arising from conditions peculiar to the moment or to themselves. The three basic causes of the disequilibrium have been: the swifter expansion of the United States from the recession of 1974–5, the failure of that country significantly to reduce its imports of oil, and the burden upon the United States of running the leading key currency – all this in the face of the two next largest industrial powers with a record of trade surpluses and domestic policy restraint.

The recovery from the recession of 1974–5 in the West was slow and fitful, but such as it was the United States led it. In 1976 the indicators showed that recovery was under way. GNP grew at 6 per cent in 1976 and at almost 5 per cent in 1977 and into 1978. With it grew American imports, particularly of oil. From the summer of 1976 the dollar was falling sharply relative to the yen and the DM and less sharply in relation to even such weak currencies as the pound and the lira.[6] The depreciation continued until, in late 1977 and early 1978, it became a slide of crisis proportions with persistent speculative selling of U.S. dollars. The American authorities, at first, persisted in their practice of benign neglect, allowing the rate to fall in the hope that at some level it would stabilise and correct the deficit in the balance of payments. During 1979 ineffectual efforts at intervention and support have been made, but in response to its basic causes the weakness persists.

The reaction of the surplus countries was anticipatable. Both Germany and Japan, fearing the effects of an under-valued dollar on their trade, took in dollars to try to check the slide. Already critical of what they regarded as America's failure to 'manage' her exchange rate they were adding to their already enormous holdings of dollars. The OPEC countries, paid as they are for their oil exports in U.S. dollars, complained that the real value of their dollar receipts were being eroded. By mid-1978 OPEC claimed that it had had to accept the equivalent of a 15 per cent drop in the price of oil as a result of the decline in the international value of the dollar. To this the Americans had only the response that some part of the responsibility for the disequilibrium lay with Germany and Japan, who were not playing their part in recovery by expanding their economies faster. As for reducing the level of oil imports, this was certainly President Carter's intention, but the appetite of the

---

[6] In 1978 the pound strengthened relative to the dollar and in 1979 maintained its position, largely from imports of short-term capital.

U.S. economy for oil, and the refusal of Congress to accept his energy policy proposals, prevented this.

One may also ask why, in the face of this polarisation of world payments, the role of international key currency did not shift away from the dollar towards the Deutsch mark? For this there were several reasons. First and strongest, the German government was determined that this should not happen. For a great trading nation with export-led prosperity there must be no such confusion between internal and external economic policies such as had bedevilled the British and American governments in managing the pound and dollar. Second, the German currency was not institutionally endowed with a banking system amenable to the role of an international currency, and finally there was tacit agreement among the senior partners of EEC that the running of an international currency was a responsibility which they would be better without. Over and above all this there was the failure of the Americans to realise the significance for them of the dollar being a key currency. They saw this role in the sixties as one conferring and confirming political power. Too late, in the seventies, they realised that it involved also responsibility and constraint.

Faced with two alternatives – abandoning his policy of economic expansion or allowing the U.S. balance of payments to worsen until the value of the dollar and the effects of U.S. deficit gave bargaining leverage to force action on the surplus countries, Carter opted for the latter. An economic summit conference was scheduled for Bonn in July 1978. At this Carter hoped to transfer some of the weight of expanding the world economy to the Germans and Japanese.

In early 1978 the European Economic Community moved again towards action in the field of monetary integration. Since the beginning of the seventies enthusiasm for this grandiose conception had ebbed and flowed with events. Now, realisation of need for a united front in dealing with the United States, and belief that a single European currency would, in all probability, be the strongest in the world, brought French and German policies for the time being into line and a new move was possible.

At Bremen in early July 1978 the leaders of EEC countries met to prepare their position for an economic summit in Bonn later in the month. The proposal agreed upon was to set up a European Monetary System by the end of 1978. The aims were to be threefold: to stabilise European currencies, to achieve the objective of European monetary integration defined by the Werner Committee and to enable Europe to play its part in strengthening the U.S. dollar. Behind the generalities of the official communiqué the real objectives were clear: to breathe new life into the EEC, languishing for lack of a defined initiative; to strengthen the West German position at the Bonn meeting, where the United States would surely demand faster expansion of the German economy to help speed world recovery; and to support the United States with pressure on Japan to reduce its trade surplus. The Bremen package was made possible by, for the moment, common objectives by the leading European powers, Germany and France. Britain, while having reservations about the currency plan, saw no reason to oppose it – at least at that stage.

The technical plan for currency union was to adapt the 'snake in the tunnel' arrangements as a basis. The major European currencies would float jointly in relation to the dollar. Between the European currencies only narrow margins were to be maintained, such margins ultimately to be so small as to create virtually fixed rates between the European currencies. To support these rates there was to be a $50 bln fund[7] from which member countries would be able to borrow currencies to intervene on the exchange markets. This intervention would be carefully co-ordinated and be carried on in European currencies rather than in dollars. The new Fund and all transactions with it would be expressed in a new European currency unit (ECU) equal to about 80 cents U.S. In the beginning it would be the accounting unit of a clearing union resembling EPU in the fifties. Ultimately it could become the European monetary unit, itself replacing the present national currencies.

The implementing of this grandiose plan would have the effect of changing weights in the world currency market. Assuming that Canada adhered to the U.S. dollar and Britain to the European group, then most of the major countries, except Japan, would be within the dual grouping. This would make it easier for the two groups to manage the exchange rate between them and would give them strong leverage in facing Japan on trade and commercial policy issues. As for shorter-range policies, the Germans were able to offer, at the Bonn meeting, to expand their economy faster and demand in return from the United States that Carter take action to cut oil imports and strengthen the dollar from the U.S. side.

The Bonn meeting gave a chance to the leading powers to work out a concerted economic plan to achieve stability in world payments. Agreement was achieved on the main monetary issues. The Germans promised to expand their economy by adding at least 1 percentage point to their growth rate. The Japanese pledged themselves to import more, export less and step up their expansion rate. The United States promised an energy policy and a check to oil imports. Only on commercial policy was there complete stalemate. Against a background of slow progress in the Tokyo Round of GATT negotiations there was American concern at the strong protectionism of the Community in refusing admission to American agricultural products. Over and above this was the group fear of the industrial countries that concessions might be wrung from them for the admission of industrial products from the developing world.

[7] Countries are to contribute 20 per cent of their dollar reserves and an equal amount of their national currency.

The Bonn Agreement was a notable one, an agreement of how, in principle, to proceed in the face of a defined set of problems. Nevertheless, it was doomed from the outset by its timing. The American economy was already on the turn. The inflation rate was rising, the rate of growth declining, wage settlements were being made at inflated rates. It was clear that the Carter energy programme was bogged down in Congress. Shortly after Bonn adverse trade figures for the United States and huge surpluses for Germany and Japan were announced. Heavy speculative pressure on the dollar in the exchange markets began. It was clear that the movers of currencies on the exchange markets had no confidence in the Carter Administration. Throughout 1979 the dollar was continuously under pressure.

On 1 January 1979 the European Monetary System (EMS) came into existence. Each member of the system has a fixed 'central exchange rate' against the new European currency unit (ECU). For each currency there is a percentage divergence indicator which determines upper and lower intervention rates at which central banks must support the currency. Thus all member currencies (except Italy, for whom special wide divergence is permitted) are pegged to the ECU, which in turn is a weighted average of all member currencies of the system. Of the nine members of EEC only Britain remains outside the scheme,[8] although Italy, as a European lame duck, has special privileges.

The move forward to the EMS had significance both for Europe and the wider world. For the Community it demonstrated determination to move towards the common currency and at least in a limited sense to meet the 1980 target date of the Werner Committee. In a wider sense the step implemented the Bremen decision of the previous summer, demonstrating to the world, and particularly the Americans, the solidarity of EEC.

With the dollar weak, the American economy sliding into recession and EMS in its infancy, 1979 brought another oil crisis. In the spring OPEC raised its oil price by more than 40 per cent and world supplies of oil were reduced by the revolution in Iran. The estimated OPEC current account surplus for 1979 is $45 bln with a cumulative surplus since 1973 of $230 bln at 1979 prices.[9] A cycle of events similar to those of 1974 appears to have been set in train. The rate of inflation rises, balances of payments of oil-importing countries worsen, recession is generalised partly from the U.S. recession and partly from the effect of the rise in oil prices diverting demand to a single factor. Once more the concomitance of inflation and recession is presented to the industrial nations, offering them a conflict of policies. Thus far the response has been to counter the inflation by disinflationary policies which show no sign of halting inflation but intensify recession. During the first part of 1979 interest rates rose

---

[8] The Republic of Ireland joined, thus for the first time requiring itself to name its currency (the punt) separately from sterling, with which the Irish pound formerly had parity.
[9] An estimate by the National Institute of Economic and Social Research, London.

in all industrial countries and by September reached 12 per cent in the United States. In November the British Minimum Lending Rate was raised to 17 per cent. As countries sought to disinflate and to protect their balances of payments, rise and counter-rise carried interest rates to levels which could not fail to diminish real investment. In face of this, currency disorder continued, with the familiar features of weakening dollar and strength for the Deutsche Mark, yen and Swiss franc. The British pound remained strong (and over-valued) as OPEC funds found a home in London – the least unsafe place for investment. The gold price rose to unprecedented levels.

At the annual meeting of the IMF in September in Belgrade pressure upon the Americans to deal with their weak currency resulted in an intensification of disinflationary measures. Following the now fashionable monetarism which motivated Western policies, restrictive monetary policy was extended from the interest-rate and credit policy to reserve ratios and direct control of the monetary supply itself; seemingly without regard for the effect which such crude weapons might have upon employment levels.

History often repeats itself, but never quite exactly. The disturbing difference between oil crises I and II appears to lie in the recycling of OPEC surpluses. In the first case these were invested by the surplus countries in the international capital markets of the West and there lent to the deficit countries. Two differences seem to appear in crisis II – one slight, one more menacing. The first lies in the greater capacity of the OPEC countries to absorb capital for their own development.[10] This, with the smaller surplus in crisis II, makes the recycling problem less threatening. The second difference is political rather than economic. In crisis I the choice of venues for OPEC investment was constrained only by a wariness in the early stages (1974) of the United States – a wariness soon dispelled. But in crisis II events are already imposing constraints which at worst threaten the whole recycling process and at best throw it upon a few countries only.[11] The unrest in Iran and the dispute in November 1979 over the seizing of the American embassy in Tehran led Iran to threaten withdrawal of all its funds from dollar holdings and the United States, in rebuttal, to place a freeze upon the with-drawal of such funds. Thus the international monetary system was directly menaced by political events. Its processes of fund-switching, which normally are smoothed by market conditions, were now seen as weapons to be deployed by one nation for the discomfiture of another. This new stochastic element in the recycling process makes it very vulnerable and renews the fears that were felt for its durability in 1974.

[10] Saudi Arabia plans to embark on a $250-bln five-year plan in 1980.

[11] Theoretically the more widely OPEC surpluses are invested the better. A single distribution centre for OPEC funds (e.g. London) would make the whole system more vulnerable. At present three-quarters of OPEC external assets are denominated in dollars and one-half are held in the United States.

(iv) CONCLUSION

Since history is a continuous process, and since all historical narratives must end at some point in time, loose ends are inevitable. It is, however, desirable to do something to tidy up these loose ends.

This book, as a history of the international economy of the West, has been concerned with three main areas: trade and its changing conditions; payments, which result from international money flows; and changing policies towards these matters, which in their turn are a reflection of the power structure between nations. We began our scrutiny of these areas in the confusion which followed the Second World War; we end it at an arbitrary point of time which can claim no finality and which has its own confusions to resolve. Let us pick out a point or two from each of these areas.

In trade we have seen an expansion which in 1945 was undreamed of. Between the industrial powers this has not only brought the advantages associated with trade as such – specialisation, diversity, a broadening of consumer choice, but it has also been a main generator of the greatest prosperity in modern economic history. For many countries, such as Germany and Japan, the rise to economic power has been trade-based; even for the laggards trade has played some part. On the positive side also has been the growing freedom, through a liberal commercial policy, which has helped to make this expansion possible. Tariff reduction, multilateral payments, a reduction of direct controls have all played their part. One of the great hopes an observer must have is that this freedom may not only be maintained but broadened and that the developed countries will progressively open their markets to the expanding industrial output of the developing countries. We need a widening of trade through this change of structure.

In the field of payments our period saw the first (and certainly the only) clean start in history. The architects of Bretton Woods gave us a system which functioned for a quarter-century and which, we have argued, is vestigial in our present arrangements. A continuous reading of the payments chapters of this book may give an impression of continual crisis, but such is not really the case. At no time since 1945 have we stood at a point at which failure to establish a new 'system' would quickly have led to financial disintegration and collapse. The narrative has really been one of continual modification to changing circumstances in a world changing faster than ever before. There is in this modification ample evidence that even makeshifts, such as those which followed the Nixon Measures of 1971 and the quickly following complications of the oil crisis, had a logic of their own and led on to new modifications, still in the main stream of development. One thing in particular has made this possible, a high degree of co-operation in international monetary affairs. Certainly there has been mercantilism, power politics and horse-trading in monetary negotiations, but disaster has always been avoided by the widespread recognition that international monetary affairs must be discussed in an international forum. The force at the centre, whether it be the leading country of a gold standard, as in the nineteenth century, or the recognition of rules of the game as in Bretton Woods, is a *sine qua non* of payments evolution. In the present, great events may be pending. Can the oldest, most politically sophisticated countries of Europe succeed in establishing monetary union? The next decade will bring the answer.

Changes in the political power structure make changes in the international economy possible. We began with the hegemony of the United States, which with a mixture of many motives led us out of the confusions of the forties and put the Western world on the way to growth and recovery, albeit under the menacing shadow of its rivalry with the other super-power. But since the sixties the United States is no longer leader of the West. The power structure has become one of groups rather than entities. The trick is to balance the groups and within the groups individual countries play their part. To be isolated from a group is to live dangerously – as Britain did when she shunned the Common Market in 1955 and the EMS in 1979, or as France still does in pursuing her own ends in the Community. Danger comes when groups generate rivalries, as between the United States and the Community within the group of industrial powers and between the industrial powers and the Third World. The ultimate success would come if the two major groups, developed and developing, could achieve working integration. In writing this book the writer has been struck by the spasmodic nature of progress in economic negotiations between powers. Negotiations are long, tenuous, often seemingly irreconcilable. Then a common pattern of aims emerges and there is some measure of agreement and a surge forward. Marshall's dictum, 'natura non facit saltum', may have been appropriate to the evolution of nineteenth-century economics, but in our own age it is stagnation, punctuated by leaps forward, which characterises the course of international economic power politics.

Index

Page numbers in italics refer to Tables.